'This book is a counter-story to Western ideas about the benefits of the pursuit of knowledge. Looking through the eyes of the colonized, cautionary tales are told from an indigenous perspective, tales designed not just to voice the voiceless but to prevent the dying – of people, of culture, of ecosystems. The book is particularly strong in situating the development of counter-practices of research within both Western critiques of Western knowledge and global indigenous movements. Informed by critical and feminist evaluations of positivism, Tuhiwai Smith urges researching back and disrupting the rules of the research game toward practices that are more respectful, ethical, sympathetic and useful vs racist practices and attitudes, ethnocentric assumptions and exploitative research. Using Kaupapa Maori, a fledgling approach toward culturally appropriate research protocols and methodologies, the book is designed primarily to develop indigenous peoples as researchers. In short, Tuhiwai Smith begins to articulate research practices that arise out of the specificities of epistemology and methodology rooted in survival struggles, a kind of research that is something other than a dirty word to those on the suffering side of history.' PATTI LATHER, PROFESSOR OF EDUCATIONAL POLICY AND LEADERSHIP, OHIO STATE UNIVERSITY AND AUTHOR OF *Getting Smart: Feminist Research and Pedagogy With/in the Postmodern* (ROUTLEDGE, 1991) AND *Troubling the Angels: Women Living With HIV/AIDS*, WITH CHRIS SMITHIES (WESTVIEW, 1997).

'Finally, a book for researchers working in indigenous context. Finally, a book especially for indigenous researchers. Linda Smith goes far beyond de-colonizing research methodology. Our contextual histories, politics, and cultural considerations are respectfully interwoven together. Our distinctive-ness remains distinct, but there are important places where our issues and methodologies intersect. Stories of research experiences, examples of projects, critical examination, and mindful reflection are woven together to make meaningful and practical designs related to indigenous issues and research.' JO-ANN ARCHIBALD, STO:LO NATION AND DIRECTOR OF THE FIRST NATIONS HOUSE OF LEARNING AT THE UNIVERSITY OF BRITISH COLUMBIA.

'A book like this is long overdue. It will be most useful for both indigenous and non-indigenous researchers in educational and non-educational institu-tions. It will empower indigenous students to undertake research which uses methods that are culturally sensitive and appropriate instead of those which they have learned about in Research Methods courses in universities which assume that research and research methods are culture-free and that researchers occupy some kind of moral high ground from which they can observe their subjects and make judgements about them.' KONAI THAMAN, PROFESSOR OF PACIFIC EDUCATION AND CULTURE, AND UNESCO CHAIR OF EDUCATION, UNIVERSITY OF THE SOUTH PACIFIC.

'Linda Tuhiwai Smith is the leading theorist on decolonization of Maori in New Zealand. This book opts for a dynamic interpretation of power relations of domination, struggle and emancipation. She uses a dual framework – the *whakapapa* of Maori knowledge and European epistemology – to interpret and capture the world of reality for a moment in time. Thus the search for truth in complex human relations is a never-ending quest.' RANGINUI WALKER, FORMERLY PROFESSOR OF MAORI STUDIES DEPARTMENT AND PRO-VICE CHANCELLOR, UNIVERSITY OF AUCKLAND.

'We have needed this book. Academic research facilitates diverse forms of economic and cultural imperialism by shaping and legitimating policies which entrench existing unjust power relations. Linda Tuhiwai Smith's powerful critique of dominant research methodologies is eloquent, informed and timely. Her distinctive proposals for an indigenous research agenda are especially valuable. Decolonization, she reminds us, cannot be limited to deconstructing the dominant story and revealing underlying texts, for none of that helps people improve their current conditions or prevents them from dying. This careful articulation of a range of research methodologies is vital, welcome and full of promise.' LAURIE ANNE WHITT, PROFESSOR OF PHILOSOPHY, MICHIGAN TECHNOLOGICAL UNIVERSITY.

'A brilliant, evocative and timely book about an issue that serves to both define and create indigenous realities. In recent years, indigenous people, often led by the emerging culturally affirmed and positioned indigenous scholars, have intensified the struggle to break free from the chains of colonialism and its oppressive legacy. In writing this book, Linda Tuhiwai Smith makes a powerful and impassioned contribution to this struggle. No budding researcher should be allowed to leave the academy without reading this book and no teacher should teach without it at their side.' BOB MORGAN, DIRECTOR, JUMBUNNA CAISER, CENTRE FOR ABORIGINAL AND TORRES STRAIT ISLANDERS, UNIVERSITY OF TECHNOLOGY, SYDNEY.

About the Author

Linda Tuhiwai Smith (Ngati Awa and Ngati Porou) is an Associate Professor in Education and Director of the International Research Institute for Maori and Indigenous Education at the University of Auckland.

Decolonizing Methodologies

Research and Indigenous Peoples

LINDA TUHIWAI SMITH

Zed Books Ltd
LONDON & NEW YORK

University of Otago Press
DUNEDIN

Decolonizing Methodologies was first published by
Zed Books Ltd, 7 Cynthia Street, London N1 9JF, UK,
and Room 400, 175 Fifth Avenue, New York, NY 10010, USA
and
University of Otago Press, PO Box 56/56 Union Street, Dunedin, New Zealand
Fax 64 3 479 8385, email university.press@stonebow.otago.ac.nz
in 1999

Distributed in the USA exclusively by
Palgrave, a division of St Martin's Press, LLC,
175 Fifth Avenue, New York, NY 10010, USA

Cover designed by Andrew Corbett.
Laserset by Long House, Cumbria, UK.
Printed and bound in Malaysia.

A catalogue record for this book
is available from the British Library.

ISBN 1 85649 623 6 Cased (Zed Books)
ISBN 1 85649 624 4 Limp (Zed Books)
ISBN 1 877133 67 1 Limp (University of Otago Press)

Contents

Acknowledgements

Ahakoa he iti, he iti pounamu
Although small, it is precious

I would like to thank the following people, individuals and organizations for their support and assistance in preparing this book. Graham Hingangaroa Smith, Kuni Jenkins, Margie Kahukura Hohepa, Patricia Maringi Johnston, Leonie Pihama, Cherryl Waerea-I-te-rangi Smith, Roger Dale, Alison Jones, Stuart McNaughton, Judith Simon, James Marshall, Betsan Martin, Kay Morris-Matthews, Michael Peters, the students of the Here Wananga programme, Research Unit for Maori Education, University of Auckland, students of Te Whare Wananga o Awanuiarangi, the University of Auckland Research Committee, indigenous colleagues from Canada, Australia, Hawa'i and the United States and others who have supported and encouraged.

For their technical support I would particularly like to thank Brenda-Liddiard Laurent, Eleanor Tedford and Tommy Perana. For valuable feedback on my writing style I thank Jenny McKnight.

For their constant support many thanks to my whanau, particularly my parents Hirini and June Mead, my sisters Aroha and Hinauri, husband Graham and daughter Kapua, sister-in-law Cherryl Wairea-I-te-rangi, my other Mum Paea and other extended family members just for being who they are.

Introduction

From the vantage point of the colonized, a position from which I write, and choose to privilege, the term 'research' is inextricably linked to European imperialism and colonialism. The word itself, 'research', is probably one of the dirtiest words in the indigenous world's vocabulary. When mentioned in many indigenous contexts, it stirs up silence, it conjures up bad memories, it raises a smile that is knowing and distrustful. It is so powerful that indigenous people even write poetry about research. The ways in which scientific research is implicated in the worst excesses of colonialism remains a powerful remembered history for many of the world's colonized peoples. It is a history that still offends the deepest sense of our humanity. Just knowing that someone measured our 'faculties' by filling the skulls of our ancestors with millet seeds and compared the amount of millet seed to the capacity for mental thought offends our sense of who and what we are.[1] It galls us that Western researchers and intellectuals can assume to know all that it is possible to know of us, on the basis of their brief encounters with some of us. It appals us that the West can desire, extract and claim ownership of our ways of knowing, our imagery, the things we create and produce, and then simultaneously reject the people who created and developed those ideas and seek to deny them further opportunities to be creators of their own culture and own nations. It angers us when practices linked to the last century, and the centuries before that, are still employed to deny the validity of indigenous peoples' claim to existence, to land and territories, to the right of self-determination, to the survival of our languages and forms of cultural knowledge, to our natural resources and systems for living within our environments.

This collective memory of imperialism has been perpetuated through the ways in which knowledge about indigenous peoples was collected, classified and then represented in various ways back to the West, and then, through the eyes of the West, back to those who have been colonized. Edward Said refers to this process as a Western discourse about the Other which is supported by 'institutions, vocabulary, scholarship, imagery, doctrines, even colonial bureaucracies and colonial styles'.[2] According to Said, this process has worked partly because of the constant interchange between the scholarly and the imaginative construction of ideas about the Orient. The scholarly construction, he argues, is supported by a corporate institution which 'makes statements about it [the Orient], authorising views of it, describing it, by teaching about it, settling it, ruling over it'.[3] In these acts both the formal scholarly pursuits of knowledge and the informal, imaginative, anecdotal constructions of the Other are intertwined with each other and with the activity of research. This book identifies research as a significant site of struggle between the interests and ways of knowing of the West and the interests and ways of resisting of the Other. In this example, the Other has been constituted with a name, a face, a particular identity, namely *indigenous peoples*. While it is more typical (with the exception of feminist research) to write about research within the framing of a specific scientific or disciplinary approach, it is surely difficult to discuss *research methodology* and *indigenous peoples* together, in the same breath, without having an analysis of imperialism, without understanding the complex ways in which the pursuit of knowledge is deeply embedded in the multiple layers of imperial and colonial practices.

Many researchers, academics and project workers may see the benefits of their particular research projects as serving a greater good 'for mankind', or serving a specific emancipatory goal for an oppressed community. But belief in the ideal that benefiting mankind is indeed a primary outcome of scientific research is as much a reflection of ideology as it is of academic training. It becomes so taken for granted that many researchers simply assume that they as individuals embody this ideal and are natural representatives of it when they work with other communities. Indigenous peoples across the world have other stories to tell which not only question the assumed nature of those ideals and the practices that they generate, but also serve to tell an alternative story: the history of Western research through the eyes of the colonized. These counter-stories are powerful forms of resistance which are repeated and shared across diverse indigenous communities. And, of course, most indigenous peoples and their communities do not differentiate scientific or 'proper' research from the forms of amateur collecting, journalistic approaches, film making or other ways of 'taking' indigenous knowledge that have occurred so casually over the centuries. The effect of travellers' tales, as pointed out by French philosopher Foucault, has contributed as much to the West's knowledge of itself as has the systematic gathering of scientific data. From some indigenous perspectives the gathering of information by scientists was as random, *ad hoc* and damaging as that undertaken by amateurs. There was no difference, from these perspectives, between 'real' or scientific research and any other visits by inquisitive and acquisitive strangers.

This book acknowledges the significance of indigenous perspectives on research and attempts to account for how, and why, such perspectives may have developed. It is written by someone who grew up within indigenous communities where stories about research and particularly about researchers (the human carriers of research) were intertwined with stories about all other forms of colonization and injustice. These were cautionary tales where the surface story was not as important as the underlying examples of cultural protocols broken, values negated, small tests failed and key people ignored. The greater danger, however, was in the creeping policies that intruded into every aspect of our lives, legitimated by research, informed more often by ideology. The power of research was not in the visits made by researchers to our communities, nor in their fieldwork and the rude questions they often asked. In fact, many individual non-indigenous researchers remain highly respected and well liked by the communities with whom they have lived. At a common sense level research was talked about both in terms of its absolute worthlessness to us, the indigenous world, and its absolute usefulness to those who wielded it as an instrument. It told us things already known, suggested things that would not work, and made careers for people who already had jobs. 'We are the most researched people in the world' is a comment I have heard frequently from several different indigenous communities. The truth of such a comment is unimportant, what does need to be taken seriously is the sense of weight and unspoken cynicism about research that the message conveys.

This cynicism ought to have been strong enough to deter any self-respecting indigenous person from being associated with research. Obviously, in this case, it has not, which leads to my other motivation for writing about indigenous peoples and research. This is a book which attempts to do something more than deconstructing Western scholarship simply by our own retelling, or by sharing indigenous horror stories about research. In a decolonizing framework, deconstruction is part of a much larger intent. Taking apart the story, revealing underlying texts, and giving voice to things that are often known intuitively does not help people to improve their current conditions. It provides words, perhaps, an insight that explains certain experiences – but it does not prevent someone from dying. It is with that sense of reality that the second part of the book has been written. Whilst indigenous communities have quite valid fears about the further loss of intellectual and cultural knowledges, and have worked to gain international attention and protection through covenants on such matters, many indigenous communities continue to live within political and social conditions that perpetuate extreme levels of poverty, chronic ill health and poor educational opportunities.[4] Their children may be removed forcibly from their care, 'adopted' or institutionalized. The adults may be as addicted to alcohol as their children are to glue, they may live in destructive relationships which are formed and shaped by their impoverished material conditions and structured by politically oppressive regimes. While they live like this they are constantly fed messages about their worthlessness, laziness, dependence and lack of 'higher' order human qualities. This applies as much to indigenous communities in First World nations as it does to indigenous communities in developing countries. Within these sorts of social realities, questions of imperialism and the effects of colonization may seem to be merely academic; sheer physical survival is far more pressing. The problem is that constant efforts by governments, states, societies and institutions to deny the historical formations of such conditions have simultaneously denied our claims to humanity, to having a history, and to all sense of hope. To acquiesce is to lose ourselves entirely and implicitly agree with all that has been said about us. To resist is to retrench in the margins, retrieve what we were and remake ourselves. The past, our stories local and global, the present, our communities, cultures, languages and social practices – all may be spaces of marginalization, but they have also become spaces of resistance and hope.

It is from within these spaces that increasing numbers of indigenous academics and researchers have begun to address social issues within the wider framework of self-determination, decolonization and social justice. This burgeoning international community of indigenous scholars and researchers is talking more widely about indigenous research, indigenous research protocols and indigenous methodologies. Its members position themselves quite clearly as indigenous researchers who are informed academically by critical and often feminist approaches to research, and who are grounded politically in specific indigenous contexts and histories, struggles and ideals. Many indigenous communities and organizations have developed policies about research, are discussing issues related to control over research activities and the knowledge that research produces, and have developed ethical guidelines and discussion documents. The second part of this book addresses some of the issues currently being discussed amongst indigenous communities that relate to our own priorities and problems. These priorities often demand an understanding of the ways in which we can ask and seek answers to our own concerns within a context in which resistance to new formations of colonization still has to be mounted and articulated. In other words, research is not an innocent or distant academic exercise but an activity that has something at stake and that occurs in a set of political and social conditions.

If in a sense this book is simply another contribution to the ways in which social science researchers in general think about methodologies and approaches to research – in this case among people and communities who hold research in high disdain – it has not been written with that intention. Rather, it is addressed more specifically to those researchers who work with, alongside and for communities who have chosen to identify themselves as indigenous. A growing number of these researchers define themselves as indigenous, although their training has been primarily within the Western academy and specific disciplinary methodologies. Many indigenous researchers have struggled individually to engage with the disconnections that are apparent between the demands of research, on one side, and the realities they encounter amongst their own and other indigenous communities, with whom they share lifelong relationships, on the other side. There are a number of ethical, cultural, political and personal issues that can present special difficulties for indigenous researchers who, in their own communities, work partially as insiders, and are often employed for this purpose, and partially as outsiders, because of their Western education or because they may work across clan, tribe, linguistic, age and gender boundaries. Simultaneously, they work within their research projects or institutions as insiders within a particular paradigm or research model, and as outsiders because they are often marginalized and perceived to be representative of either a minority or a rival interest group. Patricia Hill Collins refers to 'the outsider within' positioning of research.[5] Sometimes when in the community ('in the field') or when sitting in on research meetings it can feel like inside-out/outside-in research. More often, however, I think that indigenous research is not quite as simple as it looks, nor quite as complex as it feels! If I have one consistent message for the students I teach and the researchers I train it is that indigenous research is a humble and humbling activity.

Indigenous researchers are expected, by their communities and by the institutions which employ them, to have some form of historical and critical analysis of the role of research in the indigenous world. In general, this analysis has been acquired organically and outside of the academy. Despite the extensive literature about the life and customs of indigenous peoples, there are few critical texts on research methodologies which mention the word indigenous or its localized synonyms. Critiques by feminist scholars, by critical theorists, by black and African American scholars have provided ways of talking about knowledge and its social constructions, and about methodologies and the politics of research. But the words that apply to indigenous researchers have been inserted into the text, then read with our own world in/sight. I hope that what is written here provides space for further dialogue within a framework that privileges the indigenous presence, that uses 'the words' (such as colonialism, decolonization, self-determination), and that acknowledges our continuing existence. It has not been written, therefore, as a technical book about research for people who talk the language of research, but as a book which situates research in a much larger historical, political and cultural context and then examines its critical nature within those dynamics.

The term 'indigenous' is problematic in that it appears to collectivize many distinct populations whose experiences under imperialism have been vastly different. Other collective terms also in use refer to 'First Peoples' or 'Native Peoples', 'First Nations' or 'People of the Land', 'Aboriginals' or 'Fourth World Peoples'.[6] Some groups prefer the labels that connect us to Mother Earth, and to deeply significant spiritual relationships. While not denying the powerful world views embedded in such terms, within my own cultural framework as within others, they are not the terms that will be used here. A recent phenomenon which partly explains such a position is the Western fascination with New Age spiritual meanings which makes our own belief systems available, yet again, for further mining and exploitation. In some contexts, such as Australia and North America, the word indigenous is a way of including the many diverse communities, language groups and nations, each with their own identification within a single grouping. In other contexts, such as New Zealand, the terms 'Maori' or *tangata whenua* are used much more frequently than 'indigenous' as the universal term, while different origin and tribal terms are also used to differentiate between groups. Although the word 'Maori' is an indigenous term it has been identified as a label which defines a colonial relationship between 'Maori' and 'Pakeha', the non-indigenous settler population. For many of the world's indigenous communities there are prior terms by which they have named themselves. There are also terms by which indigenous communities have come to be known, initially perhaps as a term of insult applied by colonizers, but then politicized as a powerful signifier of oppositional identity, for example the use of the term 'Black Australia' by Aborigine activists. Inside these categories for describing or labelling are other terms that describe different layers of relationships and meanings within and between different groups. Some of these terms are about the classification systems used within the local colonial context, and others are about a prior relationship with groups whose territories now span different states.

'Indigenous peoples' is a relatively recent term which emerged in the 1970s out of the struggles primarily of the American Indian Movement (AIM), and the Canadian Indian Brotherhood. It is a term that internationalizes the experiences, the issues and the struggles of some of the world's colonized peoples.[7] The final 's' in 'indigenous peoples' has been argued for quite vigorously by indigenous activists because of the right of peoples to self-determination. It is also used as a way of recognizing that there are real differences between different indigenous peoples.[8] The term has enabled the collective voices of colonized people to be expressed strategically in the international arena. It has also been an umbrella enabling communities and peoples to come together, transcending their own colonized contexts and experiences, in order to learn, share, plan, organize and struggle collectively for self-determination on the global and local stages. Thus the world's indigenous populations belong to a network of peoples. They share experiences as peoples who have been subjected to the colonization of their lands and cultures, and the denial of their sovereignty, by a colonizing society that has come to dominate and determine the shape and quality of their lives, even after it has formally pulled out. As Wilmer has put it, 'indigenous peoples represent the unfinished business of decolonization'.[9]

The word 'indigenous' is also used in ways which are quite contrary to the definitions of the term just described, but which are legitimate meanings of the word itself. For example it is used to describe or account for the distinctiveness of colonial literary and/or feminist traditions. It has been coopted politically by the descendants of settlers who lay claim to an 'indigenous' identity through their occupation and settlement of land over several generations or simply through being born in that place – though they tend not to show up at indigenous peoples' meetings nor form alliances that support the self-determination of the people whose forebears once occupied the land that they have 'tamed' and upon which they have settled. Nor do they actively struggle as a society for the survival of indigenous languages, knowledges and cultures. Their linguistic and cultural homeland is somewhere else, their cultural loyalty is to some other place. Their power, their privilege, their history are all vested in their legacy as colonizers.

Part of the project of this book is 'researching back', in the same tradition of 'writing back' or 'talking back', that characterizes much of the post-colonial or anti-colonial literature.[10] It has involved a 'knowingness of the colonizer' and a recovery of ourselves, an analysis of colonialism, and a struggle for self-determination. Research is one of the ways in which the underlying code of imperialism and colonialism is both regulated and realized. It is regulated through the formal rules of individual scholarly disciplines and scientific paradigms, and the institutions that support them (including the state). It is realized in the myriad of representations and ideological constructions of the Other in scholarly and 'popular' works, and in the principles which help to select and recontextualize those constructions in such things as the media, official histories and school curricula. Ashis Nandy argues that the structures of colonialism contain rules by which colonial encounters occur and are 'managed'.[11] The different ways in which these encounters happen and are managed are different realizations of the underlying rules and codes which frame in the broadest sense what is possible and what is impossible. In a very real sense research has been an encounter between the West and the Other. Much more is known about one side of those encounters than is known about the other side. This book reports to some extent on views that are held and articulated by 'the other sides'. The first part of the book explores topics around the theme of imperialism, research and knowledge. They can be read at one level as a narrative about a history of research and indigenous peoples but make much more sense if read as a series of intersecting and overlapping essays around a theme.

One of the issues examined relates to the way research became institutionalized in the colonies, not just through academic disciplines, but through learned and scientific societies and scholarly networks. The transplanting of research institutions, including universities, from the imperial centres of Europe enabled local scientific interests to be organized and embedded in the colonial system. Many of the earliest local researchers were not formally 'trained' and were hobbyist researchers and adventurers. The significance of travellers' tales and adventurers' adventures is that they represented the Other to a general audience back in Europe which became fixed in the milieu of cultural ideas. Images of the 'cannibal' chief, the 'red' Indian, the 'witch' doctor, or the 'tattooed and shrunken' head, and stories which told of savagery and primitivism, generated further interest, and therefore further opportunities, to represent the Other again.

Travellers' stories were generally the experiences and observations of white men whose interactions with indigenous 'societies' or 'peoples' were constructed around their own cultural views of gender and sexuality. Observations made of indigenous women, for example, resonated with views about the role of women in European societies based on Western notions of culture, religion, race and class. Treaties and trade could be negotiated with indigenous men. Indigenous women were excluded from such serious encounters. As Memmi noted in his 'Mythical Portrait of the Colonized', the use of zoological terms to describe primitive people was one form of dehumanization.[12] These images have become almost permanent, so deeply embedded are they in the way indigenous women are discussed. 'How often do we read in the newspaper about the death or murder of a Native man, and in the same paper about the victimisation of a female Native, as though we were a species of sub-human animal life?' asks a First Nation Canadian woman, Lee Maracle. 'A female horse, a female Native, but everyone else gets to be called a man or a woman.'[13] Across the Pacific, Maori women writers Patricia Johnston and Leonie Pihama make reference to Joseph Banks's description of young Maori women who were as 'skittish as unbroke fillies'.[14] Similarly, in Australia, Aborigine women talk about a history of being hunted, raped and then killed like animals.

Travellers' tales had wide coverage. Their dissemination occurred through the popular press, from the pulpit, in travel brochures which advertised for immigrants, and through oral discourse. They appealed to the voyeur, the soldier, the romantic, the missionary, the crusader, the adventurer, the entrepreneur, the imperial public servant and the Enlightenment scholar. They also appealed to the downtrodden, the poor and those whose lives held no possibilities in their own imperial societies, and who chose to migrate as settlers. Others, also powerless, were shipped off to the colony as the ultimate prison. In the end they were all inheritors of imperialism who had learned well the discourses of race and gender, the rules of power, the politics of colonialism. They became the colonizers.

The second part of the book examines the different approaches and methodologies that are being developed to ensure that research with indigenous peoples can be more respectful, ethical, sympathetic and useful. The chapters in the second part ought not to be read as a 'how to' manual but as a series of accounts and guidelines which map a wide range of research-related issues. Feminism and the application of more critical approaches to research have greatly influenced the social sciences. Significant spaces have been opened up within the academy and within some disciplines to talk more creatively about research with particular groups and communities – women, the economically oppressed, ethnic minorities and indigenous peoples. These discussions have been informed as much by the politics of groups outside the academy as by engagement with the problems which research with real, living, breathing, thinking people actually involves. Communities and indigenous activists have openly challenged the research community about such things as racist practices and attitudes, ethnocentric assumptions and exploitative research, sounding warning bells that research can no longer be conducted with indigenous communities as if their views did not count or their lives did not matter.

In contemporary indigenous contexts there are some major research issues which continue to be debated quite vigorously. These can be summarized best by the critical questions that communities and indigenous activists often ask, in a variety of ways: Whose research is it? Who owns it? Whose interests does it serve? Who will benefit from it? Who has designed its questions and framed its scope? Who will carry it out? Who will write it up? How will its results be disseminated?[15] While there are many researchers who can handle such questions with integrity there are many more who cannot, or who approach these questions with some cynicism, as if they are a test merely of political correctness. What may surprise many people is that what may appear as the 'right', most desirable answer can still be judged incorrect. These questions are simply part of a larger set of judgements on criteria that a researcher cannot prepare for, such as: Is her spirit clear? Does he have a good heart? What other baggage are they carrying? Are they useful to us? Can they fix up our generator? Can they actually do anything?

The issues for indigenous researchers seeking to work within indigenous contexts are framed somewhat differently. If they are 'insiders' they are frequently judged on insider criteria; their family background, status, politics, age, gender, religion, as well as on their perceived technical ability. What is frustrating for some indigenous researchers is that, even when their own communities have access to an indigenous researcher, they will still select or prefer a non-indigenous researcher over an indigenous researcher. There are a number of reasons this happens, sometimes based on a deeply held view that indigenous people will never be good enough, or that indigenous researchers may divulge confidences within their own community, or that the researcher may have some hidden agenda. For quite legitimate reasons the indigenous researcher may not be the best person for the research, or may be rejected because they do not have sufficient credibility. The point being made is that indigenous researchers work within a set of 'insider' dynamics and it takes considerable sensitivity, skill, maturity, experience and knowledge to work these issues through. Non-indigenous teachers and supervisors are often ill prepared to assist indigenous researchers in these areas and there are so few indigenous teachers that many students simply 'learn by doing'. They often get hurt and fail in the process. I have heard this articulated by indigenous researchers as 'being burned' or 'being done over'. The second part of the book provides some ways for thinking about such issues.

In writing a book that focuses on research I have drawn together a range of experiences and reflections on both indigenous and research issues. I have a childhood familiarity with museums, having helped my father – a Maori anthropologist – pursue his own research in the back rooms of the Auckland War Memorial Museum and other museums in the United States. I cannot really recollect how, specifically, I helped him because many of my strongest memories are of playing hide and seek in the cupboards and corridors. I do remember quite vividly, however, the ritual of cleansing ourselves by sprinkling water over us which my mother insisted on when we returned home. My grandmother was not too thrilled with the idea of my being in a museum at all. Many other Maori people, I was aware, were scared of what lay in the cupboards, of whose bones and whose ancestors were imprisoned in those cases. Later, my first ever paid job was as an assistant working at the Peabody Museum in Salem, Massachusetts. I helped my father, when required, to photograph intricately carved Marquesan adzes which ships of the East India Company had taken back from the Pacific to Salem. My paid job was to work in the basement of the museum typing labels to put on the logbooks of ships which had sailed from New England during the American Revolution. What was especially ironic was that there I was, a 16-year-old Maori, in the basement of a museum in Salem, Massachussetts, working on material related to the American Revolution – and none of it was new to me! I had already had a strong diet of British, European and American history.

In a sense, then, I grew up in a world in which science and our own indigenous beliefs and practices coexisted. I did not become an anthropologist, and although many indigenous writers would nominate anthropology as representative of all that is truly bad about research, it is not my intention to single out one discipline over another as representative of what research has done to indigenous peoples. I argue that, in their foundations, Western disciplines are as much implicated in each other as they are in imperialism. Some, such as anthropology, made the study of us into 'their' science, others were employed in the practices of imperialism in less direct but far more devastating ways. My own academic background is in education, and in my field there is a very rich history of research which attempts to legitimate views about indigenous peoples which have been antagonistic and dehumanizing. Discussions around the concept of intelligence, on discipline, or on factors that contribute to achievement depend heavily on notions about the Other. The organization of school knowledge, the hidden curriculum and the representation of difference in texts and school practices all contain discourses which have serious implications for indigenous students as well as for other minority ethnic groups.

My own career in research began in the health field, working along-side a team of respiratory physicians, paediatricians, epidemiologists and psychologists who were trying to make sense of the ways families manage asthma in young children. As coordinator of this project I had to learn very quickly how to participate in discussions on a wide range of matters, how to gain access to some very serious bureaucratic systems such as hospital wards and emergency clinics, and how to talk about research to a range of audiences, from medical doctors to families with limited English language. I enjoyed the challenges of thinking about what things mean, about why things happen and about the different ways in which the world can be understood. I also enjoyed interviewing people and, even more, analyzing the responses they gave. While I enjoyed the hands-on level at which I was working I found that the more rewarding work involved me in trying to 'think through' a problem, 'working with' the data and bringing it together with my own readings. Mostly, however, I found that the particular issues I faced as an indigenous researcher working with indigenous research participants were never addressed by the literature, my own training or the researchers with whom I worked. Later I became involved in other research projects in education, evaluation, tribal research and community-based projects. I began to teach others about research and have since become involved in managing much larger research projects that train indigenous and non-indigenous researchers. I have spoken about research to First Nations peoples in Canada, to Hawai'ian and other Pacific Islands researchers, and to Aborigine audiences as well as to many Maori groups who have become active as research communities. I supervise indigenous students carrying out their research projects, participate in research groups and lead some of my own projects.

In positioning myself as an indigenous woman, I am claiming a genealogical, cultural and political set of experiences. My *whakapapa* or descent lines come through both my parents. Through them I belong to two different major 'tribal' groups and have close links to others.[16] In my case, these links were nurtured through my early years by my extended family relationships and particularly by my maternal grandmother. It is through my grandmother that my sense of place became so firmly grounded. That was especially important because my parents worked away from either of their tribal territories. My grandmother insisted, and my parents supported this although she gave them no choice, that I return to her as often as possible. When I had to return to my parents she would pack food parcels for me just in case they did not feed me well enough! Although she developed in me the spiritual relationships to the land, to our tribal mountain and river, she also developed a sense of quite physical groundedness, a sense of reality, and a sense of humour about ourselves. It may be those qualities that make me sceptical or cautious about the mystical, misty-eyed discourse that is sometimes employed by indigenous people to describe our relationships with the land and the universe. I believe that our survival as peoples has come from our knowledge of our contexts, our environment, not from some active beneficence of our Earth Mother. We had to know to survive. We had to work out ways of knowing, we had to predict, to learn and reflect, we had to preserve and protect, we had to defend and attack, we had to be mobile, we had to have social systems which enabled us to do these things. We still have to do these things.

Politically, my dissent lines come down through my tribal lines but also through my experiences as a result of schooling and an urban background. One of my tribes, Ngati Awa, is part of what is referred to as the *raupatu*. The *raupatu* refers to those tribes whose territories were invaded and whose lands were confiscated by the New Zealand Government last century. The grievances which have come about through the *raupatu* form the basis of our claim to the Waitangi Tribunal. That particular dissent line is part of a legacy shared by many other indigenous peoples. My other dissent lines, however, were shaped by the urban Maori activism which occurred in New Zealand in the late 1960s and early 1970s. I belonged to one group, Nga Tamatoa or 'Young Warriors', and was at one point its secretary. We had several aims, although the main two were the recognition of the Treaty of Waitangi and the compulsory teaching of our language in schools. We formed a number of different alliances with other radical groups and some of our members belonged simultaneously to two or three groups. One of my roles was to educate younger Maori students about our aims. This took me into school assemblies and to situations where young people gathered. From those beginnings I became a primary or elementary teacher, then a secondary school counsellor, a health researcher and then a lecturer at university. While my professional career was developing I also helped in the early development of Te Kohanga Reo, the Maori language nests, and was one of the group which initiated an alternative Maori elementary school movement known as Kura Kaupapa Maori. I write, therefore, from the position of an indigenous Maori woman from New Zealand. Like indigenous peoples in Australia, Canada, the United States and Western Europe I write from the context of the First World, a world described in Julian Burger's *Report from the Frontier* simply as rich.[17] Despite the very powerful issues which locate many First World indigenous peoples in Third World social conditions we still, comparatively speaking, occupy a place of privilege within the world of indigenous peoples. That does not mean that indigenous peoples from the First World have better ideas or know anything more. It may mean that such things as access to food and water can be taken for granted or that the politics of food and water can be played out in vastly different ways within the First World than is possible within developing states.

One of the many criticisms that gets levelled at indigenous

intellectuals or activists is that our Western education precludes us from writing or speaking from a 'real' and authentic indigenous position. Of course, those who do speak from a more 'traditional' indigenous point of view are criticized because they do not make sense ('speak English, what!'). Or, our talk is reduced to some 'nativist' discourse, dismissed by colleagues in the academy as naïve, contradictory and illogical. Alternatively it may be dismissed as some modernist invention of the primitive. Criticism is levelled by non-indigenous and indigenous communities. It positions indigenous intellectuals in some difficult spaces both in terms of our relations with indigenous communities and within the Western academy. It is not a new phenomenon either, the matter having been addressed previously by Frantz Fanon, for example. More recent writers have situated discussions about the intellectual within debates about post-colonialism.[18] Many indigenous intellectuals actively resist participating in any discussion within the discourses of post-coloniality. This is because post-colonialism is viewed as the convenient invention of Western intellectuals which reinscribes their power to define the world. For each indigenous intellectual who actually succeeds in the academy, however – and we are talking relatively small numbers – there is a whole array of issues about the ways we relate inside and outside of our own communities, inside and outside the academy, and between all those different worlds.

Language and the citing of texts are often the clearest markers of the theoretical traditions of a writer. In this book I draw on selected ideas, scholarship and literature. These may or may not be attributed to either Western or indigenous traditions. I say that because like many other writers I would argue that 'we', indigenous peoples, people 'of colour', the Other, however we are named, have a presence in the Western imagination, in its fibre and texture, in its sense of itself, in its language, in its silences and shadows, its margins and intersections. The selection of ideas has been informed by a preference for, and a grounding in, particular forms of analysis which are probably already evident. Like many other Maori undergraduate students who attended university in the 1970s I read some texts for my formal course of study and another set of alternative readings to keep sane, to keep connected to the rest of my life and, more importantly, to make sense of things that were happening around me. Much of that alternative reading course is now collected in anthologies labelled as cultural studies.

In addition to this literature, however, are the stories, values, practices and ways of knowing which continue to inform indigenous pedagogies. In international meetings and networks of indigenous peoples, oracy, debate, formal speech making, structured silences and other conventions which shape oral traditions remain a most important way of developing trust, sharing information, strategies, advice, contacts and ideas. In Maori language there is the expression *Kanohi kitea* or the 'seen face', which conveys the sense that being seen by the people – showing your face, turning up at important cultural events – cements your membership within a community in an ongoing way and is part of how one's credibility is continually developed and maintained.[19] In First Nations and Native American communities there are protocols of being respectful, of showing or accepting respect and reciprocating respectful behaviours, which also develop membership, credibility and reputation. In Hawai'i *kanaka Maoli,* or native Hawai'ian researchers, have talked of the many aunties, uncles and elders whose views must be sought prior to conducting any interviews in a community. In Australia Aborigine researchers speak also of the many levels of entry which must be negotiated when researchers seek information. Other indigenous researchers speak of the long-term relationships which are established and extend beyond a research relationship to one involving families, communities, organizations and networks.

Some methodologies regard the values and beliefs, practices and customs of communities as 'barriers' to research or as exotic customs with which researchers need to be familiar in order to carry out their work without causing offence. Indigenous methodologies tend to approach cultural protocols, values and behaviours as an integral part of methodology. They are 'factors' to be built in to research explicitly, to be thought about reflexively, to be declared openly as part of the research design, to be discussed as part of the final results of a study and to be disseminated back to the people in culturally appropriate ways and in a language that can be understood. This does not preclude writing for academic publications but is simply part of an ethical and respectful approach. There are diverse ways of disseminating knowledge and of ensuring that research reaches the people who have helped make it. Two important ways not always addressed by scientific research are to do with 'reporting back' to the people and 'sharing knowledge'. Both ways assume a principle of reciprocity and feedback.

Reporting back to the people is never ever a one-off exercise or a task that can be signed off on completion of the written report. Some of my students have presented their work in formal ceremonies to family and tribal councils; one has had his work positioned amongst the wreaths which have surrounded the casket of a deceased relation. I have travelled with another student back to an area where she carried out her interviews so that she could present copies of her work to the people she interviewed. The family was waiting for her; they cooked food and made us welcome. We left knowing that her work will be passed around the family to be read and eventually will have a place in the living room along with other valued family books and family photographs. Other indigenous students have presented a symposium on their research into native schools to an international conference, or given a paper to an academic audience. Some have been able to develop strategies and community-based initiatives directly from their own research projects. Some have taken a theoretical approach to a problem and through their analyses have shown new ways of thinking about issues of concern to indigenous peoples.

Sharing knowledge is also a long-term commitment. It is much easier for researchers to hand out a report and for organizations to distribute pamphlets than to engage in continuing knowledge-sharing processes. For indigenous researchers, however, this is what is expected of us as we live and move within our various communities. The old colonial adage that knowledge is power is taken seriously in indigenous communities and many processes have been discussed and enacted in order to facilitate effective ways of sharing knowledge. Indigenous communities probably know more than the dominant white community about issues raised by the Human Genome Diversity Project, for example, or the General Agreement on Tariffs and Trade (GATT) agreement. I recall, when attending the Indigenous Peoples World Conference on Education in Woollongong, New South Wales, an Aborigine woman telling me that 'we are always waiting for them [white Australia] to catch up. They still don't know.' I use the term 'sharing knowledge' deliberately, rather than the term 'sharing information' because to me the responsibility of researchers and academics is not simply to share surface information (pamphlet knowledge) but to share the theories and analyses which inform the way knowledge and information are constructed and represented. By taking this approach seriously it is possible to introduce communities and people who may have had little formal schooling to a wider world, a world which includes people who think just like them, who share in their struggles and dreams and who voice their concerns in similar sorts of ways. To assume in advance that people will not be interested in, or will not understand, the deeper issues is arrogant. The challenge always is to demystify, to decolonize.

In reading this book you may well think that it is an anti-research book on research. There is certainly a history of research of indigenous peoples which continues to make indigenous students who encounter this history very angry. Sometimes they react by deciding never to do any research; but then they go out into the community and, because of their educational background and skills they are called upon to carry out projects or feasibility studies or evaluations or to write submissions that are based on information, data, archival records and interviews with elders. They are referred to as project workers, community activists or consultants, anything but 'researchers'. They search and record, they select and interpret, they organize and re-present, they make claims on the basis of what they assemble. This is research. The processes they use can also be called methodologies. The specific tools they use to gain information can also be called methods. Everything they are trying to do is informed by a theory, regardless of whether they can talk about that theory explicitly.

Finally, a brief comment on non-indigenous researchers still researching with indigenous peoples or about indigenous issues. Clearly, there have been some shifts in the way non-indigenous researchers and academics have positioned themselves and their work in relation to the people for whom the research still counts. It is also clear, however, that there are powerful groups of researchers who resent indigenous people asking questions about their research and whose research paradigms constantly permit them to exploit indigenous peoples and their knowledges. On the positive side, in the New Zealand context, work is being carried out in terms of bicultural research, partnership research and multi-disciplinary research. Other researchers have had to clarify their research aims and think more seriously about effective and ethical ways of carrying out research with indigenous peoples. Still others have developed ways of working with indigenous peoples on a variety of projects in an ongoing and mutually beneficial way. The discussion about what that means for non-indigenous researchers and for indigenous peoples is not addressed here directly. It is not that I do not have views on the matter but rather that the present work has grown out of a concern to develop indigenous peoples as researchers. There is so little material that addresses the issues indigenous researchers face. The book is written primarily to help ourselves.

Notes

1 Thompson, A. S. (1859), *The Story of New Zealand. Past and Present – Savage and Civilised*, John Murray, London. Thompson writes that, 'This comparative smallness of the brain is produced by neglecting to exercise the higher faculties of the mind, for as muscles shrink from want of use, it is only natural that generations of mental indolence should lessen the size of brains', Vol. 1, p. 81.

2 Said, E. (1978), *Orientalism*, Vintage Books, London, p. 2.

3 *Ibid.* p. 3.

4 See, for a summary of issues, Burger, J. (1987), *Report from the Frontier. The State of the World's Indigenous Peoples*, Zed Books, London.

5 Collins, Patricia Hill (1991), 'Learning from the Outsider Within: the Sociological Significance of Black Feminist Thought', in *Beyond Methodology. Feminist Research as*

Lived Research, eds M. M. Fonow and J. A. Cook, Indiana University Press, Bloomington.

6 Aga Khan, Sadruddin, and Hassan bin Talal (1987), *Indigenous Peoples, a Global Quest for Justice: a Report for the Independent Commission on International Humanitarian Affairs*, Zed Books, London.

7 For background see *ibid.* and Wilmer, F. (1993), *The Indigenous Voice in World Politics*, Sage, California.

8 Burger, J. (1990), *The Gaia Atlas of First Peoples*, Gaia Books, London.

9 Wilmer, *The Indigenous Voice*, p. 5.

10 I am not quite sure who said it first but several writers and texts have employed this concept in their titles and writing. Salman Rushdie wrote that the 'Empire writes back to the center'. African American women writers have taken the theme of 'talking back' or 'back chat' in similar ways to which Maori women speak of 'answering back'. Also important was a critical text on racism in Britain written by the Center for Contemporary Cultural Studies, University of Birmingham (1982): *The Empire Strikes Back: Race and Racism in 1970s Britain*, Hutchinson.

11 Nandy, A. (1989), *The Intimate Enemy: Loss and Recovery of Self under Colonialism*, Oxford University Press, Delhi.

12 Memmi, A. (1965), *The Colonizer and the Colonized*, expanded edition (1991), Beacon Press Boston, pp. 79–89.

13 Maracle, L. (1996), *I Am Woman. A Native Perspective on Sociology and Feminism*, Press Gang Publishers, Vancouver, p. 21.

14 Johnston, P. and L. Pihama, (1994), 'The Marginalisation of Maori Women', in *Hecate*, Vol. 20, No. 2, pp. 83–97.

15 See for example, Smith, L. T. (1985), 'Te Rapunga I Te Ao Maori', in *Issues of Research and Maori,* eds, G. H. Smith and M. K. Hohepa, Research Unit for Maori Education, Education Department, University of Auckland.

16 The term 'tribal' is problematic in the indigenous context but is used commonly in New Zealand to refer to large kinship-based, political groupings of Maori. Our preferred name for a 'tribe' is *iwi*.

17 Burger, *Report From the Frontier*, pp. 177–208.

18 See, for example, essays by Spivak, Gayatri (1990), *The Post-Colonial Critic*, ed. S. Harasym, Routledge, New York.

19 Bishop, R. and T. Glynn (1992), 'He Kanohi Kitea: Conducting and Evaluating Educational Research', in *New Zealand Journal of Educational Studies*, Vol. 27, No. 2, pp. 125–35.

CHAPTER 1

Imperialism, History, Writing and Theory

The master's tools will never dismantle the master's house.

Audre Lorde[1]

Imperialism frames the indigenous experience. It is part of our story, our version of modernity. Writing about our experiences under imperialism and its more specific expression of colonialism has become a significant project of the indigenous world. In a literary sense this has been defined by writers like Salman Rushdie, Ngugi wa Thiong'o and many others whose literary origins are grounded in the landscapes, languages, cultures and imaginative worlds of peoples and nations whose own histories were interrupted and radically reformulated by European imperialism. While the project of creating this literature is important, what indigenous activists would argue is that imperialism cannot be struggled over only at the level of text and literature. Imperialism still hurts, still destroys and is reforming itself constantly. Indigenous peoples as an international group have had to challenge, understand and have a shared language for talking about the history, the sociology, the psychology and the politics of imperialism and colonialism as an epic story telling of huge devastation, painful struggle and persistent survival. We have become quite good at talking that kind of talk, most often amongst ourselves, for ourselves and to ourselves. 'The talk' about the colonial past is embedded in our political discourses, our humour, poetry, music, story telling and other common sense ways of passing on both a narrative of history and an attitude about history. The lived experiences of imperialism and colonialism contribute another dimension to the ways in which terms like 'imperialism' can be understood. This is a dimension that indigenous peoples know and understand well.

In this chapter the intention is to discuss and contextualise four concepts which are often present (though not necessarily clearly visible) in the ways in which the ideas of indigenous peoples are articulated;

imperialism, history, writing, and theory. These terms may seem to make up a strange selection, particularly as there are more obvious concepts such as self-determination or sovereignty which are used commonly in indigenous discourses. I have selected these words because from an indigenous perspective they are problematic. They are words which tend to provoke a whole array of feelings, attitudes and values. They are words of emotion which draw attention to the thousands of ways in which indigenous languages, knowledges and cultures have been silenced or misrepresented, ridiculed or condemned in academic and popular discourses. They are also words which are used in particular sorts of ways or avoided altogether. In thinking about knowledge and research, however, these are important terms which underpin the practices and styles of research with indigenous peoples. Decolonization is a process which engages with imperialism and colonialism at multiple levels. For researchers, one of those levels is concerned with having a more critical understanding of the underlying assumptions, motivations and values which inform research practices.

Imperialism

There is one particular figure whose name looms large, and whose spectre lingers, in indigenous discussions of encounters with the West: Christopher Columbus. It is not simply that Columbus is identified as the one who started it all, but rather that he has come to represent a huge legacy of suffering and destruction. Columbus 'names' that legacy more than any other individual.[2] He sets its modern time frame (500 years) and defines the outer limits of that legacy, that is, total destruction.[3] But there are other significant figures who symbolize and frame indigenous experiences in other places. In the imperial literature these are the 'heroes', the discoverers and adventurers, the 'fathers' of colonialism. In the indigenous literature these figures are not so admired; their deeds are definitely not the deeds of wonderful discoverers and conquering heroes. In the South Pacific, for example it is the British explorer James Cook, whose expeditions had a very clear scientific purpose and whose first encounters with indigenous peoples were fastidiously recorded. Hawai'ian academic Haunani Kay Trask's list of what Cook brought to the Pacific includes: 'capitalism, Western political ideas (such as predatory individualism) and Christianity. Most destructive of all he brought diseases that ravaged my people until we were but a remnant of what we had been on contact with his pestilent crew.'[4] The French are remembered by Tasmanian Aborigine Greg Lehman, 'not [for] the intellectual hubbub of an emerging anthrologie or even with the swish of their travel-weary frocks. It is with an arrogant death that they presaged their appearance....'[5] For many communities there were waves of different sorts of Europeans; Dutch, Portuguese, British, French, whoever had political ascendancy over a region. And, in each place, after figures such as Columbus and Cook had long departed, there came a vast array of military personnel, imperial administrators, priests, explorers, missionaries, colonial officials, artists, entrepreneurs and settlers, who cut a devastating swathe, and left a permanent wound, on the societies and communities who occupied the lands named and claimed under imperialism.

The concepts of imperialism and colonialism are crucial ones which are used across a range of disciplines, often with meanings which are taken for granted. The two terms are interconnected and what is generally agreed upon is that colonialism is but one expression of imperialism. Imperialism tends to be used in at least four different ways when describing the form of European imperialism which 'started' in the fifteenth century: (1) imperialism as economic expansion; (2) imperialism as the subjugation of 'others'; (3) imperialism as an idea or spirit with many forms of realization; and (4) imperialism as a discursive field of knowledge. These usages do not necessarily contradict each other; rather, they need to be seen as analyses which focus on different layers of imperialism. Initially the term was used by historians to explain a series of developments leading to the economic expansion of Europe. Imperialism in this sense could be tied to a chronology of events related to 'discovery', conquest, exploitation, distribution and appropriation.

Economic explanations of imperialism were first advanced by English historian J. A. Hobson in 1902 and by Lenin in 1917.[6] Hobson saw imperialism as being an integral part of Europe's economic expansion. He attributed the later stages of nineteenth-century imperialism to the inability of Europeans to purchase what was being produced and the need for Europe's industrialists to shift their capital to new markets which were secure. Imperialism was the system of control which secured the markets and capital investments. Colonialism facilitated this expansion by ensuring that there was European control, which necessarily meant securing and subjugating the indigenous populations. Like Hobson, Lenin was concerned with the ways in which economic expansion was linked to imperialism, although he argued that the export of capital to new markets was an attempt to rescue capitalism because Europe's workers could not afford what was being produced.

A second use of the concept of imperialism focuses more upon the exploitation and subjugation of indigenous peoples. Although economic explanations might account for why people like Columbus were funded to explore and discover new sources of wealth, they do not account for the devastating impact on the indigenous peoples whose lands were invaded. By the time contact was made in the South Pacific, Europeans, and more particularly the British, had learned from their previous encounters with indigenous peoples and had developed much more sophisticated 'rules of practice'.[7] While these practices ultimately lead to forms of subjugation, they also lead to subtle nuances which give an unevenness to the story of imperialism, even within the story of one indigenous society. While in New Zealand all Maori tribes, for example, lost the majority of their lands, not all tribes had their lands confiscated, were invaded militarily or were declared to be in rebellion. Similarly, while many indigenous nations signed treaties, other indigenous communities have no treaties. Furthermore, legislated identities which regulated who was an Indian and who was not, who was a *metis*, who had lost all status as an indigenous person, who had the correct fraction of blood quantum, who lived in the regulated spaces of reserves and communities, were all worked out arbitrarily (but systematically), to serve the interests of the colonizing society. The specificities of imperialism help to explain the different ways in which indigenous peoples have struggled to recover histories, lands, languages and basic human dignity. The way arguments are framed, the way dissent is controlled, the way settlements are made, while certainly drawing from international precedents, are also situated within a more localized discursive field.

A third major use of the term is much broader. It links imperialism to the spirit which characterized Europe's global activities. MacKenzie defines imperialism as being 'more than a set of economic, political and military phenomena. It is also a complex ideology which had widespread cultural, intellectual and technical expressions'.[8] This view of imperialism locates it within the Enlightenment spirit which signalled the transformation of economic, political and cultural life in Europe. In this wider Enlightenment context, imperialism becomes an integral part of the development of the modern state, of science, of ideas and of the 'modern' human person. In complex ways imperialism was also a mode through which the new states of Europe could expand their economies, through which new ideas and discoveries could be made and harnessed, and through which Europeans could develop their sense of Europeanness. The imperial imagination enabled European nations to imagine the possibility that new worlds, new wealth and new possessions existed that could be discovered and controlled. This imagination was realized through the promotion of science, economic expansion and political practice.

These three interpretations of imperialism have reflected a view from the imperial centre of Europe. In contrast, a fourth use of the term has been generated by writers whose understandings of imperialism and colonialism have been based either on their membership of and experience within colonized societies, or on their interest in understanding imperialism from the perspective of local contexts. Although these views of imperialism take into account the other forms of analysis, there are some important distinctions. There is, for example, a greater and more immediate need to understand the complex ways in which people were brought within the imperial system, because its impact is still being felt, despite the apparent independence gained by former colonial territories. The reach of imperialism into 'our heads' challenges those who belong to colonized communities to understand how this occurred, partly because we perceive a need to decolonize our minds, to recover ourselves, to claim a space in which to develop a sense of authentic humanity. This analysis of imperialism has been referred to more recently in terms such as 'post-colonial discourse', the 'empire writes back' and/or 'writing from the margins'. There is a more political body of writing, however, which extends to the revolutionary, anticolonial work of various activists (only some of whom, such as Frantz Fanon, actually wrote their ideas down) that draws also upon the work of black and African American writers and other minority writers whose work may have emerged out of a concern for human and civil rights, the rights of women and other forms of oppression.

Colonialism became imperialism's outpost, the fort and the port of imperial outreach. Whilst colonies may have started as a means to secure ports, access to raw materials and efficient transfer of commodities from point of origin to the imperial centre, they also served other functions. It was not just indigenous populations who had to be subjugated. Europeans also needed to be kept under control, in service to the greater imperial enterprise. Colonial outposts were also cultural sites which preserved an image or represented an image of what the West or 'civilization' stood for. Colonies were not exact replicas of the imperial centre, culturally, economically or politically. Europeans resident in the colonies were not culturally homogeneous, so there were struggles within the colonizing community about its own identity. Wealth and class status created very powerful settler interests which came to dominate the politics of a colony. Colonialism was, in part, an image of imperialism, a particular realization of the imperial imagination. It was also, in part, an image of the future nation it would become. In this image lie images of the Other, stark contrasts and subtle nuances, of the ways in which the indigenous communities were perceived and dealt with, which make the stories of colonialism part of a grander narrative and yet part also of a very local, very specific experience.

A constant reworking of our understandings of the impact of imperialism and colonialism is an important aspect of indigenous cultural politics and forms the basis of an indigenous language of critique. Within this critique there have been two major strands. One draws upon a notion of authenticity, of a time before colonization in which we were intact as indigenous peoples. We had absolute authority over our lives; we were born into and lived in a universe which was entirely of our making. We did not ask, need or want to be 'discovered' by Europe. The second strand of the language of critique demands that we have an analysis of how we were colonized, of what that has meant in terms of our immediate past and what it means for our present and future. The two strands intersect but what is particularly significant in indigenous discourses is that solutions are posed from a combination of the time before, *colonized time*, and the time before that, *pre-colonized time*. Decolonization encapsulates both sets of ideas.

There are, however, new challenges to the way indigenous peoples think and talk about imperialism. When the word globalization is substituted for the word imperialism, or when the prefix 'post' is attached to colonial, we are no longer talking simply about historical formations which are still lingering in our consciousness. Globalization and conceptions of a new world order represent different sorts of challenges for indigenous peoples. While being on the margins of the world has had dire consequences, being incorporated within the world's marketplace has different implications and in turn requires the mounting of new forms of resistance. Similarly, post-colonial discussions have also stirred some indigenous resistance, not so much to the literary reimagining of culture as being centred in what were once conceived of as the colonial margins, but to the idea that colonialism is over, finished business. This is best articulated by Aborigine activist Bobbi Sykes, who asked at an academic conference on post-colonialism, 'What? Post-colonialism? Have they left?' There is also, amongst indigenous academics, the sneaking suspicion that the fashion of post-colonialism has become a strategy for reinscribing or reauthorizing the privileges of non-indigenous academics because the field of 'post-colonial' discourse has been defined in ways which can still leave out indigenous peoples, our ways of knowing and our current concerns.

Research within late-modern and late-colonial conditions continues relentlessly and brings with it a new wave of exploration, discovery, exploitation and appropriation. Researchers enter communities armed with goodwill in their front pockets and patents in their back pockets, they bring medicine into villages and extract blood for genetic analysis. No matter how appalling their behaviours, how insensitive and offensive their personal actions may be, their acts and intentions are always justified as being for the 'good of mankind'. Research of this nature *on* indigenous peoples is still justified by the ends rather than the means, particularly if the indigenous peoples concerned can still be positioned as ignorant and undeveloped (savages). Other researchers gather traditional herbal and medicinal remedies and remove them for analysis in laboratories around the world. Still others collect the intangibles: the belief systems and ideas about healing, about the universe, about relationships and ways of organizing, and the practices and rituals which go alongside such beliefs, such as sweat lodges, massage techniques, chanting, hanging crystals and wearing certain colours. The global hunt for new knowledges, new materials, new cures, supported by international agreements such as the General Agreement on Tariffs and Trade (GATT) brings new threats to indigenous communities. The ethics of research, the ways in which indigenous communities can protect themselves and their knowledges, the understandings required not just of state legislation but of international agreements – these are the topics now on the agenda of many indigenous meetings.

On Being Human

The faculty of imagination is not strongly developed among them, although they permitted it to run wild in believing absurd superstitions.

(A. S. Thompson, 1859)[9]

One of the supposed characteristics of primitive peoples was that we could not use our minds or intellects. We could not invent things, we could not create institutions or history, we could not imagine, we could not produce anything of value, we did not know how to use land and other resources from the natural world, we did not practice the 'arts' of civilization. By lacking such virtues we disqualified ourselves, not just from civilization but from humanity itself. In other words we were not 'fully human'; some of us were not even considered partially human. Ideas about what counted as human in association with the power to define people as human or not human were already encoded in imperial and colonial discourses prior to the period of imperialism covered here.[10] Imperialism provided the means through which concepts of what counts as human could be applied systematically as forms of classification, for example through hierarchies of race and typologies of different societies. In conjunction with imperial power and with 'science', these classification systems came to shape relations between imperial powers and indigenous societies.

Said has argued that the 'oriental' was partially a creation of the West, based on a combination of images formed through scholarly and imaginative works. Fanon argued earlier that the colonized were brought into existence by the settler and the two, settler and colonized, are

mutual constructions of colonialism. In Fanon's words 'we know each
other well'.[11] The European powers had by the nineteenth century
already established systems of rule and forms of social relations which
governed interaction with the indigenous peoples being colonized. These
relations were gendered, hierarchical and supported by rules, some
explicit and others masked or hidden. The principle of 'humanity' was
one way in which the implicit or hidden rules could be shaped. To
consider indigenous peoples as not fully human, or not human at all,
enabled distance to be maintained and justified various policies of either
extermination or domestication. Some indigenous peoples ('not human'),
were hunted and killed like vermin, others ('partially human'), were
rounded up and put in reserves like creatures to be broken in, branded
and put to work.

The struggle to assert and claim humanity has been a consistent
thread of anti-colonial discourses on colonialism and oppression. This
struggle for humanity has generally been framed within the wider
discourse of humanism, the appeal to human 'rights', the notion of a
universal human subject, and the connections between being human and
being capable of creating history, knowledge and society. The focus on
asserting humanity has to be seen within the anti-colonial analysis of
imperialism and what were seen as imperialism's dehumanizing imperatives which were structured into language, the economy, social relations
and the cultural life of colonial societies. From the nineteenth century
onwards the processes of dehumanization were often hidden behind
justifications for imperialism and colonialism which were clothed within
an ideology of humanism and liberalism and the assertion of moral
claims which related to a concept of civilized 'man'. The moral justifications did not necessarily stop the continued hunting of Aborigines in
the early nineteenth century nor the continued ill-treatment of different
indigenous peoples even today.

Problems have arisen, however, within efforts to struggle for
humanity by overthrowing the ideologies relating to our supposed lack
of humanity. The arguments of Fanon, and many writers since Fanon,
have been criticized for essentializing our 'nature', for taking for granted
the binary categories of Western thought, for accepting arguments
supporting cultural relativity, for claiming an authenticity which is overly
idealistic and romantic, and for simply engaging in an inversion of the
colonizer/colonized relationship which does not address the complex
problems of power relations. Colonized peoples have been compelled
to define what it means to be human because there is a deep understanding of what it has meant to be considered not fully human, to be
savage. The difficulties of such a process, however, have been bound
inextricably to constructions of colonial relations around the binary of

colonizer and colonized. These two categories are not just a simple opposition but consist of several relations, some more clearly oppositional than others. Unlocking one set of relations most often requires unlocking and unsettling the different constituent parts of other relations. The binary of colonizer/colonized does not take into account, for example, the development of different layerings which have occurred within each group and across the two groups. Millions of indigenous peoples were ripped from their lands over several generations and shipped into slavery. The lands they went to as slaves were lands already taken from another group of indigenous peoples. Slavery was as much a system of imperialism as was the claiming of other peoples' territories. Other indigenous peoples were transported to various outposts in the same way as interesting plants and animals were reclimatized, in order to fulfil labour requirements. Hence there are large populations in some places of non-indigenous groups, also victims of colonialism, whose primary relationship and allegiance is often to the imperial power rather than to the colonized people of the place to which they themselves have been brought. To put it simply, indigenous peoples as commodities were transported to and fro across the empire. There were also sexual relations between colonizers and colonized which led to communities who were referred to as 'half-castes' or 'half-breeds', or stigmatized by some other specific term which often excluded them from belonging to either settler or indigenous societies. Sometimes children from 'mixed' sexual relationships were considered at least half-way civilized; at other times they were considered worse than civilized. Legislation was frequently used to regulate both the categories to which people were entitled to belong and the sorts of relations which one category of people could have with another.

Since the Second World War wars of independence and struggles for decolonization by former parts of European empires have shown us that attempts to break free can involve enormous violence: physical, social, economic, cultural and psychological. The struggle for freedom has been viewed by writers such as Fanon as a necessarily, inevitably violent process between 'two forces opposed to each other by their very nature'.[12] Fanon argues further that 'Decolonization which sets out to change the order of the world is, obviously, a programme of complete disorder.'[13] This introduces another important principle embedded in imperialism, that of order. The principle of order provides the underlying connection between such things as: the nature of imperial social relations; the activities of Western science; the establishment of trade; the appropriation of sovereignty; the establishment of law. No great conspiracy had to occur for the simultaneous developments and activities which took place under imperialism because imperial activity was driven by fundamentally similar underlying principles. Nandy refers to these principles as the 'code' or 'grammar' of imperialism.[14] The idea of code suggests that there is a deep structure which regulates and legitimates imperial practices.

The fact that indigenous societies had their own systems of order was dismissed through what Albert Memmi referred to as a series of negations: they were not fully human, they were not civilized enough to have systems, they were not literate, their languages and modes of thought were inadequate.[15] As Fanon and later writers such as Nandy have claimed, imperialism and colonialism brought complete disorder to colonized peoples, disconnecting them from their histories, their landscapes, their languages, their social relations and their own ways of thinking, feeling and interacting with the world. It was a process of systematic fragmentation which can still be seen in the disciplinary carve-up of the indigenous world: bones, mummies and skulls to the museums, art work to private collectors, languages to linguistics, 'customs' to anthropologists, beliefs and behaviours to psychologists. To discover how fragmented this process was one needs only to stand in a museum, a library, a bookshop, and ask where indigenous peoples are located. Fragmentation is not a phenomenon of postmodernism as many might claim. For indigenous peoples fragmentation has been the consequence of imperialism.

Writing, History and Theory

A critical aspect of the struggle for self-determination has involved questions relating to our history as indigenous peoples and a critique of how we, as the Other, have been represented or excluded from various accounts. Every issue has been approached by indigenous peoples with a view to *re*writing and *re*righting our position in history. Indigenous peoples want to tell our own stories, write our own versions, in our own ways, for our own purposes. It is not simply about giving an oral account or a genealogical naming of the land and the events which raged over it, but a very powerful need to give testimony to and restore a spirit, to bring back into existence a world fragmented and dying. The sense of history conveyed by these approaches is not the same thing as the discipline of history, and so our accounts collide, crash into each other.

Writing or literacy, in a very traditional sense of the word, has been used to determine the breaks between the past and the present, the beginning of history and the development of theory.[16] Writing has been viewed as the mark of a superior civilization and other societies have been judged, by this view, to be incapable of thinking critically and objectively, or having distance from ideas and emotions. Writing is part of theorizing and writing is part of history. Writing, history and theory, then, are key sites in which Western research of the indigenous world have come together. As we saw at the beginning of this chapter, however, from another perspective writing and especially writing theory are very intimidating ideas for many indigenous students. Having been immersed in the Western academy which claims theory as thoroughly Western, which has constructed all the rules by which the indigenous world has been theorized, indigenous voices have been overwhelmingly silenced. The act, let alone the art and science, of theorizing our own existence and realities is not something which many indigenous people assume is possible. Frantz Fanon's call for the indigenous intellectual and artist to create a new literature, to work in the cause of constructing a national culture after liberation still stands as a challenge. While this has been taken up by writers of fiction, many indigenous scholars who work in the social and other sciences struggle to write, theorize and research as indigenous scholars.

Is History Important for Indigenous Peoples?

This may appear to be a trivial question as the answer most colonized people would give, I think, is that 'yes, history is important'. But I doubt if what they would be responding to is the notion of history which is understood by the Western academy. Poststructuralist critiques of history which draw heavily on French poststructural thought have focused on the characteristics and understandings of history as an Enlightenment or modernist project. Their critique is of both liberal and Marxist concepts of history. Feminists have argued similarly (but not necessarily from a poststructuralist position) that history is the story of a specific form of domination, namely of patriarchy, literally 'his-story'.

While acknowledging the critical approaches of poststructuralist theory and cultural studies the arguments which are debated at this level are not new to indigenous peoples. There are numerous oral stories which tell of what it means, what it feels like, to be present while your history is erased before your eyes, dismissed as irrelevant, ignored or rendered as the lunatic ravings of drunken old people. The negation of indigenous views of history was a critical part of asserting colonial ideology, partly because such views were regarded as clearly 'primitive' and 'incorrect' and mostly because they challenged and resisted the mission of colonization.

Indigenous peoples have also mounted a critique of the way history is told from the perspective of the colonizers. At the same time, however, indigenous groups have argued that history is important for understanding the present and that reclaiming history is a critical and essential aspect of decolonization. The critique of Western history argues that history is a modernist project which has developed alongside imperial beliefs about the Other. History is assembled around a set of interconnected ideas which I will summarize briefly here. I have drawn on a wide range of discussions by indigenous people and by writers such as Robert Young, J. Abu-Lughod, Keith Jenkins, C. Steadman.[17]

1. The idea that history is a totalizing discourse

The concept of totality assumes the possibility and the desirability of being able to include absolutely all known knowledge into a coherent whole. In order for this to happen, classification systems, rules of practice and methods had to be developed to allow for knowledge to be selected and included in what counts as history.

2. The idea that there is a universal history

Although linked to the notion of totality, the concept of universal assumes that there are fundamental characteristics and values which all human subjects and societies share. It is the development of these universal characteristics which are of historical interest.

3. The idea that history is one large chronology

History is regarded as being about developments over time. It charts the progress of human endeavour through time. Chronology is important as a method because it allows events to be located at a point in time. The actual time events take place also makes them 'real' or factual. In order to begin the chronology a time of 'discovery' has to be established. Chronology is also important for attempting to go backwards and explain how and why things happened in the past.

4. The idea that history is about development

Implicit in the notion of development is the notion of progress. This assumes that societies move forward in stages of development much as an infant grows into a fully developed adult human being. The earliest phase of human development is regarded as primitive, simple and emotional. As societies develop they become less primitive, more civilized, more rational, and their social structures become more complex and bureaucratic.

5. The idea that history is about a self-actualizing human subject

In this view humans have the potential to reach a stage in their development where they can be in total control of their faculties. There is an order of human development which moves, in stages, through the

fulfilment of basic needs, the development of emotions, the development of the intellect and the development of morality. Just as the
individual moves through these stages, so do societies.

6. The idea that the story of history can be told in one coherent narrative

This idea suggests that we can assemble all the facts in an ordered way
so that they tell us the truth or give us a very good idea of what really
did happen in the past. In theory it means that historians can write a
true history of the world.

7. The idea that history as a discipline is innocent

This idea says that 'facts' speak for themselves and that the historian
simply researches the facts and puts them together. Once all the known
facts are assembled they tell their own story, without any need of a
theoretical explanation or interpretation by the historian. This idea also
conveys the sense that history is pure as a discipline, that is, it is not
implicated with other disciplines.

8. The idea that history is constructed around binary categories

This idea is linked to the historical method of chronology. In order for
history to begin there has to be a period of beginning and some criteria
for determining when something begins. In terms of history this was
often attached to concepts of 'discovery', the development of literacy,
or the development of a specific social formation. Everything before
that time is designated as prehistorical, belonging to the realm of myths
and traditions, 'outside' the domain.

9. The idea that history is patriarchal

This idea is linked to the notions of self-actualization and development,
as women were regarded as being incapable of attaining the higher
orders of development. Furthermore they were not significant in terms
of the ways societies developed because they were not present in the
bureaucracies or hierarchies where changes in social or political life were
being determined.

Other key ideas

Intersecting this set of ideas are some other important concepts.
Literacy, as one example, was used as a criterion for assessing the
development of a society and its progress to a stage where history can
be said to begin. Even places such as India, China and Japan, however,
which were very literate cultures prior to their 'discovery' by the West,
were invoked through other categories which defined them as

uncivilized. Their literacy, in other words, did not count as a record of legitimate knowledge.

The German philosopher Hegel is usually regarded as the 'founding father' of history in the sense outlined here. This applies to both Liberal and Marxist views.[18] Hegel conceived of the fully human subject as someone capable of 'creating (his) own history'. However, Hegel did not simply invent the rules of history. As Robert Young argues, 'the entire Hegelian machinery simply lays down the operation of a system already in place, already operating in everyday life'.[19] It should also be self-evident that many of these ideas are predicated on a sense of Otherness. They are views which invite a comparison with 'something/someone else' which exists *on the outside*, such as the oriental, the 'Negro', the 'Jew', the 'Indian', the 'Aborigine'. Views about the Other had already existed for centuries in Europe, but during the Enlightenment these views became more formalized through science, philosophy and imperialism, into explicit systems of classification and 'regimes of truth'. The racialization of the human subject and the social order enabled comparisons to be made between the 'us' of the West and the 'them' of the Other. History was the story of people who were regarded as *fully human*. Others who were not regarded as human (that is, capable of self-actualization) were prehistoric. This notion is linked also to Hegel's master–slave construct which has been applied as a psychological category (by Freud) and as a system of social ordering.

A further set of important ideas embedded in the modernist view of history relates to the origins (causes) and nature of social change. The Enlightenment project involved new conceptions of society and of the individual based around the precepts of rationalism, individualism and capitalism. There was a general belief that not only could individuals remake themselves but so could societies. The modern industrial state became the point of contrast between the pre-modern and the modern. History in this view began with the emergence of the rational individual and the modern industrialized society. However, there is something more to this idea in terms of how history came to be conceptualized as a method. The connection to the industrial state is significant because it highlights what was regarded as being worthy of history. The people and groups who 'made' history were the people who developed the underpinnings of the state – the economists, scientists, bureaucrats and philosophers. That they were all men of a certain class and race was 'natural' because they were regarded (naturally) as fully rational, self-actualizing human beings capable, therefore, of creating social change, that is history. The day-to-day lives of 'ordinary' people, and of women, did not become a concern of history until much more recently.

Contested Histories

For indigenous peoples, the critique of history is not unfamiliar, although it has now been claimed by postmodern theories. The idea of contested stories and multiple discourses about the past, by different communities, is closely linked to the politics of everyday contemporary indigenous life. It is very much a part of the fabric of communities that value oral ways of knowing. These contested accounts are stored within genealogies, within the landscape, within weavings and carvings, even within the personal names that many people carried. The means by which these histories were stored was through their systems of knowledge. Many of these systems have since been reclassified as oral *traditions* rather than histories.

Under colonialism indigenous peoples have struggled against a Western view of history and yet been complicit with that view. We have often allowed our 'histories' to be told and have then become outsiders as we heard them being retold. Schooling is directly implicated in this process. Through the curriculum and its underlying theory of know-ledge, early schools redefined the world and where indigenous peoples were positioned within the world. From being direct descendants of sky and earth parents, Christianity positioned some of us as higher-order savages who deserved salvation in order that we could become children of God. Maps of the world reinforced our place on the periphery of the world, although we were still considered part of the Empire. This included having to learn new names for our own lands. Other symbols of our loyalty, such as the flag, were also an integral part of the imperial curriculum.[20] Our orientation to the world was already being redefined as we were being excluded systematically from the writing of the history of our own lands. This on its own may not have worked were it not for the actual material redefinition of our world which was occurring simultaneously through such things as the renaming and 'breaking in' of the land, the alienation and fragmentation of lands through legislation, the forced movement of people off their lands, and the social consequences which resulted in high sickness and mortality rates.

Indigenous attempts to reclaim land, language, knowledge and sovereignty have usually involved contested accounts of the past by colonizers and colonized. These have occurred in the courts, before various commissions, tribunals and official enquiries, in the media, in Parliament, in bars and on talkback radio. In these situations contested histories do not exist in the same cultural framework as they do when tribal or clan histories, for example, are being debated within the indigenous community itself. They are not simply struggles over 'facts' and 'truth'; the rules by which these struggles take place are never clear (other than that we as the indigenous community know they are going to be stacked against us); and we are not the final arbiters of what really counts as the truth.

It is because of these issues that I ask the question, 'Is history in its modernist construction important or not important for indigenous peoples?' For many people who are presently engaged in research on indigenous land claims the answer would appear to be self-evident. We assume that when 'the truth comes out' it will prove that what happened was wrong or illegal and that therefore the system (tribunals, the courts, the government) will set things right. We believe that history is also about justice, that understanding history will enlighten our decisions about the future. *Wrong*. History is also about power. In fact history is mostly about power. It is the story of the powerful and how they became powerful, and then how they use their power to keep them in positions in which they can continue to dominate others. It is because of this relationship with power that we have been excluded, marginalized and 'Othered'. In this sense history is not important for indigenous peoples because a thousand accounts of the 'truth' will not alter the 'fact' that indigenous peoples are still marginal and do not possess the power to transform history into justice.

This leads then to several other questions. The one which is most relevant to this book is the one which asks, ' Why then has revisiting history been a significant part of decolonization?' The answer, I suggest, lies in the intersection of indigenous approaches to the past, of the modernist history project itself and of the resistance strategies which have been employed. Our colonial experience traps us in the project of modernity. There can be no 'postmodern' for us until we have settled some business of the modern. This does not mean that we do not understand or employ multiple discourses, or act in incredibly contra-dictory ways, or exercise power ourselves in multiple ways. It means that there is unfinished business, that we are still being colonized (and know it), and that we are still searching for justice.

Coming to know the past has been part of the critical pedagogy of decolonization. To hold alternative histories is to hold alternative knowledges. The pedagogical implication of this access to alternative knowledges is that they can form the basis of alternative ways of doing things. Transforming our colonized views of our own history (as written by the West), however, requires us to revisit, site by site, our history under Western eyes. This in turn requires a theory or approach which helps us to engage with, understand and then act upon history. It is in this sense that the sites visited in this book begin with a critique of a Western view of history. Telling our stories from the past, reclaiming the past, giving testimony to the injustices of the past are all strategies which are commonly employed by indigenous peoples struggling for justice. On the international scene it is extremely rare and unusual when indigenous accounts are accepted and acknowledged as valid interpretations of what has taken place. And yet, the need to tell our stories remains the powerful imperative of a powerful form of resistance.

Is Writing Important for Indigenous Peoples?

As I am arguing, every aspect of the act of producing knowledge has influenced the ways in which indigenous ways of knowing have been represented. Reading, writing, talking, these are as fundamental to academic discourse as science, theories, methods, paradigms. To begin with reading, one might cite the talk in which Maori writer Patricia Grace undertook to show that 'Books Are Dangerous'.[21] She argues that there are four things that make many books dangerous to indigenous readers: (1) they do not reinforce our values, actions, customs, culture and identity; (2) when they tell us only about others they are saying that we do not exist; (3) they may be writing about us but are writing things which are untrue; and (4) they are writing about us but saying negative and insensitive things which tell us that we are not good. Although Grace is talking about school texts and journals, her comments apply also to academic writing. Much of what I have read has said that we do not exist, that if we do exist it is in terms which I cannot recognize, that we are no good and that what we think is not valid.

Leonie Pihama makes a similar point about film. In a review of *The Piano* she says: 'Maori people struggle to gain a voice, struggle to be heard from the margins, to have our stories heard, to have our descriptions of ourselves validated, to have access to the domain within which we can control and define those images which are held up as reflections of our realities.'[22] Representation is important as a concept because it gives the impression of 'the truth'. When I read texts, for example, I frequently have to orientate myself to a text world in which the centre of academic knowledge is either in Britain, the United States or Western Europe; in which words such as 'we', 'us', 'our', 'I' actually exclude me. It is a text world in which (if what I am interested in rates a mention) I have learned that I belong *partly* in the Third World, *partly* in the 'Women of Colour' world, *partly* in the black or African world. I read myself into these labels *partly* because I have also learned that, although there may be commonalities, they still do not entirely account for the experiences of indigenous peoples.

So, reading and interpretation present problems when we do not see ourselves in the text. There are problems, too, when we do see ourselves but can barely recognize ourselves through the representation. One problem of being trained to read this way, or, more correctly, of learning to read this way over many years of academic study, is that we can adopt uncritically similar patterns of writing. We begin to write about ourselves as indigenous peoples as if we really were 'out there', the 'Other', with all the baggage that this entails. Another problem is that academic writing is a form of selecting, arranging and presenting knowledge. It privileges sets of texts, views about the history of an idea, what issues count as significant; and, by engaging in the same process uncritically, we too can render indigenous writers invisible or unimportant while reinforcing the validity of other writers. If we write without thinking critically about our writing, it can be dangerous. Writing can also be dangerous because we reinforce and maintain a style of discourse which is never innocent. Writing can be dangerous because sometimes we reveal ourselves in ways which get misappropriated and used against us. Writing can be dangerous because, by building on previous texts written about indigenous peoples, we continue to legitimate views about ourselves which are hostile to us. This is particularly true of academic writing, although journalistic and imaginative writing reinforce these 'myths'.

These attitudes inform what is sometimes referred to as either the 'Empire writes back' discourse or post-colonial literature. This kind of writing assumes that the centre does not necessarily have to be located at the imperial centre.[23] It is argued that the centre can be shifted ideologically through imagination and that this shifting can recreate history. Another perspective relates to the ability of 'native' writers to appropriate the language of the colonizer as the language of the colonized and to write so that it captures the ways in which the colonized actually use the language, their dialects and inflections, and in the way they make sense of their lives. Its other importance is that it speaks to an audience of people who have also been colonized. This is one of the ironies of many indigenous peoples' conferences where issues of indigenous language have to be debated in the language of the colonizers. Another variation of the debate relates to the use of literature to write about the terrible things which happened under colonialism or as a consequence of colonialism. These topics inevitably implicated the colonizers *and their literature* in the processes of cultural domination.

Yet another position, espoused in African literature by Ngugi wa Thiong'o, was to write in the languages of Africa. For Ngugi wa Thiong'o, to write in the language of the colonizers was to pay homage to them, while to write in the languages of Africa was to engage in an anti-imperialist struggle. He argued that language carries culture and the language of the colonizer became the means by which the 'mental universe of the colonized' was dominated.[24] This applied, in Ngugi wa Thiong'o's view, particularly to the language of writing. Whereas oral languages were frequently still heard at home, the use of literature in association with schooling resulted in the alienation of a child from the child's history, geography, music and other aspects of culture.[25]

In discussing the politics of academic writing, in which research writing is a subset, Cherryl Smith argues that 'colonialism, racism and cultural imperialism do not occur only in society, outside of the gates of universities'.[26] Academic writing, she continues, is a way of '"writing back" whilst at the same time writing to ourselves'.[27] The act of 'writing back' and simultaneously writing to ourselves is not simply an inversion of how we have learned to write academically.[28] The different audiences to whom we speak makes the task somewhat difficult. The scope of the literature which we use in our work contributes to a different framing of the issues. The oral arts and other forms of expression set our landscape in a different frame of reference. Our understandings of the academic disciplines within which we have been trained also frame our approaches. Even the use of pronouns such as 'I' and 'we' can cause difficulties when writing for several audiences, because while it may be acceptable now in academic writing, it is not always acceptable to indigenous audiences.[29]

Edward Said also asks the following questions: 'Who writes? For whom is the writing being done? In what circumstances? These it seems to me are the questions whose answers provide us with the ingredients making a politics of interpretation.'[30] These questions are important ones which are being asked in a variety of ways within our communities. They are asked, for example, about research, policy making and curriculum development. Said's comments, however, point to the problems of interpretation, in this case of academic writing. 'Who' is doing the writing is important in the politics of the Third World and African America, and indeed for indigenous peoples; it is even more important in the politics of how these worlds are being represented 'back to' the West. Although in the literary sense the imagination is crucial to writing, the use of language is not highly regarded in academic discourses which claim to be scientific. The concept of imagination, when employed as a sociological tool, is often reduced to a way of seeing and understanding the world, or a way of understanding how people either construct the world or are constructed by the world. As Toni Morrison argues, however, the imagination can be a way of sharing the world.[31] This means, according to Morrison, struggling to find the language to do this and then struggling to interpret and perform within that shared imagination.

Writing Theory

Research is linked in all disciplines to theory. Research adds to, is generated from, creates or broadens our theoretical understandings.

Indigenous peoples have been, in many ways, oppressed by theory. Any consideration of the ways our origins have been examined, our histories recounted, our arts analysed, our cultures dissected, measured, torn apart and distorted back to us will suggest that theories have not looked sympathetically or ethically at us. Writing research is often considered marginally more important than writing theory, providing it results in tangible benefits for farmers, economists, industries and sick people. For indigenous peoples, most of the theorizing has been driven by anthropological approaches. These approaches have shown enormous concern for our origins as peoples and for aspects of our linguistic and material culture.

The development of theories by indigenous scholars which attempt to explain our existence in contemporary society (as opposed to the 'traditional' society constructed under modernism) has only just begun. Not all these theories claim to be derived from some 'pure' sense of what it means to be indigenous, nor do they claim to be theories which have been developed in a vacuum separated from any association with civil and human rights movements, other nationalist struggles or other theoretical approaches. What is claimed, however, is that new ways of theorizing by indigenous scholars are grounded in a real sense of, and sensitivity towards, what it means to be an indigenous person. As Kathie Irwin urges, 'We don't need anyone else developing the tools which will help us to come to terms with who we are. We can and will do this work. Real power lies with those who design the tools – it always has. This power is ours'.[32] Contained within this imperative is a sense of being able to determine priorities, to bring to the centre those issues of our own choosing, and to discuss them amongst ourselves.

I am arguing that theory at its most simple level is important for indigenous peoples. At the very least it helps make sense of reality. It enables us to make assumptions and predictions about the world in which we live. It contains within it a method or methods for selecting and arranging, for prioritising and legitimating what we see and do. Theory enables us to deal with contradictions and uncertainties. Perhaps more significantly, it gives us space to plan, to strategize, to take greater control over our resistances. The language of a theory can also be used as a way of organising and determining action. It helps us to interpret what is being told to us, and to predict the consequences of what is being promised. Theory can also protect us because it contains within it a way of putting reality into perspective. If it is a good theory it also allows for new ideas and ways of looking at things to be incorporated constantly without the need to search constantly for new theories.

A dilemma posed by such a thorough critical approach to history, writing and theory is that whilst we may reject or dismiss them, this does not make them go away, nor does the critique necessarily offer the alternatives. We live simultaneously within such views while needing to pose, contest and struggle for the legitimacy of oppositional or alternative histories, theories and ways of writing. At some points there is, there has to be, dialogue across the boundaries of oppositions. This has to be because we constantly collide with dominant views while we are attempting to transform our lives on a larger scale than our own localized circumstances. This means struggling to make sense of our own world while also attempting to transform what counts as important in the world of the powerful.

Part of the exercise is about recovering our own stories of the past. This is inextricably bound to a recovery of our language and epistemological foundations. It is also about reconciling and reprioritizing what is really important about the past with what is important about the present. These issues raise significant questions for indigenous communities who are not only beginning to fight back against the invasion of their communities by academic, corporate and populist researchers, but to think about, and carry out research, on their own concerns. One of the problems discussed in this first section of this book is that the methodologies and methods of research, the theories that inform them, the questions which they generate and the writing styles they employ, all become significant acts which need to be considered carefully and critically before being applied. In other words, they need to be 'decolonized'. Decolonization, however, does not mean and has not meant a total rejection of all theory or research or Western knowledge. Rather, it is about centring our concerns and world views and then coming to know and understand theory and research from our own perspectives and for our own purposes.

As a site of struggle research has a significance for indigenous peoples that is embedded in our history under the gaze of Western imperialism and Western science. It is framed by our attempts to escape the penetration and surveillance of that gaze whilst simultaneously reordering and reconstituting ourselves as indigenous human beings in a state of ongoing crisis. Research has not been neutral in its objectification of the Other. Objectification is a process of dehumanization. In its clear links to Western knowledge research has generated a particular relationship to indigenous peoples which continues to be problematic. At the same time, however, new pressures which have resulted from our own politics of self-determination, of wanting greater participation in, or control over, what happens to us, and from changes in the global environment, have meant that there is a much more active and knowing engagement in the activity of research by indigenous peoples. Many indigenous groups, communities and organisations are thinking about, talking about, and carrying out research activities of various kinds. In this chapter I have suggested that it is important to have a critical understanding of some of the tools of research – not just the obvious technical tools but the conceptual tools, the ones which make us feel uncomfortable, which we avoid, for which we have no easy response.

I lack imagination you say
No. I lack language.
The language to clarify
my resistance to the literate....

Cherrie Moraga[33]

Notes

1 Lorde, Audre (1979), 'The Master's Tools will Never Dismantle the Master's House', comments at 'The personal and the Political' panel, Second Sex Conference, reproduced in Moraga, C. and G. Anzaldua (1981), *This Bridge Called My Back*, Kitchen Table Women of Color Press, New York, pp. 98–101.

2 See Sale, K. (1990), *The Conquest of Paradise, Christopher and the Columbian Legacy*, Alfred Knopf, New York.

3 See Churchill, W. (1994), *Indians Are Us? Culture and Genocide in North America*, Common Courage Press, Maine.

4 Trask, H. K. (1993), *From a Native Daughter*, Common Courage Press, Maine, p. 7.

5 Lehman, G. (1996), 'Life's Quiet Companion', paper, Riawunna Centre for Aboriginal Studies, University of Tasmania, Hobart, Australia.

6 Giddens, A. (1989), *Sociology*, Polity Press, Cambridge, pp. 530–3.

7 The term 'rules of practice' comes from Foucault. See, for this encounter, Salmond, A. (1991), *Two Worlds, First Meetings Between Maori and Europeans 1642–1772*, Viking, Auckland.

8 Mackenzie, J. R. (1990), *Imperialism and the Natural World*, Manchester University Press, England.

9 Thompson, A. S. (1859), *The Story of New Zealand: Past and Present, Savage and Civilized*, John Murray, London, p. 82.

10 Goldberg, D. T. (1993), *Racist Culture, Philosophy and the Politics of Meaning*, Blackwell, Oxford. See also Sardar, Z., A. Nandy and W. Davies (1993), *Barbaric Others, A Manifesto of Western Racism*, Pluto Press, London.

11 Fanon, Frantz (1990), *The Wretched of the Earth*, Penguin, London.

12 *Ibid.*, pp. 27–8.

13 *Ibid.*, p. 27.

14 Nandy, A. (1989), *The Intimate Enemy: Loss and Recovery of Self Under Colonialism*, Oxford University Press, Delhi.

15 Memmi, A. (1991), *The Colonizer and the Colonized*, Beacon Press, Boston, p. 83.

16 For a critique of these views refer to Street, B. V. (1984), *Literacy in Theory and Practice*, Cambridge University Press, New York.

17 I have drawn on a wide range of discussions both by indigenous people and by various writers such as Robert Young, J. Abu-Lughod, Keith Jenkins and C. Steadman. See, for example, Young, R. (1990), *White Mythologies, Writing, History*

and the West, Routledge, London; Abu-Lughood, J. (1989), 'On the Remaking of History. How to Reinvent the Past', in *Remaking History,* Dia Art Foundation, Bay Press, Seattle, pp. 111–29; Steadman, C. (1992), 'Culture, Cultural Studies and the Historians', in *Cultural Studies,* eds G. Nelson, P. A. Treicher and L. Grossberg, Routledge, New York, pp. 613–20; Trask, *From a Native Daughter.*

18 Young, *White Mythologies.*

19 *Ibid.* p. 3.

20 Mangan, J. (1993), *The Imperial Curriculum – Racial Images and Education in the British Colonial Experience,* Routledge, London.

21 Grace, P. (1985), 'Books are Dangerous', paper presented at the Fourth Early Childhood Convention, Wellington, New Zealand.

22 Pihama, L. (1994), 'Are Films Dangerous? A Maori Woman's Perspective on *The Piano*', *Hecate,* Vol. 20, No. 2, p. 241.

23 Ashcroft, B., G. Griffiths and H. Tiffin (1989), *The Empire Writes Back, Theory and Practice in Post-colonial Literatures,* Routledge, London.

24 Thiong'o, Ngugi Wa (1986), *Decolonizing the Mind: The Politics of Language in African Literature,* James Currey, London.

25 *Ibid.*

26 Smith, C.W. (1994), 'Kimihia Te Matauranga: Colonization and Iwi Development', MA thesis, University of Auckland, New Zealand, p. 13.

27 *Ibid.,* p. 13.

28 van Dijk, T. A. (1989), *Elite Discourses and Racism,* Sage Publications, Newbury Park, California.

29 Smith, L. T. (1994), 'In Search of a Language and a Shareable Imaginative World: E Kore Taku Moe, E Riro i a Koe', *Hecate,* Vol. 20, No. 2, pp. 162–74.

30 Said, E. (1983), 'Opponents, Audiences, Constituencies and Community', in *The Politics of Interpretation,* ed. W. J. T. Mitchell, University of Chicago Press, Chicago, p. 7.

31 Morrison, T. (1993), *Playing in the Dark: Whiteness and the Literary Imagination,* Vintage Books, New York.

32 Irwin, K. (1992), 'Towards Theories of Maori Feminisms', in *Feminist Voices: Women's Studies Texts for Aotearoa/New Zealand,* ed. R. du Plessis, Oxford University Press, Auckland, p. 5.

33 Moraga, Cherrie (1983), quoted by G. Anzaldua, in 'Speaking Tongues: a Letter to 3rd World Women Writers', in *This Bridge Called My Back,* p. 166.

CHAPTER 2

Research Through Imperial Eyes

Many critiques of research have centred around the theory of knowledge known as empiricism and the scientific paradigm of positivism which is derived from empiricism. Positivism takes a position that applies views about how the natural world can be examined and understood to the social world of human beings and human societies. Understanding is viewed as being akin to measuring. As the ways we try to understand the world are reduced to issues of measurement, the focus of understanding becomes more concerned with procedural problems. The challenge then for understanding the social world becomes one developing operational definitions of phenomena which are reliable and valid. The analysis in this chapter begins with a much broader brushstroke. Most indigenous criticisms of research are expressed within the single terms of 'white research', 'academic research' or 'outsider research'. The finer details of how Western scientists might name themselves are irrelevant to indigenous peoples who have experienced unrelenting research of a profoundly exploitative nature. From an indigenous perspective Western research is more than just research that is located in a positivist tradition. It is research which brings to bear, on any study of indigenous peoples, a cultural orientation, a set of values, a different conceptualization of such things as time, space and subjectivity, different and competing theories of knowledge, highly specialized forms of language, and structures of power.

In this chapter I argue that what counts as Western research draws from an 'archive' of knowledge and systems, rules and values which stretch beyond the boundaries of Western science to the system now referred to as the West. Stuart Hall makes the point that the West is an idea or concept, a language for imagining a set of complex stories, ideas, historical events and social relationships. Hall suggests that the concept of the West functions in ways which (1) allow 'us' to characterize and *classify* societies into categories, (2) condense complex images of other societies through a *system of representation*, (3) provide a standard *model of comparison*, and (4) provide *criteria of evaluation* against which other societies can be ranked.[1] These are the procedures by which indigenous peoples and their societies were coded into the Western system of knowledge.

Research contributed to, and drew from, these systems of classification, representation and evaluation. The cultural archive did not embody a unitary system of knowledge but should be conceived of as containing multiple traditions of knowledge and ways of knowing. Some knowledges are more dominant than others, some are submerged and outdated. Some knowledges are actively in competition with each other and some can only be formed in association with others. Whilst there may not be a unitary system there are 'rules' which help make sense of what is contained within the archive and enable 'knowledge' to be recognized. These rules can be conceived of as rules of classification, rules of framing and rules of practice.[2] Although the term 'rules' may sound like a set of fixed items which are articulated in explicit ways as regulations, it also means rules which are masked in some way and which tend to be articulated through implicit understandings of how the world works. Power is expressed at both the explicit and implicit levels. Dissent, or challenges to the rules, is manageable because it also conforms to these rules, particularly at the implicit level. Scientific and academic debate in the West takes place within these rules. Two major examples of how this works can be found in Marxism and Western feminism. Arguably, Western feminism has provided a more radical challenge to knowledge than Marxism because of its challenge to epistemology: not just the body of knowledge and world view, but the science of how knowledge can be understood. Even Western feminism, however, has been challenged, particularly by women of colour, for conforming to some very fundamental Western European world views, value systems and attitudes towards the Other. Indigenous peoples would probably claim to know much of this implicitly but in this chapter some fundamental ideas related to understandings of being human, of how humans relate to the world, are examined. Differences between Western and indigenous conceptions of the world have always provided stark contrasts. Indigenous beliefs were considered shocking, abhorrent and barbaric and were prime targets for the efforts of missionaries. Many of those beliefs still persist; they are embedded in indigenous languages and stories and etched in memories.

The Cultural Formations of Western Research

Forms of imperialism and colonialism, notions of the Other, and theories about human nature existed long before the Enlightenment in

Western philosophy. Some scholars have argued that the key tenets of what is now seen as Western civilization are based on black experiences and a black tradition of scholarship, and have simply been appropriated by Western philosophy and redefined as Western epistemology.[3] Western knowledges, philosophies and definitions of human nature form what Foucault has referred to as a cultural archive and what some people might refer to as a 'storehouse' of histories, artefacts, ideas, texts and/or images, which are classified, preserved, arranged and represented back to the West. This storehouse contains the fragments, the regions and levels of knowledge traditions, and the 'systems' which allow different and differentiated forms of knowledge to be retrieved, enunciated and represented in new contexts.[4] Although many colonized peoples refer to the West, usually with a term of their own, as a cohesive system of people, practices, values and languages, the cultural archive of the West represents multiple traditions of knowledge. Rather, there are many different traditions of knowledge and moments of history in which philosophical ideas are sometimes reformed or transformed, in which new knowledges lead to new sets of ideas.

Foucault also suggests that the archive reveals 'rules of practice' which the West itself cannot necessarily describe because it operates within the rules and they are taken for granted. Various indigenous peoples would claim, indeed do claim, to be able to describe many of those rules of practice as they have been 'revealed' and/or perpetrated on indigenous communities. Hall has suggested that the Western cultural archive functions in ways which allow shifts and transformations to happen, quite radically at times, without the archive itself, and the modes of classifications and systems of representation contained within it, being destroyed. This sense of what the idea of the West represents is important here because to a large extent theories about research are underpinned by a cultural system of classification and representation, by views about human nature, human morality and virtue, by conceptions of space and time, by conceptions of gender and race. Ideas about these things help determine what counts as real. Systems of classification and representation enable different traditions or fragments of traditions to be retrieved and reformulated in different contexts as discourses, and then to be played out in systems of power and domination, with real material consequences for colonized peoples. Nandy, for example, discusses the different phases of colonization, from 'rapacious bandit-kings' intent on exploitation, to 'well-meaning middle class liberals' intent on salvation as a legitimation of different forms of colonization.[5] These phases of colonization, driven by different economic needs and differing ideologies of legitimation, still had real consequences for the nations, communities and groups of indigenous people being colonized.

These consequences have led Nandy to describe colonization as a 'shared culture' for those who have been colonized and for those who have colonized. This means, for example, that colonized peoples share a language of colonization, share knowledge about their colonizers, and, in terms of a political project, share the same struggle for decolonization. It also means that colonizers, too, share a language and knowledge of colonization.

The Intersections of Race and Gender

David Theo Goldberg argues that one of the consequences of Western experiences under imperialism is that Western ways of viewing, talking about and interacting with the world at large are intricately embedded in racialized discourses.[6] Notions of difference are discussed in Greek philosophy, for example, as ways of rationalizing the essential characteristics and obligations of slaves.[7] Medieval literature and art represent fabulous monsters and half-human, half-animal creatures from far-off places. According to Goldberg, concern about these images led to 'observers [being] overcome by awe, repulsion and fear of the implied threat to spiritual life and the political state'.[8] Goldberg argues that whilst these early beliefs and images 'furnished models that modern racism would assume and transform according to its own lights', there was no explicit category or space in medieval thought for racial differentiation.[9] What did happen, according to Goldberg, was that the 'savage' was internalized as a psychological and moral space within the individual that required 'repression, denial and disciplinary restraint'.[10] In Goldberg's analysis, modernity and the philosophy of liberalism (which underpins modernist discourses) transformed these fragments of culture into an explicit racialized discourse. Race, as a category, was linked to human reason and morality, to science, to colonialism and to the rights of citizenship in ways that produced the racialized discourse and racist practices of modernity.[11]

Western concepts of race intersect in complex ways with concepts of gender. Gender refers not just to the roles of women and how those roles are constituted but to the roles of men and of the relations between men and women. Ideas about gender difference and what that means for a society can similarly be traced back to the fragmented artefacts and representations of Western culture, and to different and differentiated traditions of knowledge. The desired and undesired qualities of women for example, as mothers, daughters and wives, were inscribed in the texts of the Greeks and Romans, sculptured, painted and woven into medieval wall hangings, and performed through oral poetry. Different historical ideas about men and women were enacted through social institutions such as marriage, family life, the class system and ecclesiastic orders.[12] These institutions were underpinned by economic systems, notions of property and wealth, and were increasingly legitimated in the West through Judaeo-Christian beliefs. Economic changes from feudal to capitalist modes of production influenced the construction of the 'family' and the relations of women and men in Western societies. Gender distinctions and hierarchies are also deeply encoded in Western languages. It is impossible to speak without using this language, and, more significantly for indigenous peoples, it is impossible to translate or interpret our societies into English, French or Castilian, for example, without making gendered distinctions.

The process of en-gendering descriptions of the Other has had very real consequences for indigenous women in that the ways in which indigenous women were described, objectified and represented by Europeans in the nineteenth century has left a legacy of marginalization within indigenous societies as much as within the colonizing society. In New Zealand many of these issues are the subject of a claim brought by a group of prominent Maori women to the Waitangi Tribunal. The Waitangi Tribunal was established to hear the claims by Maori relating to contraventions of the Treaty of Waitangi.[13] Before this Tribunal, the Maori women taking the claim are having to establish and argue, using historical texts, research and oral testimonies, that the Crown has ignored the *rangatiratanga*, or chiefly and sovereign status, of Maori women. To argue this, the claimants are compelled to prove that Maori women were as much *rangatira* (chiefs) as Maori men. At a very simple level the 'problem' is a problem of translation. *Rangatiratanga* has generally been interpreted in English as meaning chieftainship and sovereignty, which in colonialism was a 'male thing'.

This claim illustrates the complexities which Stuart Hall raised. Several different and differentiated sets of ideas and representations are to be 'retrieved' and 'enunciated' in the historically specific context of this claim. In summary these may be classified as: (1) a legal framework inherited from Britain, which includes views about what constitutes admissible evidence and valid research; (2) a 'textual' orientation, which will privilege the written text (seen as expert and research-based) over oral testimonies (a concession to indigenous 'elders'); (3) views about science, which will allow for the efficient selection and arrangement of 'facts'; (4) 'rules of practice' such as 'values' and 'morals', which all parties to the process are assumed to know and to have given their 'consent' to abide by, for example, notions of 'goodwill' and 'truth telling'; (5) ideas about subjectivity and objectivity which have already determined the constitution of the Tribunal and its 'neutral' legal framework, but which will continue to frame the way the case is heard; (6) ideas about time and space, views related to history, what constitutes the appropriate length of a hearing, 'shape' of a claim, size of the panel; (7) views about human nature, individual accountability and culpability; (8) the selection of speakers and experts, who speaks for whom, whose knowledge is presumed to be the 'best fit' in relation to a set of proven 'facts'; and (9) the politics of the Treaty of Waitangi and the way those politics are managed by politicians and other agencies such as the media. Within each set of ideas are systems of classification and representation; epistemological, ontological, juridical, anthropological and ethical, which are coded in such ways as to 'recognize' each other and either mesh together, or create a cultural 'force field' which can screen out competing and oppositional discourses. Taken as a whole system, these ideas determine the wider rules of practice which ensure that Western interests remain dominant.

Conceptualizations of the Individual and Society

Social science research is based upon ideas, beliefs and theories about the social world. While it is acknowledged that people always live in some form of social organization (for example, a family unit, an efficient hunting and gathering unit, a pastoral unit, and increasingly larger and more effective and sophisticated variations of those basic units), Western forms of research also draw on cultural ideas about the human 'self' and the relationship between the individual and the groups to which he or she may belong. Such ideas explore both the internal workings of an individual and the relationships between what an individual is and how an individual behaves. These ideas suggest that relationships between or among groups of people are basically causal and can be observed and predicted. Some earlier accounts of how and why individuals behave as they do were based on ideas which often began with a creation story to explain the presence of people in their specific environment and on understandings of human behaviour as being connected to some form of external force, such as spiritually powerful beings, 'gods' or sacred objects. Human activity was seen to be caused by factors outside the control of the individual. Early European societies would not have made much distinction between human beings and their natural environment. Classical Greek philosophy is regarded as the point at which ideas about these relationships changed from 'naturalistic' explanations to humanistic explanations. Naturalistic explanations linked nature and life as one and humanistic explanations separate people out from the world around them, and place humanity on a higher plane (than animals and plants) because of such characteristics as language and reason.[14] Socrates, Plato and Aristotle are regarded as the founders of this humanistic tradition of knowledge. Human nature, that is, the essential characteristics of an individual person, is an overarching concern of Western philosophy even though 'human' and 'nature' are also seen to be in opposition to each other. Education, research and other scholarly traditions have emerged from or been framed by debates relating to human nature. The separation between mind and body, the investing of a human person with a soul, a psyche and a consciousness, the distinction between sense and reason, definitions of human virtue and morality, are cultural constructs. These ideas have been transformed as philosophers have incorporated new insights and discoveries, but the underlying categories have remained in place. From Aristotle and Plato, in Greek philosophy, the mind–body distinction was heavily Christianized by Aquinas. French philosopher Descartes developed this dualism further, making distinctions which would relate to the separate disciplines required to study the body (physiology) and the mind (psychology). His distinctions are now referred to as the Cartesian dualism. Hegel reasoned that the split was dialectical, meaning that there was a contradictory interplay between the two ideas and the form of debate required to develop these ideas. It must be remembered, however, that concepts such as the mind or the intellect, the soul, reason, virtue and morality are not in themselves 'real' or biological parts of a human body. Whilst the workings of a mind may be associated in Western thinking primarily with the human brain, the mind itself is a concept or an idea. In Maori world views, for example, the closest equivalent to the idea of a 'mind' or intellect is associated with the entrails and other parts of the body. The head was considered *tapu* for other reasons.

 What makes ideas 'real' is the system of knowledge, the formations of culture, and the relations of power in which these concepts are located. What an individual is – and the implications this has for the way researchers or teachers, therapists or social workers, economists or journalists, might approach their work – is based on centuries of philosophical debate, principles of debate and systems for organizing whole societies predicated on these ideas. These ideas constitute reality. Reality cannot be constituted without them. When confronted by the alternative conceptions of other societies, Western reality became reified as representing something 'better', reflecting 'higher orders' of thinking, and being less prone to the dogma, witchcraft and immediacy of people and societies which were so 'primitive'. Ideological appeals to such things as literacy, democracy and the development of complex social structures, make this way of thinking appear to be a universal truth and a necessary criterion of civilized society. Although eighteenth- and nineteenth-century forms of colonization brought Christian beliefs about the soul and human morality to indigenous peoples, these concepts were discussed in Western traditions prior to Christianity. Christianity, when organized into a system of power, brought to bear on these basic concepts a focus of systematic study and debate which could then be used to regulate all aspects of social and spiritual life.

The individual, as the basic social unit from which other social organizations and social relations form, is another system of ideas which needs to be understood as part of the West's cultural archive. Western philosophies and religions place the individual as the basic building block of society. The transition from feudal to capitalist modes of production simply emphasized the role of the individual. Concepts of social development were seen as the natural progression and replication of human development. The relationship between the individual and the group, however, was a major theoretical problem for philosophy. This problem tended to be posed as a dialectic or tension between two irreconcilable notions. Hegel's dialectic on the self and society has become the most significant model for thinking about this relationship. His master–slave construct has served as a form of analysis which is both psychological and sociological, and in the colonial context highly political.

Rousseau has a particular influence over the way indigenous peoples in the South Pacific came to be regarded, because of his highly romanticized and idealized view of human nature. It is to Rousseau that the idea of the 'noble savage' is attributed. This view linked the natural world to an idea of innocence and purity, and the developed world to corruption and decay. It was thought that the people who lived in the idyllic conditions of the South Pacific, close to nature, would possess 'noble' qualities from which the West could relearn and rediscover what had been lost. This romanticized view was particularly relevant to the way South Pacific women were represented, especially the women of Tahiti and Polynesia. The view soon lost favour, or was turned around into the 'ignoble savage', when it was found that these idealized humans actually indulged in 'barbaric' and 'savage' customs and were capable of what were viewed as acts of grave injustice and 'despicability'.

Just as in the psychological traditions the individual has been central, so within sociological traditions the individual is assumed to be the basic unit of a society. A major sociological concern becomes a struggle over the extent to which individual consciousness and reality shapes, or is shaped by, social structure. During the nineteenth century this view of the individual and society became heavily influenced by social Darwinism. This meant, for example, that a society could be viewed as a 'species' of people with biological traits.[15] 'Primitive' societies could be ranked according to these traits, predictions could be made about their survival and ideological justifications could be made about their treatment. Early sociology came to focus on the belief systems of these 'primitive' people and the extent to which they were capable of thought and of developing 'simple' ideas about religion. This focus was intended to enhance the understandings of Western society by showing how simple societies developed the building blocks of classification systems and modes of thought. These systems, it was believed, would demonstrate how such social phenomena as language developed. This in turn would enable distinctions to be made between categories which were fixed – that is, the structural underpinnings of society – and categories which people could create, that is, the cultural aspects of the life-world. It also reinforced, through contrasting associations or oppositional categories, how superior the West was.

Conceptions of Space

Similar claims can be made about other concepts, such as time and space. These concepts are particularly significant for some indigenous languages because the language makes no clear or absolute distinction between the two: for example, the Maori word for time or space is the same. Other indigenous languages have no related word for either space or time, having instead a series of very precise terms for parts of these ideas, or for relationships between the idea and something else in the environment. There are positions within time and space in which people and events are located, but these cannot necessarily be described as distinct categories of thought. Western ideas about time and space are encoded in language, philosophy and science. Philosophical conceptions of time and space have been concerned with: (1) the relationships between the two ideas, that is, whether space and time are absolute categories or whether they exist relationally; and (2) the measurement of time and space.[16] Space came to be seen as consisting of lines which were either parallel or elliptical. From these ideas, ways of thinking which related to disciplines of study emerged (for example, mapping and geography, measurement and geometry, motion and physics). These distinctions are generally part of a taken-for-granted view of the world. Spatialized language is frequently used in both everyday and academic discourses.

Henri Lefebvre argues that the notion of space has been 'appropriated by mathematics' which has claimed an ideological position of dominance over what space means.[17] Mathematics has constructed a language which attempts to define with absolute exactness the parameters, dimensions, qualities and possibilities of space. This language of space influences the way the West thinks about the world beyond earth (cosmology), the ways in which society is viewed (public/private space, city/country space), the ways in which gender roles were defined (public/domestic, home/work) and the ways in which the social world of people could be determined (the market place, the theatre).[18] Compartmentalized, space can be better defined and measured.

Conceptions of space were articulated through the ways in which people arranged their homes and towns, collected and displayed objects of significance, organized warfare, set out agricultural fields and arranged gardens, conducted business, displayed art and performed drama, separated out one form of human activity from another. Spatial arrangements are an important part of social life. Western classifications of space include such notions as architectural space, physical space, psychological space, theoretical space and so forth. Foucault's metaphor of the cultural archive is an architectural image. The archive not only contains artefacts of culture, but is itself an artefact and a construct of culture. For the indigenous world, Western conceptions of space, of arrangements and display, of the relationship between people and the landscape, of culture as an object of study, have meant that not only has the indigenous world been represented in particular ways back to the West, but the indigenous world view, the land and the people, have been radically transformed in the spatial image of the West. In other words, indigenous space has been colonized. Land, for example, was viewed as something to be tamed and brought under control. The landscape, the arrangement of nature, could be altered by 'Man': swamps could be drained, waterways diverted, inshore areas filled, not simply for physical survival, but for further exploitation of the environment or making it 'more pleasing' aesthetically. Renaming the land was probably as powerful ideologically as changing the land. Indigenous children in schools, for example, were taught the new names for places that they and their parents had lived in for generations. These were the names which appeared on maps and which were used in official communications. This newly named land became increasingly disconnected from the songs and chants used by indigenous peoples to trace their histories, to bring forth spiritual elements or to carry out the simplest of ceremonies. More significantly, however, space was appropriated from indigenous cultures and then 'gifted back' as reservations, reserved pockets of land for indigenous people who once possessed all of it.

Other artefacts and images of indigenous cultures were also classified, stored and displayed in museum cases and boxes, framed by the display cases as well as by the categories of artefacts with which they were grouped. Some images became part of the postcard trade and the advertising market or were the subject of Western artistic interpretations of indigenous peoples. Still other 'live' and performing examples were put 'on stage' as concert parties to entertain Europeans. Indigenous cultures became framed within a language and a set of spatialized representations.[19]

A specific example of the colonization of an indigenous architectural space and of indigenous spatial concepts can be found in the story of the Mataatua, a carved Maori house built in 1875 as a wedding gift from one tribal group to another. The New Zealand Government negotiated and gained agreement to send the Mataatua to the British Empire Exhibition at Sydney in 1879. The house was displayed according to the aesthetic and economic sense of the exhibition's curators:

> Finding that it would cost at least 700 pounds to erect it in the ordinary manner as a Maori house, the walls were reversed so that the carvings showed on the outside; and the total cost, including painting and roofing with Chinese matting was reduced to 165 pounds.[20]

A 'Maori House', displayed inside-out and lined with Chinese matting was seen as an important contribution by New Zealand to the Sydney Exhibition. As argued by its original owners,

> the house itself had undergone a transformation as a result of being assimilated into a British Empire Exhibition. It changed from being a 'living' meeting house which the people used and had become an ethnological curiosity for strange people to look at the wrong way and in the wrong place.[21]

Having gained agreement for this single purpose, the New Zealand government then appropriated the house and sent it to England, where it was displayed at the South Kensington Museum, stored for forty years at the Victoria and Albert Museum, displayed again at the Wembley British Empire Exhibition in 1924, shipped back to New Zealand for a South Seas Exhibition in Dunedin in 1925, and then 'given', by the government, to the Otago Museum. Ngati Awa, the owners of this house, have been negotiating for its return since 1983. This has now been agreed upon by the New Zealand government after a case put to the Waitangi Tribunal, and the 'door lintel' of the Mataatua has been returned as a symbolic gesture prior to the return of the entire house over the next two years.

Space is often viewed in Western thinking as being static or divorced from time. This view generates ways of making sense of the world as a 'realm of stasis', well-defined, fixed and without politics.[22] This is particularly relevant in relation to colonialism. The establishment of military, missionary or trading stations, the building of roads, ports and bridges, the clearing of bush and the mining of minerals all involved processes of marking, defining and controlling space. There is a very specific spatial vocabulary of colonialism which can be assembled around three concepts: (1) the line, (2) the centre, and (3) the outside. The 'line' is important because it was used to map territory, to survey land, to establish boundaries and to mark the limits of colonial power. The 'centre' is important because orientation to the centre was an orientation to the system of power. The 'outside' is important because it positioned territory and people in an oppositional relation to the colonial centre; for indigenous Australians to be in an 'empty space' was to 'not exist'. That vocabulary in New Zealand is depicted in Table 2.1:

Table 2.1 The spatial vocabulary of colonialism in nineteenth-century *Aotearoa*

The Line	The Centre	The Outside
maps	mother country	empty land
charts	London	*terra nullius*
roads	magistrate's residence	uninhabited
boundaries	redoubt, stockade, barracks	unoccupied
pegs	prison	uncharted
surveys	mission station	reserves
claims	Parliament	*Maori pa*
fences	store	*Kainga*
hedges	Church	*Marae*
stone walls	Europe	burial grounds
tracks	port	background
genealogies	foreground	hinterland
perimeters	flagpole	

Conceptions of Time

Time is associated with social activity, and how other people organized their daily lives fascinated and horrified Western observers. The links between the industrial revolution, the Protestant ethic, imperialism and science can be discussed in terms of time and the organization of social life. Changes in the mode of production brought about by the industrial revolution, an emerging middle class able to generate wealth and make distinctions in their lives between work, leisure, education and religion, and a working-class evangelical movement which linked work to salvation contributed to a potent cultural mix. In Africa, the Americas and the Pacific, Western observers were struck by the contrast in the way time was used (or rather, not used or organized) by indigenous peoples. Representations of 'native life' as being devoid of work habits, and of native people being lazy, indolent, with low attention spans, is part of a colonial discourse that continues to this day. There were various explanations advanced for such indolence; a hot climate, for example, was viewed as a factor. Often it was a simple association between race and indolence, darker skin peoples being considered more 'naturally' indolent.

An example of how integral time is to social life can be found in the journals of Joseph Banks. Banks accompanied Cook on his first voyages to the South Pacific. The Royal Society supervised the Greenwich Observatory which eventually set the world-wide standard of time measurement (Greenwich mean time) and was instrumental in organizing Cook's voyage to Tahiti in 1769 to observe the transit of Venus. Throughout this journey Banks kept a detailed diary which documents his observations and reflections upon what he saw. The diary was a precise organization of his life on board ship, not only a day by day account, but an account which included weather reports, lists of plants and birds collected, and details on the people he encountered. Life on board the *Endeavour* was organized according to the rules and regulations of the British Admiralty, an adaptation of British time. Not only did the diary measure time, but there were scientific instruments on board which also measured time and place. As an observer, Banks saw the Pacific world through his own sense of time, his observations were prefaced by phrases such as, 'at daybreak', 'in the evening', 'by 8 o'clock', 'about noon', 'a little before sunset'.[23] He confessed, however – after describing in detail such things as dress, ornaments, tattooing, house construction and lay-out, clothing, gardens, net making, the women, food, religion and language, and after describing visits he and a companion made at particular times to observe the people eating, carrying out their daily activities and sleeping – that he was unable to get a 'complete idea' of how the people divided time.

The connection between time and 'work' became more important after the arrival of missionaries and the development of more systematic colonization. The belief that 'natives' did not value work or have a sense of time provided ideological justification for exclusionary practices which reached across such areas as education, land development and employment. The evangelical missionaries who arrived in the Pacific had a view of salvation in which were embedded either lower middle-class English or puritanical New England work practices and values. It was hard work to get to heaven and 'savages' were expected to work extra hard to qualify to get into the queue. This also meant wearing 'decent' clothes designed more for hard labour in cold climates, eating 'properly' at 'proper' meal times (before and after work) and reorganizing family patterns to enable men to work at some things and women to support them.

Lineal views of both time and space are important when examining Western ideas about history. Here, the Enlightenment is a crucial point in time. Prior to this period of Western development was an era likened to a period of 'darkness' (the 'Age of Darkness') which 'coincided' with the rise of power to the east. This era was followed by reformation within the Church of Rome. During these periods of time, which are social 'constructions' of time, society was said to be feudal, belief systems were based on dogma, monarchs ruled by divine authority, and literacy was confined to the very few. People lived according to myths and stories which hid the 'truth' or were simply not truths. These stories were kept alive by memory. The Enlightenment has also been referred to as the 'Age of Reason'. During this period history came to be viewed as a more reasoned or scientific understanding of the past. History could be recorded systematically and then retrieved through recourse to written texts. It was based on a lineal view of time and was linked closely to notions of progress. Progress could be 'measured' in terms of technological advancement and spiritual salvation. Progress is evolutionary and teleological and is present in both liberal and Marxist ideas about history.

Different orientations towards time and space, different positioning within time and space, and different systems of language for making space and time 'real' underpin notions of past and present, of place and of relationships to the land. Ideas about progress are grounded within ideas and orientations towards time and space. What has come to count as history in contemporary society is a contentious issue for many indigenous communities because it is not only the story of domination; it is also a story which assumes that there was a 'point in time' which was 'prehistoric'. The point at which society moves from prehistoric to historic is also the point at which tradition breaks with modernism. Traditional indigenous knowledge ceased, in this view, when it came into contact with 'modern' societies, that is the West. What occurred at this point of culture contact was the beginning of the end for 'primitive' societies. Deeply embedded in these constructs are systems of classification and representation which lend themselves easily to binary oppositions, dualisms, and hierarchical orderings of the world.

One of the concepts through which Western ideas about the individual and community, about time and space, knowledge and research, imperialism and colonialism can be drawn together is the concept of distance. The individual can be distanced, or separated, from the physical environment, the community. Through the controls over time and space the individual can also operate at a distance from the universe. Both imperial and colonial rule were systems of rule which stretched from the centre outwards to places which were far and distant. Distance again separated the individuals in power from the subjects they governed. It was all so impersonal, rational and extremely effective. In research the concept of distance is most important as it implies a neutrality and objectivity on behalf of the researcher. Distance is measurable. What it has come to stand for is objectivity, which is not measurable to quite the same extent.

Research 'through imperial eyes' describes an approach which assumes that Western ideas about the most fundamental things are the only ideas possible to hold, certainly the only rational ideas, and the only ideas which can make sense of the world, of reality, of social life and of human beings. It is an approach to indigenous peoples which still conveys a sense of innate superiority and an overabundance of desire to bring progress into the lives of indigenous peoples – spiritually, intellectually, socially and economically. It is research which from indigenous perspectives 'steals' knowledge from others and then uses it to benefit the people who 'stole' it. Some indigenous and minority group researchers would call this approach simply racist. It is research which is imbued with an 'attitude' and a 'spirit' which assumes a certain ownership of the entire world, and which has established systems and forms of governance which embed that attitude in institutional practices. These practices determine what counts as legitimate research and who count as legitimate researchers. Before assuming that such an attitude has long since disappeared, it is often worth reflecting on who would make such a claim, researchers or indigenous peoples? A recent attempt (fortunately unsuccessful) to patent an indigenous person in the New Guinea Highlands might suggest that there are many groups of indigenous peoples who are still without protection when it comes to the activities of research.[24] Although in this particular case the attempt was unsuccessful, what it demonstrated yet again is that there are people out there who in the name of science and progress still consider indigenous peoples as specimens, not as humans.

Notes

1 Hall, S. (1992), 'The West and the Rest: Discourse and Power', Chapter 6 of *Formations of Modernity,* eds S. Hall and B. Gielben, Polity Press and Open University, Cambridge, pp. 276–320.

2 Bernstein, B. (1971), 'On the Classification and Framing of Knowledge', in *Knowledge and Control. New Directions for the Sociology of Education,* ed. M. F. D. Young, Collier Macmillan, London, pp. 47–69.

3 See for example, Bernal, M. (1991), *Black Athena, The Afroasiatic Roots of Civilisation,* Vintage, London.

4 Foucault, M. (1972), *The Archaeology of Knowledge,* trans. A. Sheridan Smith, Pantheon, New York.

5 Nandy, A. (1989), *The Intimate Enemy: Loss and Recovery of Self Under Colonialism,*

Oxford University Press, Delhi, p. xi.

6 Goldberg, D. T. (1993), *Racist Culture, Philosophy and the Politics of Meaning*, Blackwell, Oxford.

7 *Ibid.*, p. 23.

8 *Ibid.*, p. 23.

9 *Ibid.*, p. 23.

10 *Ibid.*, p. 23.

11 *Ibid.*, pp. 41–60.

12 Erler, M. and M. Kowaleski (1988), *Women and Power in the Middle Ages*, University of Georgia Press, Athens.

13 The Treaty of Waitangi was signed between Maori chiefs and the British Crown in 1840. The Waitangi Tribunal was established by Parliament under The Treaty of Waitangi Act 1975. This Act established the Tribunal with the brief of hearing claims by Maori that the Crown had contravened the principles of the Treaty of Waitangi. This applied to recent grievances. The Tribunal was given powers to recommend actions to the Crown. The Act was amended in 1985 in order to extend the scope of claims back to 1840.

14 Brennan, J. F. (1991), *Racist Culture, The History and Systems of Psychology*, third edition, Prentice Hall International, New Jersey.

15 Goldberg, *Racist Culture*, pp. 62–9.

16 In the fifth century Zeno, for example, posited a series of paradoxes which centred around two ideas, one which suggests that space and time are continuous, and one which suggests that they are made up of divisible parts. Others have argued since Zeno that there can be no such thing as 'empty' space because, if it is empty, it does not exist.

17 Lefebvre, H. (1991), *The Production of Space*, Blackwell, USA.

18 See for example, Williams, R. (1973), *The Country and the City*, Paladin, London. See also Fanon, Frantz (1967), *The Wretched of the Earth*, Penguin, London, p. 30. Fanon talks about 'zones' where natives live and 'zones' where settlers live. For him, the border between the two are clear and there is no possibility of reconciliation.

19 See also, Gidley, M., ed. (1994), *Representing Others, White Views of Indigenous Peoples*, University of Exeter Press.

20 Appendices to the Journals of the New Zealand House of Representatives, 1880, H5: 2.

21 Te Runanga o Ngati Awa (1990), *Nga Karoretanga o Mataatua Whare. The Wanderings of the Carved House, Mataatua*, Ngati Awa Research Report 2, Whakatane, New Zealand.

22 Massey, D. (1993), 'Politics and Space/Time', in *Place and the Politics of Identity*, eds M. Keith, and S. Pile, Routledge, London, pp. 141–61.

23 Beaglehole, J. C. (1962), *The Endeavour Journal of Joseph Banks*, Angus and Robertson, Sydney.

24 See account of this attempt in *Third World Resurgence*, No. 63, p. 30.

CHAPTER 3

Colonizing Knowledges

We have a history of people putting Maori under a microscope in the same way a scientist looks at an insect. The ones doing the looking are giving themselves the power to define.

Merata Mita[1]

In the previous chapter the metaphor of an archive was used to convey the sense by which the West drew upon a vast history of itself and multiple traditions of knowledge which incorporate cultural views of reality, of time and space. This chapter argues that the form of imperialism which indigenous peoples are confronting now emerged from that period of European history known as the Enlightenment. The Enlightenment provided the spirit, the impetus, the confidence, and the political and economic structures that facilitated the search for new knowledges. The project of the Enlightenment is often referred to as 'modernity' and it is that project which is claimed to have provided the stimulus for the industrial revolution, the philosophy of liberalism, the development of disciplines in the sciences and the development of public education. Imperialism underpinned and was critical to these developments. Whilst imperialism is often thought of as a system which drew everything back into the centre, it was also a system which distributed materials and ideas outwards. Said's notion of 'positional superiority' is useful here for conceptualizing the ways in which know-ledge and culture were as much part of imperialism as raw materials and military strength. Knowledge was also there to be discovered, extracted, appropriated and distributed. Processes for enabling these things to occur became organized and systematic. They not only informed the field of study referred to by Said as 'Orientalism' but other disciplines of knowledge and 'regimes of truth'. It is through these disciplines that the indigenous world has been *re*presented to the West and it is through these disciplines that indigenous peoples often *re*search for the fragments

of ourselves which were taken, catalogued, studied and stored. It is not
the intention of this chapter to tell the history of Western knowledge
but rather to draw that history down into the colonized world, show the
relationship between knowledge, research and imperialism, and then
discuss the ways in which it has come to structure our own ways of
knowing, through the development of academic disciplines and through
the education of colonial elites and indigenous or 'native' intellectuals.
Western knowledge and science are 'beneficiaries' of the colonization of
indigenous peoples. The knowledge gained through our colonization has
been used, in turn, to colonize us in what Ngugi wa Thiong'o calls the
colonization 'of the mind'.[2]

Establishing the Positional Superiority of Western Knowledge

The project of modernity signalled the end of feudalism and absolutist
authority, legitimated by divine rule, and announced the beginning of
the modern state. The new state formation had to meet the requirements
of an expanding economy based on major improvements in production.
The industrial revolution changed and made new demands upon the
individual and the political system. The modern state was wrested from
the old regime of absolutist monarchs by the articulation of liberal
political and economic theories.[3] As a system of ideas, liberalism focuses
on the individual, who has the capacity to reason, on a society which
promotes individual autonomy and self-interest, and on a state which
has a rational rule of law which regulates a public sphere of life, but
which allows individuals to pursue their economic self-interest. Once it
was accepted that humans had the capacity to reason and to attain this
potential through education, through a systematic form of organizing
knowledge, then it became possible to debate these ideas in rational and
'scientific' ways.

The development of scientific thought, the exploration and
'discovery' by Europeans of other worlds, the expansion of trade, the
establishment of colonies, and the systematic colonization of indigenous
peoples in the eighteenth and nineteenth centuries are all facets of the
modernist project. Modernism is more than a re-presentation of
fragments from the cultural archive in new contexts. 'Discoveries' about
and from the 'new' world expanded and challenged ideas the West held
about itself.[4] The production of knowledge, new knowledge and
transformed 'old' knowledge, ideas about the nature of knowledge and
the validity of specific forms of knowledge, became as much
commodities of colonial exploitation as other natural resources.[5]
Indigenous peoples were classified alongside the flora and fauna;
hierarchical typologies of humanity and systems of representation were

fuelled by new discoveries; and cultural maps were charted and territories claimed and contested by the major European powers. Hence some indigenous peoples were ranked above others in terms of such things as the belief that they were 'nearly human', 'almost human' or 'sub-human'. This often depended on whether it was thought that the peoples concerned possessed a 'soul' and could therefore be 'offered' salvation and whether or not they were educable and could be offered schooling. These systems for organizing, classifying and storing new knowledge, and for theorizing the meanings of such discoveries, constituted research. In a colonial context, however, this research was undeniably also about power and domination. The instruments or technologies of research were also instruments of knowledge and instruments for legitimating various colonial practices.

The imaginary line between 'east' and 'west', drawn in 1493 by a Papal Bull, allowed for the political division of the world and the struggle by competing Western states to establish what Said has referred to as a 'flexible positional superiority' over the known, and yet to become known, world.[6] This positional superiority was contested at several levels by European powers. These imaginary boundaries were drawn again in Berlin in 1934 when European powers sat around the table once more to carve up Africa and other parts of 'their' empires. They continue to be redrawn. Imperialism and colonialism are the specific formations through which the West came to 'see', to 'name' and to 'know' indigenous communities. The cultural archive with its systems of representation, codes for unlocking systems of classification, and fragmented artefacts of knowledge enabled travellers and observers to make sense of what they saw and to represent their new-found knowledge back to the West through the authorship and authority of their representations.

Whilst colonialism at an economic level, including its ultimate expression through slavery, opened up new materials for exploitation and new markets for trade, at a cultural level, ideas, images and experiences about the Other helped to shape and delineate the essential differences between Europe and the rest. Notions about the Other, which already existed in the European imagination, were recast within the framework of Enlightenment philosophies, the industrial revolution and the scientific 'discoveries' of the eighteenth and nineteenth centuries. When discussing the scientific foundations of Western research, the indigenous contribution to these foundations is rarely mentioned. To have acknowledged their contribution would, in terms of the rules of research practice, be as legitimate as acknowledging the contribution of a variety of plant, a shard of pottery or a 'preserved head of a native' to research. Furthermore, according to Bazin, 'Europeans could not even imagine that other people could ever have done things before or better than themselves'.[7] The objects of research do not have a voice and do not contribute to research or science. In fact, the logic of the argument would suggest that it is simply impossible, ridiculous even, to suggest that the object of research can contribute to anything. An object has no life force, no humanity, no spirit of its own, so therefore 'it' cannot make an active contribution. This perspective is not deliberately insensitive; it is simply that the rules did not allow such a thought to enter the scene. Thus, indigenous Asian, American, Pacific and African forms of knowledge, systems of classification, technologies and codes of social life, which began to be recorded in some detail by the seventeenth century, were regarded as 'new discoveries' by Western science.[8] These discoveries were commodified as property belonging to the cultural archive and body of knowledge of the West.[9]

The eighteenth and nineteenth centuries also constituted an era of highly competitive 'collecting'. Many indigenous people might call this 'stealing' rather than 'collecting'. This included the collecting of territories, of new species of flora and fauna, of mineral resources and of cultures. James Clifford, for example, refers to ethnography as a science which was

> [a] form of culture collecting … [which] highlights the ways that diverse experiences and facts are selected, gathered, detached from their original temporal occasions, and given enduring value in a new arrangement. Collecting – at least in the West, where time is generally thought to be linear and irreversible – implies a rescue of phenomena from inevitable historical decay or loss.[10]

The idea that collectors were actually rescuing artefacts from decay and destruction, and from indigenous peoples themselves, legitimated practices which also included commercial trade and plain and simple theft. Clearly, in terms of trade indigenous peoples were often active participants, in some cases delivering 'made to order' goods. The different agendas and rivalries of indigenous groups were also known to have been incorporated into the commercial activities of Europeans. Hence, muskets could be traded and then used to pursue traditional enemies or one group of people could be used to capture and assist in the enslavement of another group who were also their traditional rivals. Indigenous property is still said to be housed in 'collections', which in turn are housed either in museums or private galleries, and art and artefacts are often grouped and classified in the name of their 'collector'. These collections have become the focus of indigenous peoples' attempts to reclaim ancestral remains and other cultural items (known in the West as 'artefacts') belonging to their people.

It is important to remember, however, that colonialism was not just about collection. It was also about re-arrangement, re-presentation and re-distribution. For example, plant species were taken by Joseph Banks for the Royal Botanic Gardens at Kew. Here they could be 'grown, studied, and disbursed to the colonial stations, a centre of plant transfers on the scientific level, and of the generation and publication of know-ledge about plants'.[11] The British Empire became a global laboratory for research and development. New species of plants and animals were introduced to the colonies to facilitate development and to 'strengthen' indigenous species. This point is worth remembering as it contrasts with the view, sometimes referred to as a diffusionist explanation, that knowledge, people, flora and fauna simply disbursed themselves around the world. This botanical colonization had already been successfully carried out in other places: for example, maize, sweet potatoes, and tobacco from South America had been widely distributed. In the centre of this collection and distribution network was the imperial 'home' country. The colonies were peripheral satellites which gained access to these new knowledges and technologies through 'recourse to the writings of authors in the centre'.[12] One effect of this system of redistribution was the interference caused by new species to the ecologies of their new environments and the eventual extinction of several species of bird and animal life.[13] In the case of New Zealand, Cherryl Smith argues that, ecologically, the indigenous world was colonized by weeds.[14]

Among the other significant consequences of ecological imperialism – carried by humans, as well as by plants and animals – were the viral and bacterial diseases which devastated indigenous populations. This devastation or genocide was, in the accounts of many indigenous peoples, used deliberately as a weapon of war. Stories are told in Canada, for example, of blankets used by smallpox victims being sent into First Nation communities while the soldiers and settlers camped outside waiting for the people to die. There were several ideologies which legitimated the Western impact on indigenous health and well-being. These supported racial views already in place but which in the later nineteenth century became increasingly legitimated by the 'scientific' views of social Darwinism. The concept of the 'survival of the fittest', used to explain the evolution of species in the natural world, was applied enthusiastically to the human world. It became a very powerful belief that indigenous peoples were inherently weak and therefore, at some point, would die out. There were debates about how this could be prevented, for example, through miscegenation and cultural assimilation, and whether this, in fact, was 'desirable'. Judgements on these issues circled back or depended upon prior considerations as to whether the indigenous group concerned had souls, could be saved, and also could be redeemed culturally. Influential debates on these matters by Catholic scholars such as Bartolome de Las Casas took place during the sixteenth century. In nineteenth-century New Zealand some of the debates delved right down into the supposed fecundity rates of indigenous women and the better prospects for racial survival if miscegenation occurred. There were very serious scientific views put forward to account for the demise of the indigenous populations. Some views included: sterility caused by the 'licentiousness' of the women, a vegetable diet, infanticide and abortion. Other causes were put down to a sense of 'hopelessness' and lack of spirit, which came about through contact with 'civilization'.[15]

But there were also state policies (federal, provincial and local) of 'benign neglect' which involved minimal intervention (the 'infected blanket' strategy) while people suffered and died. There were also more proactive policies based around such ideas as 'Manifest Destiny' which sanctioned the taking of indigenous lands by any means.[16] Ward Churchill and other indigenous writers classify these actions as part of the Columbian legacy of genocide.[17] In relation to the diseases and disease which the West is said to have introduced to indigenous peoples, the bigger question has always been the extent to which the impact of disease is an inevitable consequence of contact with the West. The significance of the issues which this question raises emerges when we examine, in a later chapter, the world-wide search currently being undertaken amongst indigenous populations for genetic solutions to Western diseases. Aborigine activist Bobbi Sykes has an 'acid test' for the Western impact on indigenous health which consists of two lists: one a list of diseases introduced by Europeans to Aboriginal people, the other a list of diseases introduced by Aboriginal people to Europeans. There are no items listed on the second list. That empty space tells a very potent story.[18]

The globalization of knowledge and Western culture constantly reaffirms the West's view of itself as the centre of legitimate knowledge, the arbiter of what counts as knowledge and the source of 'civilized' knowledge. This form of global knowledge is generally referred to as 'universal' knowledge, available to all and not really 'owned' by anyone, that is, until non-Western scholars make claims to it. When claims like that are made history is revised (again) so that the story of civilization remains the story of the West. For this purpose, the Mediterranean world, the basin of Arabic culture and the lands east of Constantinople are conveniently appropriated as part of the story of Western civilization, Western philosophy and Western knowledge.[19] Through imperialism, however, these cultures, peoples and their nation states were repositioned as 'oriental', or 'outsider' in order to legitimate the imposition of colonial rule. For indigenous peoples from other places, the real lesson to be learned is that we have no claim whatsoever to civilization. It is something which has been introduced from the West, by the West, to indigenous peoples, for our benefit and for which we should be duly grateful.

The nexus between cultural ways of knowing, scientific discoveries, economic impulses and imperial power enabled the West to make ideological claims to having a superior civilization. The 'idea' of the West became a reality when it was re-presented back to indigenous nations through colonialism. By the nineteenth century colonialism not only meant the imposition of Western authority over indigenous lands, indigenous modes of production and indigenous law and government, but the imposition of Western authority over all aspects of indigenous knowledges, languages and cultures. This authority incorporated what Said refers to as alliances between the ideologies, 'clichés', general beliefs and understandings held about the Orient and the views of 'science' and philosophical theories.[20]

For many indigenous peoples the major agency for imposing this positional superiority over knowledge, language and culture was colonial education. Colonial education came in two basic forms: missionary or religious schooling (which was often residential) followed later by public and secular schooling. Numerous accounts across nations now attest to the critical role played by schools in assimilating colonized peoples, and in the systematic, frequently brutal, forms of denial of indigenous languages, knowledges and cultures. Not all groups of indigenous peoples, however, were permitted to attend school – some groups being already defined in some way as 'ineducable' or just plain troublesome and delinquent. Furthermore, in many examples the indigenous language was used as the medium of instruction and access to the colonizing language was denied specifically. This policy was designed to deny opportunities to participate as citizens.

Colonial education was also used as a mechanism for creating new indigenous elites. It was not the only mechanism for producing elite groups, as the traditional hierarchies within an indigenous society who converted to the colonial ideology also formed part of the elite group. Schooling helped identify talented students who were then groomed for more advanced education. Many of these students were sent away to boarding schools while others were sent to the metropolitan centre in Europe for their university studies. In these settings, and through their learning, students acquired the tastes, and sampled some of the benefits and privileges, of living within the metropolitan culture. Their elite status came about through the alignment of their cultural and economic interests with those of the colonizing group rather than with those of their own society.

School knowledge systems however, were informed by a much more comprehensive system of knowledge which linked universities, scholarly societies and imperial views of culture. Hierarchies of knowledge and theories which had rapidly developed to account for the discoveries of the new world were legitimated at the centre. Schools simply reproduced domesticated versions of that knowledge for uncritical consumption. Although colonial universities saw themselves as being part of an international community and inheritors of a legacy of Western knowledge, they were also part of the historical processes of imperialism. They were established as an essential part of the colonizing process, a bastion of civilization and a sign that a colony and its settlers had 'grown up'. Attempts to 'indigenize' colonial academic institutions and/or individual disciplines within them have been fraught with major struggles over what counts as knowledge, as language, as literature, as curriculum and as the role of intellectuals, and over the critical function of the concept of academic freedom.[21]

Colonizing the Disciplines

Academic knowledges are organized around the idea of disciplines and fields of knowledge. These are deeply implicated in each other and share genealogical foundations in various classical and Enlightenment philosophies. Most of the 'traditional' disciplines are grounded in cultural world views which are either antagonistic to other belief systems or have no methodology for dealing with other knowledge systems. Underpinning all of what is taught at universities is the belief in the concept of science as the all-embracing method for gaining an understanding of the world. Some of these disciplines, however, are more directly implicated in colonialism in that either they have derived their methods and understandings from the colonized world or they have tested their ideas in the colonies. How the colonized were governed, for example, was determined by previous experiences in other colonies and by the prevailing theories about race, gender, climate and other factors generated by 'scientific' methods. Classification systems were developed specifically to cope with the mass of new knowledge generated by the discoveries of the 'new world'. New colonies were the laboratories of Western science. Theories generated from the exploration and exploitation of colonies, and of the people who had prior ownership of these lands, formed the totalizing appropriation of the Other.

Robert Young argues that Hegel

articulates a philosophical structure of the appropriation of the other as a form of knowledge which uncannily simulates the project of nineteenth century imperialism; the construction of knowledges which all operate

through forms of expropriation and incorporation of the other mimics at
a conceptual level the geographical and economic absorption of the non-
European world by the West.[22]

David Goldberg claims that notions of the Other are more deeply
embedded in classical philosophy but became racialized within the
framework of liberalism and the ideas about people and society which
developed as disciplines through liberalism.[23] In an interesting discussion
on the discourses which employ the word 'civilization', John Laffey
suggests that the word 'civilization' entered Anglo-French usage in the
second part of the eighteenth century, enabling the distinction to be
drawn between those who saw themselves as civilized and those who
they then regarded as the 'savages' abroad and at home.[24] As a standard
of judgement, according to Laffey, the word 'civilized' became more
defined with the help of Freud and more specialized in the way different
disciplines employed the concept. One such use was comparative and
allowed for comparisons between children and savages or children and
women, for example. This way of thinking was elaborated further into
psychological justifications for the distinctions between the civilized and
the uncivilized. Freud's influence on the way disciplines developed in
relation to colonialism is further explored by Marianna Torgovnick, who
examines the links between Freud and anthropology in her analysis of
Malinowski's book 'The Sexual Life of Savages'.[25] According to
Turgovnick,

> Freud's explanation of the human psyche in terms of sexuality under-
> girded their endeavors and influenced the structure of many ethnographic
> enquiries at this stage of the discipline's development even when those
> enquiries suggested (as they often did) modifications of Freudian
> paradigms, such as the Oedipus complex.[26]

Other key intellectuals have also been referred to as not so innocent
philosophers of the truth. Henry Louis Gates Jr names Kant, Bacon,
Hume, Jefferson and Hegel as 'great intellectual racialists' who have been
influential in defining the role of literature and its relationship to
humanity, 'The salient sign of the black person's humanity ... would be
the mastering of the very essence of Western civilization, the very
foundation of the complex fiction upon which white Western culture
has been constructed....'[27]

Of all the disciplines, anthropology is the one most closely associated
with the study of the Other and with the defining of primitivism.[28] As
Adam Kuper argued, 'The anthropologists took this primitive society as
their special subject, but in practice primitive society proved to be their
own society (as they understood it) seen in a distorting mirror.[29] The

ethnographic 'gaze' of anthropology has collected, classified and represented other cultures to the extent that anthropologists are often the academics popularly perceived by the indigenous world as the epitome of all that it is bad with academics. Haunani Kay Trask accuses anthropologists of being 'takers and users' who 'exploit the hospitality and generosity of native people'.[30] Trinh T. Minh-ha makes similar references to anthropology and anthropologists, including those whose intent now is to train Third World anthropologists. 'Gone out of date,' she says, 'then revitalised, the mission of civilizing savages mutates into the imperative of "making equal".'[31] In writing a history of geography, Livingstone refers to this discipline as the 'science of imperialism par excellence'.[32] His comment relates to geographical studies into such things as the mapping of racial difference, the links which were drawn between climate and mental abilities, the use of map makers in French colonies for military intelligence and the development of acclimatization societies.[33] As suggested above in the Introduction, history is also implicated in the construction of totalizing master discourses which control the Other. The history of the colonies, from the perspective of the colonizers, has effectively denied other views of what happened and what the significance of historical 'facts' may be to the colonized. 'If history is written by the victor,' argues Janet Abu-Lughod, 'then it must, almost by definition, "deform" the history of the others.'[34] Donna Awatere claims that, 'The process of recording what happened automatically favours the white occupiers because they won. In such a way a whole past is "created" and then given the authority of truth.'[35] These comments have been echoed wherever indigenous peoples have had the opportunity to 'talk back' to the academic world.

While disciplines are implicated in each other, particularly in their shared philosophical foundations, they are also insulated from each other through the maintenance of what are known as disciplinary boundaries. Basil Bernstein has shown how this works in his paper on the 'classification and framing of knowledge'.[36] Insulation enables disciplines to develop independently. Their histories are kept separate and 'pure'. Concepts of 'academic freedom', the 'search for truth' and 'democracy' underpin the notion of independence and are vigorously defended by intellectuals. Insularity protects a discipline from the 'outside', enabling communities of scholars to distance themselves from others and, in the more extreme forms, to absolve themselves of responsibility for what occurs in other branches of their discipline, in the academy and in the world.

In the context of research and at a very pragmatic level researchers from different projects and different research teams can be in and out of the same community (much in the way many government social services are in and out of family homes), showing 'as a collective' little responsibility for the overall impact of their activities. At other levels criticism of individual researchers and their projects is deflected by the argument that those researchers are different in some really significant 'scientific' way from others. How indigenous communities are supposed to work this out is a mystery. There are formal organizations of disciplines, researchers and communities of scholars, many of which have ethical guidelines. These organizations are based on the idea that scholars consent to participate within them as scholars, as professionals, or as ethical human beings. Not all who carry out research in indigenous communities belong to, or are bound by, such collegial self-discipline.

Disciplining the Colonized

The concept of discipline is even more interesting when we think about it not simply as a way of organizing systems of knowledge but also as a way of organizing people or bodies. Foucault has argued that discipline in the eighteenth century became 'formulas of domination' which were at work in schools, hospitals and military organizations.[37] Techniques of detail were developed to maintain discipline over the body. The colonizing of the Other through discipline has a number of different meanings. In terms of the way knowledge was used to discipline the colonized it worked in a variety of ways. The most obvious forms of discipline were through exclusion, marginalization and denial. Indigenous ways of knowing were excluded and marginalized. This happened to indigenous views about land, for example, through the forced imposition of individualized title, through taking land away for 'acts of rebellion', and through redefining land as 'waste land' or 'empty land' and then taking it away. Foucault suggests that one way discipline was distributed was through enclosure. This is the other side of exclusion in that the margins are enclosures: reserved lands are enclosures, schools enclose, but in order to enclose they also exclude, there is something on the outside. Discipline is also partitioned, individuals separated and space compartmentalized. This allowed for efficient supervision and for simultaneous distinctions to be made between individuals. This form of discipline worked at the curriculum level, for example, as a mechanism for selecting out 'native' children and girls for domestic and manual work. It worked also at the assessment level, with normative tests designed around the language and cultural capital of the white middle classes.

The deepest memory of discipline, however, is of the sheer brutality meted out to generations of indigenous communities. Aborigine parents in Australia had their children forcibly removed, sent away beyond reach and 'adopted'.[38] Native children in Canada were sent to residential schools at an age designed to systematically destroy their language and memories of home. There is a growing body of testimony from First Nations people in Canada which tells of years of abuse, neglect and viciousness meted out to young children by teachers and staff in schools run by various religious denominations.[39] These forms of discipline were supported by paternalistic and racist policies and legislation; they were accepted by white communities as necessary conditions which had to be met if indigenous people wanted to become citizens (of their own lands). These forms of discipline affected people physically, emotionally, linguistically and culturally. They were designed to destroy every last remnant of alternative ways of knowing and living, to obliterate collective identities and memories and to impose a new order. Even after the Second World War, when the post-colonial period was beginning according to some cultural studies theorists, many indigenous peoples around the world were still not recognized as humans, let alone citizens. The effect of such discipline was to silence (for ever in some cases) or to suppress the ways of knowing, and the languages for knowing, of many different indigenous peoples. Reclaiming a voice in this context has also been about reclaiming, reconnecting and reordering those ways of knowing which were submerged, hidden or driven underground.

Colonialism and 'Native' Intellectuals

The position within their own societies of 'native' intellectuals who have been trained in the West has been regarded by those involved in nationalist movements as very problematic. Much of the discussion about intellectuals in social and cultural life, and their participation in anti-colonial struggles, is heavily influenced by Marxist revolutionary thought, is framed in the language of oppositional discourse, and was written during the post-war period when struggles for independence were under way.[40] Included within the rubric of 'intellectual' by liberation writers such as Frantz Fanon are also artists, writers, poets, teachers, clerks, officials, the petit bourgeoisie and other professionals engaged in producing 'culture'. Their importance in nationalist movements is related to their abilities to reclaim, rehabilitate and articulate indigenous cultures, and to their implicit leadership over 'the people' as voices which can legitimate a new nationalist consciousness.

At the same time, however, these same producers and legitimators of culture are the group most closely aligned to the colonizers in terms of their class interests, their values and their ways of thinking. This view was restated in 1984 by Donna Awatere who wrote that '[Colonial Maori] ... are noticeable because they have succeeded as white in some section of white culture; economically, through the arts, at sport, through religion, the universities, the professions.'[41] There were concerns that native intellectuals may have become estranged from their own cultural values to the point of being embarrassed by, and hostile towards, all that those values represented. In his introduction to Cesaire's *Return to My Native Land* Mazisi Kunene wrote that, 'those [students] who returned despised and felt ashamed of their semi-literate or illiterate parents who spoke inelegant patois'.[42] In New Zealand the few Maori who were trained at universities in the last part of the nineteenth century are generally viewed positively as individuals who retained a love for their culture and language and who were committed in the context of the times to the survival of indigenous people. What is problematic is that this group of men have been named by the dominant non-indigenous population as individuals who represent 'real' leadership. They have been idealized as the 'saviours of the people' and their example remains as a 'measure' of real leadership.

As Fanon has argued, the problem of creating and legitimating a national culture 'represents a special battlefield'[43] and intellectuals are important to this battle in a number of different ways. In recognizing that intellectuals were trained and enculturated in the West, Fanon identifies three levels through which 'native' intellectuals can progress in their journey 'back over the line'.[44] First there is a phase of proving that intellectuals have been assimilated into the culture of the occupying power. Second comes a period of disturbance and the need for the intellectuals to remember who they actually are, a time for remembering the past. In the third phase the intellectuals seek to awaken the people, to realign themselves with the people and to produce a revolutionary and national literature.[45] In this phase the 'native writer progressively takes on the habit of addressing his [sic] own people'.[46]

Fanon was writing about Algeria and the structure of French colonialism in Africa. He himself was trained in France as a psychiatrist and was influenced by European philosophies. One of the problems of connecting colonialism in New Zealand with its formations elsewhere is that New Zealand, like Canada and Australia, was already privileged as a white dominion within the British Empire and Commonwealth, with the indigenous populations being minorities. Whilst geographically on the margins of Europe, they were economically and culturally closely attached to Britain. Within these states the indigenous people were absolute minorities. The settlers who came arrived as permanent migrants. For indigenous peoples in these places this meant a different kind of experience with colonialism and different possibilities for decolonization. What it also points to is that indigenous intellectuals have emerged from different colonial and indigenous systems. In the

Pacific Islands, for example, scholars come from majority cultures and independent island nations but they have also been incorporated at a regional level into the metropolitan cultures of Australia and New Zealand.[47] Hau'ofa argues that 'the ruling classes of the South Pacific are increasingly culturally homogeneous. They speak the same language, which is English; they share the same ideologies and the same material life styles....'[48]

Currently the role of the 'native' intellectual has been reformulated not in relation to nationalist or liberationary discourses but in relation to the 'post-colonial' intellectual. Many intellectuals who position themselves as 'post-colonial' move across the boundaries of indigenous and metropolitan, institution and community, politics and scholarship. Their place in the academy is still highly problematic. Gayatri Spivak, who writes as a post-colonial Asian/Indian intellectual working in the United States, argues that Third World intellectuals have to position themselves strategically as intellectuals within the academy, within the Third World or indigenous world, and within the Western world in which many intellectuals actually work. The problem, she argues, for Third World intellectuals remains the problem of being taken seriously.

> For me, the question 'Who should speak?' is less crucial than 'Who will listen?'. 'I will speak for myself as a Third World person' is an important position for political mobilisation today. But the real demand is that, when I speak from that position, I should be listened to seriously; not with that kind of benevolent imperialism....[49]

Spivak acknowledges that the task of changing the academy is difficult: 'I would say that if one begins to take a whack at shaking the structure up, one sees how much more consolidated the opposition is.'[50]

The role of intellectuals, teachers, artists and writers in relation to indigenous communities is still problematic, and the rhetoric of liberation still forms part of indigenous discourses. Indigenous communities continue to view education in its Western, modern, sense as being critical to development and self-determination. While criticizing indigenous people who have been educated at universities, on one hand, many indigenous communities will struggle and save to send their children to university on the other. There is a very real ambivalence in indigenous communities towards the role of Western education and those who have been educated in universities. This is reflected in many contexts in struggles over leadership, representation and voice between those perceived as 'traditional' and those seen either as the 'radicals' or simply as having Western credentials. In Australia, the term 'flash blacks' encompasses both those who are well educated and those who have high-flying jobs. In New Zealand one struggle over the value of Western education was played out in the 1980s through a process of reprivileging of 'elders' and a reification of elders as the holders of all traditional knowledge and a parallel deprivileging of the younger, frequently much better educated members (in a Western sense) of an *iwi* (tribe). Maori academics who work away from their tribal territories can easily be criticised because they live away from home, and are perceived therefore as being distanced from the people. At the same time they are drawn into tribal life whenever a crisis occurs or there are additional demands for specialist knowledge and skills. The bottom line, however, is that in very fundamental ways they still remain members of an *iwi* with close relations to families and other community ties.

The 'Authentic, Essentialist, Deeply Spiritual' Other

At a recent international conference held in New Zealand to discuss issues related to indigenous intellectual and cultural property rights, the local newspapers were informed and invited to interview some of the delegates. One news reporter thought it would be a good idea to have a group photograph, suggesting that it would be a very colourful feature for the newspaper to highlight. When she and the photographer turned up at the local *marae* (cultural centre) they were so visibly disappointed at the motley display of track suits, jeans and other items of 'modern' dress, that they chose not to take a photograph. 'Oh, I forgot to come as a native', joked one of the delegates. 'My feathers got confiscated at the airport when I arrived.' 'I suppose my eyes are too blue.' 'Are we supposed to dress naked?' As we have seen, the notion of 'authentic' is highly contested when applied to, or by, indigenous peoples. 'Authorities' and outside experts are often called in to verify, comment upon, and give judgements about the validity of indigenous claims to cultural beliefs, values, ways of knowing and historical accounts. Such issues are often debated vigorously by the 'public', (a category which usually means the dominant group), leading to an endless parading of 'nineteenth century' views of race and racial difference. Questions of who is a 'real indigenous' person, what counts as a 'real indigenous leader', which person displays 'real cultural values' and the criteria used to assess the characteristics of authenticity are frequently the topic of conversation and political debate. These debates are designed to fragment and marginalize those who speak for, or in support of, indigenous issues. They frequently have the effect also of silencing and making invisible the presence of other groups within the indigenous society like women, the urban non-status tribal person and those whose ancestry or 'blood quantam' is 'too white'.[51] In Tasmania, where experts had already determined that Aborigines were 'extinct', the voices of those who still speak as Aboriginal Tasmanians are interpreted as some political invention of a people who no longer exist and who therefore no longer have claims.

Recent poststructural and psychoanalytical feminist theorists have argued against the claims made by earlier generations of feminists that women as a group were different, because their essence as women was fundamentally, undeniably different, and that therefore their 'sisterhood' would be a natural meeting place for all women. Pedagogically, essentialism was attacked because of its assumption that, because of this essence, it was necessary to be a woman and to experience life as a woman before one could analyse or understand women's oppression. Third World women and women of colour also attacked this assumption because it denied the impact of imperialisms, racism and local histories on women, who were different from white women who lived in First World nations. The concept of authentic, which is related to essentialism, was also deconstructed but more so from psychoanalytic perspectives because the concept assumed that if we strip away the oppressions and psychological consequences of oppression we would find a 'pure' and authentic 'self'. One of the major problems with the way words are defined is that these debates are often held by academics in one context, within a specific intellectual discourse, and then appropriated by the media and popular press to serve a more blatant ideological and racist agenda.[52] As Trinh T. Minh-ha put it when writing of anthropologists in particular, 'But once more *they* spoke. *They* decide who is "racism-free or anti-colonial", and they seriously think they can go on formulating criteria for us....'[53]

In the colonized world, however, these terms are not necessarily employed in the same way that First World academics may have used them. The term 'authentic', for example, was an oppositional term used in at least two different ways. First, it was used as a form of articulating what it meant to be dehumanized by colonization; and, second, for reorganizing 'national consciousness' in the struggles for decolonization. The belief in an authentic self is framed within humanism but has been politicized by the colonized world in ways which invoke simultaneous meanings; it does appeal to an idealized past when there was no colonizer, to our strengths in surviving thus far, to our language as an uninterrupted link to our histories, to the ownership of our lands, to our abilities to create and control our own life and death, to a sense of balance among ourselves and with the environment, to our authentic selves as a people. Although this may seem overly idealized, these symbolic appeals remain strategically important in political struggles. Furthermore the imputing of a Western psychological 'self', which is a highly individualized notion, to group consciousness as it is centred in many colonized societies, is not a straightforward translation of the individual to the group, although this is often the only way that Westerners can come to understand what may constitute a group. The purpose of commenting on such a concept is that what counts as 'authentic' is used by the West as one of the criteria to determine who really is indigenous, who is worth saving, who is still innocent and free from Western contamination. There is a very powerful tendency in research to take this argument back to a biological 'essentialism' related to race, because the idea of culture is much more difficult to control. At the heart of such a view of authenticity is a belief that indigenous cultures cannot change, cannot recreate themselves and still claim to be indigenous. Nor can they be complicated, internally diverse or contradictory. Only the West has that privilege.

The concept of essentialism is also discussed in different ways within the indigenous world. It is accepted as a term which is related to humanism and is seen therefore in the same way as the idea of authenticity. In this use of the word, claiming essential characteristics is as much strategic as anything else, because it has been about claiming human rights and indigenous rights. But the essence of a person is also discussed in relation to indigenous concepts of spirituality. In these views, the essence of a person has a genealogy which can be traced back to an earth parent, usually glossed as an Earth Mother. A human person does not stand alone, but shares with other animate and, in the Western sense, 'inanimate' beings, a relationship based on a shared 'essence' of life. The significance of place, of land, of landscape, of other things in the universe, in defining the very essence of a people, makes for a very different rendering of the term essentialism as used by indigenous peoples.

The arguments of different indigenous peoples based on spiritual relationships to the universe, to the landscape and to stones, rocks, insects and other things, seen and unseen, have been difficult arguments for Western systems of knowledge to deal with or accept. These arguments give a partial indication of the different world views and alternative ways of coming to know, and of being, which still endure within the indigenous world. Concepts of spirituality which Christianity attempted to destroy, then to appropriate, and then to claim, are critical sites of resistance for indigenous peoples. The values, attitudes, concepts and language embedded in beliefs about spirituality represent, in many cases, the clearest contrast and mark of difference between indigenous peoples and the West. It is one of the few parts of ourselves which the West cannot decipher, cannot understand and cannot control ... yet.

Notes

1 Mita, M. (1989), 'Merata Mita On...', in the *New Zealand Listener*, 14 October, p. 30.

2 Ngugi Wa Thiong'o (1986), *Decolonizing the Mind: the Politics of Language in African Literature*, James Currey, London.

3 Jaggar, A. (1983), *Feminist Politics and Human Nature*, Harvester Press, Sussex.

4 Hall, S. (1992), 'The West and the Rest: Discourse and Power', Chapter 6 of *Formations of Modernity*, eds S. Hall and B. Gielben, Polity Press and Open University, Cambridge, pp. 276–320.

5 Goonatilake, S. (1982), 'Colonies: Scientific Expansion (and Contraction)', in *Review*, Vol. 5, No. 3, Winter, pp. 413–36.

6 Said, E. (1978), *Orientalism*, Vintage Books, New York, p. 7.

7 Bazin, M. (1993), 'Our Sciences, Their Science', in *Race and Class*, Vol. 34, No. 2, pp. 35–6.

8 Goonatilake, 'Colonies'.

9 Adas, M. (1989), *Machines as the Measure of Man. Science, Technology and Ideologies of Western Dominance*, Cornell University Press, Ithaca.

10 Clifford, J. (1988), *The Predicament of Culture, Twentieth Century Ethnography, Literature, and Art*, Harvard University Press, Cambridge, p. 231. See also on the topic of collection, Ames, M. (1986), *Museums, The Public and Anthropology*, University of Columbia Press, London.

11 Brockway, L. H. (1979), *Science and Colonial Expansion. The Role of the British Royal Botanical Gardens*, Academic Press, New York, p. 187.

12 Goonatilake, 'Colonies', p. 432.

13 Crosby, A. W. (1986), 'Biotic Change in Nineteenth Century New Zealand', in *Review*, Vol. 9, No. 3, Winter, pp. 325–37.

14 Smith, C. W. (1994), 'Kimihia te Matauranga, Colonization and Iwi Development', MA thesis, University of Auckland, p. 23.

15 Pool, D. L. (1977), *The Maori Population of New Zealand 1769–1971*, Auckland University Press and Oxford University Press, Auckland, pp. 75–105.

16 Churchill, W. (1994), *Indians Are Us? Culture and Genocide in Native North America*, Common Courage Press, Maine.

17 *Ibid.*, pp. 28–42.

18 Sykes, R. B. (1989), *Black Majority*, Hudson Hawthorn, Victoria, p. 185.

19 Bernal, M. (1991), *Black Athena, The Afroasiatic Roots of Classical Civilization*, Vintage, London.

20 Said, E. *Orientalism*, pp. 205–6.

21 See, for examples of these debates in relation to indigenous issues, Ngugi wa Thiong'o (1986), *Decolonizing the Mind. The Politics of Language in African Literature*, James Currey, London, and Haunani Kay Trask (1993), *From a Native Daughter*, Common Courage Press, Maine.

22 Young, R. (1990), *White Mythologies, Writing, History and the West*, Routledge, London, p. 3.

23 Goldberg, D. T. (1993), *Racist Culture: Philosophy and the Politics of Meaning*, Blackwell, Oxford.

24 Laffey, J. F. (1993), *Civilization and its Discontented*, Black Rose Books, New York.

25 Torgovnick, M. (1990), *Gone Primitive: Savage Intellects, Modern Lives*, University of Chicago Press, Chicago.

26 *Ibid.*, p. 7.

27 Gates, H. L. (1994), 'Authority (White) Power and the (Black) Critic: It's All

Greek to Me', in *Culture/Power/History*, eds N. Dirks, G. Eley and S. B. Ortner, Princeton University Press, New Jersey.

28 Stocking, G. Jr (1987), *Victorian Anthropology*, The Free Press, London.

29 Kuper, A. (1988), *The Invention of Primitive Society*, Routledge, London, p. 5.

30 Trask, H. K. (1993), *From a Native Daughter*, Common Courage Press, Maine.

31 Minh-ha, Trinh T. (1989), *Woman, Native, Other*, Indiana University Press, Bloomington, p. 59.

32 Livingstone, D. (1992), *The Geographical Tradition*, Blackwell, Oxford.

33 *Ibid.*, p. 216.

34 Abu-Lughod, J. (1989), 'On the Remaking of History: How to Reinvent the Past', in *Remaking History*, Dia Art Foundation, Bay Press, Seattle, p. 118.

35 Awatere, D. (1983), 'Awatere on Intellectuals: Academic Fragmentation or Visionary Unity', article in *Craccum*, Auckland University Students' Association, 3 May, Auckland, pp. 6–7.

36 Bernstein, B. (1971), 'On the Classification and Framing of Knowledge' in *Knowledge and Control: New Directions for the Sociology of Education*, ed. M. F. D. Young, Collier Macmillan, London, pp. 47–69.

37 Foucault, M. (1977), *Discipline and Punish: The Birth of the Prison*, trans. A. Sheridan, Penguin, London, p. 137.

38 This practice is known popularly as the 'stolen children' policy but an official inquiry was conducted by the Australian government called 'A National Inquiry into the Separation of Aboriginal and Torres Strait Islander Children from Their Families'. This was completed in 1997.

39. A government commission to investigate the abuses in the residential school system for Indian children was recently completed by the Canadian government. For further background read Furness, E. (1995), *Victims of Benevolence: The Dark Legacy of the Williams Lake Residential School*, Arsenal Pulp Press, Vancouver; Haig-Brown, C. (1988), *Resistance and Renewal: Surviving the Indian Residential School*, Tillacum Library, Vancouver in L. Taine, ed. (1993), *Residential Schools: the Stolen Years*, University of Saskatechewan Press, Saskatson.

40 Gramsci's views on the intellectual have been influential, among other Marxist views. So too have the existentialist views of Jean Paul Sartre who wrote the introduction to Fanon's book, *The Wretched of the Earth*. A critique of these influences on Fanon, in particular, can be read in Young, *White Mythologies*.

41 Awatere, D. (1984), Maori Sovereignty, Broadsheet, Auckland, p. 83.

42 Cesaire, A. (1969), *Return to My Native Land*, translated by John Berger and Ana Bostock, introduction by Mazisi Kunene, Penguin Books, Harmondsworth, p. 24.

43 Fanon, F. (1990), *The Wretched of the Earth*, Penguin, London, p. 193.

44 *Ibid.*, pp. 178–9.

45 *Ibid.*, p. 179.

46 *Ibid.*, p. 193.

47 Hau'ofa, E. (1987), 'The New South Pacific Society: Integration and Independence', in *Class and Culture in the South Pacific*, eds A. Hooper, S. Britton, R. Crocombe, J. Huntsman and C. Macpherson, Centre for Pacific Studies, University of Auckland, Institute for Pacific Studies, University of the South Pacific, pp. 1–15.

48 *Ibid.*, p. 3.

49 Spivak, G. (1990), 'Questions of Multiculturalism', in *The Post-Colonial Critic: Interviews, Strategies, Dialogues*, ed. S. Harasayam, Routledge, New York, pp. 59–60.

50 Spivak, G. (1990), 'Criticism, Feminism and the Institution', in *The Post-Colonial Critic*, p. 6.
51 'Blood quantum' refers to the 'amount' of native blood one has and is used in places such as Hawai'i to determine eligibility access to Hawai'ian lands and identity. It is based on racial beliefs that the more indigenous peoples inter-married the more assimilated or 'watered down' they became. Conversely if they did not inter-marry they remained 'pure'.
52 Similar debates occur over a word such as 'invention', where anthropologists may talk to each other about the invention of culture; the media can then accuse indigenous people of inventing culture to serve their own interests *at the expense of the dominant group*. This occurred in New Zealand over an article written by A. Hanson (1991), 'The Making of the Maori: Culture Invention and its Logic', in *American Anthropologist*, pp. 890–902. One of the larger daily newspapers took the article and turned it into the following headline: 'US EXPERT SAYS MAORI CULTURE INVENTED', *Dominion*, Saturday 24 February.
53 Minh-ha, Trin T., *Woman, Native, Other,* p. 59.

CHAPTER 4

Research Adventures
on Indigenous Land

As mentioned earlier, travellers' tales and other anecdotal ways of representing indigenous peoples have contributed to the general impressions and the milieu of ideas that have informed Western knowledge and Western constructions of the Other. There has been recent theorising of the significance of travel, and of location, on shaping Western understandings of the Other and producing more critical understandings of the nature of theory.[1] bell hooks, in describing black representations of whiteness, writes of these journeys as being acts of terror which have become part of our memory.[2] While travelling theory may focus on the location of those who travel, the attention here is on the people whose bodies, territories, beliefs and values have been travelled *through*. One particular genre of travellers' tales relates to the 'adventures' experienced in the new world, in Indian country, or Maoriland, or some other similarly named territory. These adventures were recounted with some relish; they told stories of survival under adversity and recorded eye witness accounts of fabulous, horrible, secret, never-seen-before-by-a-European ceremonies, rituals or events. From an indigenous perspective all early Westerners were travellers who came with a mission (scientific, religious or entrepreneurial), rather than with a sense of adventure, and many decided to stay. The sense of adventure and spirit which is contained in histories of science and biographies of scientists are a good example of how wondrous and exciting the discoveries of 'new scientific knowledge' from the new world were perceived in the West. Missionaries and traders also conveyed that sense of adventure in their accounts. For missionaries there was the huge and exciting minefield of lost and fallen souls who needed rescuing. The savagery, abhorrence and 'despicability' of the natives challenged their very vocabulary. For traders, the opportunities were equally immense, their field of operations covering vast continents and oceans.

Although always ethnocentric and patriarchal, travellers' accounts remain interesting because of the details and sometimes perceptive (and on occasions reflective) comments made by some writers of the events they were recording. There was a consciousness expressed in some accounts of the 'need' to record what was seen in the interests of expanding knowledge and of the need to write things down before too many changes occurred to the peoples being observed. There were also artistic representations of indigenous peoples that had wide appeal to audiences in Europe. Many travellers, including women, were aristocratic and had the resources to travel; they were available for speaking engagements on their return home.[3] Various scientific societies and gentlemen's clubs were keen to discuss and debate the travel exploits of such people. The more romanticized versions of travellers fed the public imagination with tales of daring and gallantry. An example of this is the story of Pocahontas.

This chapter discusses some of the ways in which the more informal systems for collecting information on and about indigenous societies became more formally constituted and institutionalised within the New Zealand colonial context. One of the reasons why this is important is that the more formal these systems became, the more authoritative and influential they were. What may have begun as early fanciful, ill-informed opinions or explanations of indigenous life and customs quickly entered the language and became ways of representing and relating to indigenous peoples. In the case of religious missionaries the viewpoints expressed were designed as much to justify further financial support from their central base as to justify any ideological motivations. The more horrendous and evil the people, the stronger the imperative was to carry out God's work. Many of these early travellers' views are now taken for granted as facts and have become embedded in the language and attitudes of non-indigenous people towards indigenous peoples. They continue to frame the discourses on indigenous issues of a particular society and account in part for the very specific use of language, including terms of abuse, the sorts of issues which are selected for debate and even the types of resistance being mounted by indigenous peoples.

It is through both the organization of interested people into learned societies and the institutionalization of their ideas and attitudes that the directions and priorities of research into indigenous peoples have been shaped. The role in this process of well-intentioned officials, missionaries, traders and travellers, who became familiar with indigenous customs, languages and made important friends, is a complex one. They were often identified as 'friends' of the natives to be used, reviled, sometimes honoured by their own societies and by their indigenous host society. They often formed relationships with indigenous women, had children, were gifted lands and things of value. Others became more serious scholars intent on recording the details of what they viewed as a dying culture. Many also reinvented themselves, so to speak, beginning their adventures perhaps as traders and ending them as highly-respected 'orientalists'. Others built their careers as government soldiers intent on killing resistant indigenous populations and then became teachers or surveyors, magistrates or settler-elected politicians.

They Came, They Saw, They Named, They Claimed

In the Pacific context, research on indigenous Maori by Europeans began in a systematic way from Cook's first voyage. Prior to that time Abel Tasman's observations and encounters with Maori (which were not happy ones) had infiltrated into the general consciousness of Europeans as travellers' tales.[4] Maori were represented as savages and, according to Salmond, his descriptions 'gave Maori a bloodthirsty reputation in Europe'.[5] Tasman is also credited as the man who 'discovered' and 'named' New Zealand. Although Salmond argues that 'not much can be learned about Maori life from this voyage',[6] Tasman and his crew nevertheless signalled the start of recorded observations of Maori which has since led some Maori to claim that we 'are the most researched people in the world'.[7] Similar claims are made by other indigenous people who can trace back even further the beginnings of their recorded encounters.

Cook's voyages to New Zealand are more important to Maori in that the link to science and research was much more explicit. His first voyage was funded partially by the Royal Society in order that the transit of Venus could be observed in Tahiti. The journey also included the southern places already known as New Zealand and Australia. Joseph Banks was regarded highly as a botanist and sailed with Cook, taking his own small entourage of eight people. His observations of plant life and his penchant for collecting plants and birds also included observations of Maori and the potential of New Zealand as a colony. Banks's journal covers a number of topics which were of great interest at that time and was full of comparisons with other places known to the British. The ease with which comparisons could be made reinforce the imperial eye with which Banks saw the land and all that was part of it. While at one level this ability could be called knowledge, it was imperial knowledge that measured everything new against what was known by Banks himself. He noted the quality of the natural resources and commented on the 'immense quantity of woodland, which was yet uncleared, but promised great returns to the people who would take the trouble of Clearing it'.[8] He noted the 'properest place we have yet seen for establishing a colony' along what he called the River Thames. 'The River Thames would furnish plenty of fish, and the soil make ample returns of any European Vegetables sown in it.'[9] After describing the landscape, insects and butterflies, sea animals, birds, vegetables, cultivated plants and fruits, Banks described the people – the men, then the women – with the same detached eye. He comments on their appearances and their dispositions, still making comparisons with other 'Islanders' (South Sea Islanders) they had previously met. He goes on to write about their clothing, their houses, their food, their technology, their weaponry, death ceremonies, religion and language. He commented on what he liked and on what disgusted him, and made suppositions which attempted to explain what he considered 'curious'. In short, his work constituted a pre-ethnography of those sections of Maori society which Banks encountered.

Unlike Tasman, who visited only one coastline, Cook circum-navigated New Zealand and proceeded to rename the entire country at will. This renaming was at one level entirely arbitrary, responding to the fortunes or misfortunes of those on board the ship and to the impressions gained from out at sea of the land they were observing. Other names, however, recalled the geography and people of Britain. These names and the landmarks associated with them were inscribed on maps and charts and thus entered into the West's archive as the spoils of discovery. The renaming of the world has never stopped. After the Treaty of Waitangi was signed in 1840 and settlement by British settlers became more intensive, townships, streets and regions were renamed after other parts of the British Empire. Some towns took on names which reflected Britain's battles in other parts of its Empire, such as India, or Britain's heroes from its various conquests of other nations. Naming the world has been likened by Paulo Freire to claiming the world and claiming those ways of viewing the world that count as legitimate.[10]

If the first encounters with Europeans were ones in which indigenous people were observed as research objects, what did that mean for Maori? Salmond argues that these observations, or what she refers to as 'interpretative encounters', occurred both ways, with Maori people exercising a considerable degree of agency over how they saw these first Europeans and pursuing their own agenda.[11] The master narrative has been the one established from European accounts, while Maori inter-pretations remained as oral stories. The difficulty with trying to extract specific reactions to 'research' is that, for the most part, Maori people involved did not 'know', in the sense that we would now expect them to know, that they were being researched. Research could not be disconnected from other European activities. 'Researchers' were also missionaries, amateur botanists, surveyors, officials, traders – any European, in fact, who was able to write or draw pictures. Indeed, many Europeans managed to combine several occupations into one life. Colenso, for example, began life in New Zealand as a printer, was ordained as a minister and then awarded medals as a botanist. In between his ordination and honours as a botanist he had a child with a Maori woman while still married, was defrocked, and then reinstated as a minister.[12]

During the Land Wars which took place in New Zealand in the 1860s the multiple roles of colonists became far more problematic for some tribes, as military men who led campaigns against Maori then became resident magistrates or land commissioners who presided over the alienation of Maori land, or interpreters in trials or land dealings, or, in later life, 'reliable' and respected sources on Maori beliefs and customs.[13] Their authority as experts in Maori things was vested in the whole structure of colonialism so that while engaging in very colonial operations with Maori, they also carried out investigations into Maori life which later were published under their names. Through their publications they came to be seen by the outside world as knowledgeable, informed and relatively 'objective'. Their 'informants' were relegated to obscurity, their colonial activities seen as unproblematic, and their chronic ethnocentrism viewed as a sign of the times.

At one level, all the Europeans who wrote about their travels, their time in residence and their experiences with indigenous peoples contributed to the larger research encounter which occurred between the colonizing world and indigenous worlds. For example, there were a number of books published in the nineteenth century which told the stories of life in the New Zealand colony and of contact with Maori through the eyes of British colonists. These 'adventures' idealized some aspects of life in the colony and obviously, as autobiographies, put the authors at the centre of events. At the same time, the actual experience the writers had and their encounters with 'real life savages' continually fed the imaginations of people 'back home'. On the basis of these stories and the hard-sell of settlement companies, new migrants set off for their own adventures in the colonies armed with all their newly acquired misinformation about the availability of land, indigenous land, and the opportunity to make new lives.

Those observers of indigenous peoples whose interest was of a more 'scientific' nature could be regarded as being far more dangerous in that they had theories to prove, evidence and data to gather and specific languages by which they could classify and describe the indigenous world. So, for example, skulls were measured and weighed to prove that 'primitive' minds were smaller than the European mind.[14] This was the 'science' of craniometry.[15] Other stories are told of burial caves being 'discovered' and examined for the precious 'artefacts' which were left with the dead, of carved houses being dismantled and shipped to England, of dried and shrunken heads sold and exported back to museums. This side of the research encounter, with the inducements that sometimes went with the exchange of 'artefacts', has left a long-lasting resentment among indigenous peoples, who are now attempting to have items and the remains of ancestors returned to their own people.

On the Road to ... Research

Some amateur scientists developed a passion for their work which extended to more systematic studies of indigenous peoples. In New Zealand George Grey, Percy Smith and Elsdon Best – among a number of other collectors and appreciators of Maori knowledge – represent the kinds of increasingly systematic research encounters which occurred between Maori and Europeans in the nineteenth and early twentieth centuries. These encounters remain influential in that they also involved an attitude to indigenous peoples which was a complex mixture of colonial exploitation and fostered dependence. They had a deep sympathy towards Maori people as an ideal while being hostile towards those Maori who fell short of this construct. They were also driven by the need to collect volumes of material. Sir George Grey, who served as a colonial official in Australia, New Zealand and South Africa, is described by Stocking as a 'benevolent administrative despot [with an] iron willed personality' and a 'systematic propagator of Anglo-Saxon imperialism in a period of colonial retrenchment'.[16] Stocking also refers to Grey, however, as 'one of the more perceptive ethnographers of his day and author of some of the most influential ethnographic work this century'.[17] As Governor, Grey collected around him a number of Maori chiefs and confidants. Much of his material on Maori was gathered from his close friendships with chiefs whose names mean little to the non-Maori audience and whose knowledge has been rendered entirely invisible.

Both Percy Smith and Elsdon Best were colonial officials who surveyed Maori land on one hand and observed Maori life on the other. Percy Smith, who was older than Best, eventually became Surveyor General. Elsdon Best has been acknowledged as a New Zealand-born ethnologist of high standing in the scientific community because of his years of meticulous study of Maori culture. He spent some time in the Armed Constabulary and was sent to Taranaki to 'put down' the passive resistance of Te Whiti. His senior officer and brother-in-law, Captain Gudgeon, and Percy Smith, who was also at Taranaki, later became the founding members of the Polynesian Society. Percy Smith became Best's mentor and after Best left the Armed Constabulary he followed Smith to the heavily forested and isolated Urewera in the eastern Bay of Plenty in 1895 to assist in the building of a road through the lands of Tuhoe. Best remained in the Urewera until 1910. In 1900 he became a health inspector in the Mataatua District and then became the ethnologist at the Dominion Museum. Most of Best's research was carried out among the people of Tuhoe.

Best's research amongst Tuhoe is probably the most significant early work on Maori because it was clearly conceived by Best as research, and followed many of the conventions now associated with social science. This includes systematic note taking, checking and rechecking of sources, interviews with informants and, eventually, the publication of results. At the same time, however, he was not involved with Tuhoe simply as a researcher. He was employed initially as paymaster-storeman for the road works and was expected to ease the communications between the road workers, who were British, and the chiefs of Tuhoe, who did not actually desire to have a road built through their lands.[18] He was to play this intermediary role between Maori and colonial officials for the rest of his life. Colonial officials clearly saw Best as a 'friend of the Maori', but how Maori, particularly Tuhoe, regarded him has been left largely to anecdote and unrecorded stories.[19]

Revisiting some of Best's material suggests that the people of Tuhoe did react to Best, the researcher, in a number of ways. There were acts of openness and generosity as well as occasions of hostility and resistance. Best, for his part, was deeply committed to his pursuit of knowledge, but was also generous and willing to learn from his mistakes. He either paid or gave a 'gift' to some of his informants. It is unclear where this practice came from; it is possible to interpret it in terms of established Maori values of gifting or in a less sympathetic context of bribery. On the other hand, Best had to work hard to gain the trust of the learned 'experts' known as *tohunga*. According to Elsdon Craig, his nephew and biographer, there were a number of incidents which shed some light on how the people dealt with the researcher. Best was determined to get access to the forms of knowledge held by *tohunga* which were more 'sacred', and at one level he was an opportunist who exploited friendships with chiefs and *tohunga*. In return, it appears that he was treated with respect; his mistakes were forgiven and his intense questioning answered with patience. Some of the things Best experienced are still important today in Maori contexts; for example, the use of spiritual 'chants' known as *karakia* to protect knowledge and to open a discussion about sacred things. Meetings or *hui* were called to discuss collectively relevant issues or concerns. There were also the 'little tests and barriers' that were put before Best (just as Best tested their knowledge). Many of the 'strategies' employed by the people need to be considered within a context. First, this was a context in which Maori, even Tuhoe who had been cut off from much contact with Europeans, no longer had control over their own lives or lands and were dealing with hostile officials. A friend such as Best was an important friend to have in the circumstances. Second, the strong belief was held at the time that the Maori race was dying, or that civilization was occurring so rapidly that the 'traditional' needed to be recorded as rapidly as possible before it became polluted or lost. The exchange of highly sacred forms of knowledge for sheer physical survival seems to be a pragmatic solution to the encroachment of colonization, but it did not occur as a full-scale divulging of things held to be important. Best did give up on some pursuits but put his change of tack down to the lack of importance of the topic, not his failure to discover anything.

Best gained his knowledge from the *tohunga* of Tuhoe, and some from other tribes. He sought the most knowledgeable and most respected *tohunga* who had access to the kind of knowledge he thought would reveal the most profound aspects of primitive culture. Their knowledge existed within a much wider cultural framework which was under attack by the colonial urge to civilize and assimilate Maori. In 1907 *tohunga* were outlawed through the Tohunga Suppression Act which sought to prevent *tohunga* from practising 'quackery'. While Best lives on as an expert, the names of his informants and the rest of their knowledge lie buried in manuscripts and archives.

Organizing Research

Scientific and learned societies were very important for the organization of science in eighteenth-century Europe.[20] This was a new development based on similar systems for the organization of other cultural activities such as salons, gentlemen's clubs and religious orders. The Royal Society of London and the Paris Academy were established in the 1660s as were a few others.[21] They grew partly in resistance to the role universities then played as religious institutions, where science was expected to conform to theological prescriptions. For the most part these earlier models were associated with wealthy patrons and private capital as their source of funding. By the eighteenth century, however, scientific societies had become associated with secular government and received support from government sources.[22] This shift allowed for the systematic exchange and distribution of ideas and for the growth of some form of consensus among a community of scientists. The disciplines, particularly those in the social sciences, were being formed around this consensual groupings of scientists.

In the nineteenth century the scientific drive assumed that there were universal models of human society and human nature, and that societies deemed to be more primitive could contribute to science by showing the most simple, most fundamental systems of social organization. Learned societies were an important part of the way these ideas were organized and then redistributed. Certainly in New Zealand, fellows and members of various societies came, looked, named and then wrote about their own encounters with the flora, fauna and people they met. Societies developed within New Zealand in the latter part of the nineteenth century to further assist these scholarly pursuits. Learned societies exerted some form of ethical control over their members, partly by encouraging the view that they were good scholars with open minds, and mostly by insisting that they should be gentlemen with the 'right conduct'.[23] Access to the status of gentleman and scholar was based on class divisions and wealth. The significance of these societies for indigenous peoples, however, is that they defined, produced and reproduced 'culture': not just scientific culture, but the culture of knowledge, the culture of elitism, the culture of patriarchy.

Joseph Banks was already a member of the Royal Society when he set forth on Cook's first voyage to the South Pacific in 1769. In fact the Royal Society partially funded the voyage and Banks was wealthy enough to bring four servants with him. This scientific interest in the Pacific began with Roggeveen's voyage, funded by the Dutch West India Company in 1721. These earlier expeditions were driven by several different objectives from the search for a treasure-filled El Dorado and other trade possibilities to scientific interest in, and speculations about, the nature of human beings, exploring in particular Rousseau's view of the noble savage. With colonization as a primary objective, in the nineteenth century scientific interest shifted, according to Sorrenson, towards more ethnographic descriptions.[24] Implied in the urgency for describing indigenous cultures was the sense that these cultures were becoming 'contaminated' by contact with the West and were likely to die out. Literary and learned societies were established alongside other settler activities, and by the 1860s there were a number of such societies functioning in New Zealand. These culminated in 1867 with the passing of legislation establishing the New Zealand Institute and a public museum. This occurred before the establishment of the University of New Zealand. The *Transactions and Proceedings of the New Zealand Institute* provided the first scholarly New Zealand journal for the publication of research on Maori.

The Polynesian Society was established in 1892. Percy Smith's initial proposal conforms to the view that central to the scientific endeavour there was the need for a community of scientists, and for a system of communication which allowed for the production of ideas. Smith saw the need for a Society which would allow for 'communication, co-operation and mutual criticism between those interested in studying Polynesian anthropology, ethnology, philology, history, manners and customs of the Oceanic races, and preservation of all that relates to such subjects in a permanent form'.[25] The comparative emphasis was reflected in the membership, with the first patron being the Hawai'ian Queen Lili'iokalani. Two other Hawai'ian women joined and in fact the Hawai'ian women appear to be the only women members when the Polynesian Society was established. There were two Maori men and a Samoan who were also invited to join.

Percy Smith and Elsdon Best exerted considerable influence over the way Maori histories were theorized. Their theories on the origin of Maori can be summarized in two 'orthodoxies' which have become taken for granted despite being challenged and discredited. Percy Smith is regarded as having established the chronology of Maori migration through a method of analysing Maori genealogies and attributing an 'average' life span to each generation. Through this 'method', dates and time spans were established and the myth of the 'Great Fleet' entered the way the Maori past has been framed historically and geographically. This 'myth' says that the main group of Maori people arrived in New Zealand in about 1300 AD in a Great Fleet of canoes. Elsdon Best was a supporter of the idea that there were some Maori whose origins were more 'Melanesian' and who, as a people, must have been conquered and assimilated by the more aggressive Maori of Polynesian ancestry. This belief reinforced the second major myth, namely the myth of the Moriori. This 'myth' says that there was a more peaceful group of people in New Zealand before the Maori arrived and because Maori were naturally more aggressive they conquered and wiped out the Moriori. The power of these two 'myths' lies partly in the fact that they have shaped the understandings about Maori of generations of both indigenous and non-indigenous school children, and partly in that they have also shaped academic discourses on Maori by scholars set on proving or disproving various origin theories. The greater ideological significance of the myths, however, is that they support and give legitimacy to the role of conquest and migration in colonization. By 'demonstrating' that conquest and then migration were integral to indigenous patterns of settlement it suggested that these were natural and universal processes of human settlement which, under Western modes of colonization, were much more civilized and humane – for which the indigenous Maori ought to be duly grateful.

Academic research on Maori became oriented to such debates and obsessed with describing various modes of cultural decay. The 'fatal impact' of the West on indigenous societies generally has been theorized as a phased progression from: (1) initial discovery and contact, (2) population decline, (3) acculturation, (4) assimilation, (5) 'reinvention' as a hybrid, ethnic culture. While the terms may differ across various theoretical paradigms the historical descent into a state of nothingness and hopelessness has tended to persist. Indigenous perspectives also show a phased progression, more likely to be articulated as: (1) contact and invasion, (2) genocide and destruction, (3) resistance and survival (4) recovery as indigenous peoples. The sense of hope and optimism is a characteristic of contemporary indigenous politics which is often criticized, by non-indigenous scholars, because it is viewed as being overly idealistic.

While Western theories and academics were describing, defining and explaining cultural demise, however, indigenous peoples were having their lands and resources systematically stripped by the state; were becoming ever more marginalized; and were subjected to the layers of colonialism imposed through economic and social policies. This failure of research, and of the academic community, to address the real social issues of Maori was recalled in later times when indigenous disquiet became more politicized and sophisticated. Very direct confrontations took place between Maori and some academic communities. Such confrontations have also occurred in Australia and other parts of the indigenous world, resulting in much more active resistances by communities to the presence and activities of researchers.

Trading the Other

In a recent newspaper headline a New Zealand politician is quoted as saying, in reference to a highly politicized debate on the funding of Maori television, that 'Maori should be paid in blankets'.[26] Apart from providing, yet again, a very good example of the power and persistence of colonial discourses, the comment illustrates the economic under-pinnings of cultural imperialism. There is a direct relationship between the expansion of knowledge, the expansion of trade and the expansion of empire. That relationship continues, although in the reframed discourse of globalization it is referred to as the relationship between the expansion of technology/information, the expansion of economic opportunities and the expansion of 'the market'. Although much has been written about the development of trade and the role of traders and trading companies in imperialism, including the role of indigenous entrepreneurs in the process, the indigenous world is still coming to grips with the extent to which the 'trade' of human beings, artefacts, curios, art works, specimens and other cultural items has scattered our remains across the globe. The term 'trade' assumes at the very least a two-way transaction between those who sold and those who bought. It further assumes that human beings and other cultural items were commodities or goods and were actually available 'for sale'. For indigenous peoples those assumptions are not held. From indigenous perspectives territories, peoples and their possessions were stolen, not traded.[27]

Many indigenous responses to Western 'trading' practices have generally been framed by the Western juridical system and have had to argue claims on the basis of proven theft, or of outrageously unjust rates of exchange (one hundred blankets and fifty beads do not buy one hundred million hectares of land for the rest of eternity). The more difficult claims have attempted to establish recognition of indigenous spirituality in Western law. Even when evidence is overwhelmingly in favour of an indigenous case, there are often statutes of limitation which determine how far back in time a claim can reach, or there are international agreements between states, or some institutions just refuse in principle to consider the possibility that an indigenous group have a claim at all. The legacy, however, of the fragmentation and alienation of a cultural 'estate' over hundreds of years is that the material connection between people, their place, their languages, their beliefs and their practices has been torn apart.

The real critical question in this discussion relates to the commercial nature of knowledge 'transfer', regardless of what knowledge is collected or how that knowledge has been collected or is represented. In this sense, the people and their culture, the material and the spiritual, the exotic and the fantastic, became not just the stuff of dreams and imagination, or stereotypes and eroticism but of the first truly global commercial enterprise: *trading the Other*. This trade had its origins before the Enlightenment, but capitalism and Western culture have transformed earlier trade practices (such as feudal systems of tribute), through the development of native appetites for goods and foreign desires for the strange; the making of labour and consumer markets; the protection of trade routes, markets and practices; and the creation of systems for protecting the power of the rich and maintaining the powerlessness of the poor. Trading the Other is a vast industry based on the positional superiority and advantages gained under imperialism. It is concerned more with ideas, language, knowledge, images, beliefs and fantasies than any other industry. Trading the Other deeply, intimately, defines Western thinking and identity. As a trade, it has no concern for the peoples who originally produced the ideas or images, or with how and why they produced those ways of knowing. It will not, indeed, cannot, return the raw materials from which its products have been made. It no longer has an administrative Head Office with regional offices to which indigenous peoples can go, queue for hours and register complaints which will not be listened to or acted upon.

In its contemporary formations trading the Other is, for bell hooks in an essay called 'Eating the Other', a 'commodification of otherness', which, she argues, 'has been so successful because it is offered as a new delight, more intense, more satisfying than normal ways of doing and feeling'.[28] hooks also points out how easily and dangerously trading the Other can be incorporated into black politics where communities of resistances are replaced by communities of consumption. Maori academic Graham Smith lists some of the new ways in which Maori indigenous culture is being prepared for trade in the 'new right' economic framework that dominates the New Zealand scene. These include the commodification of such things as: treaty rights, identity, traditional knowledge, traditional customs, traditional organizations, land titles, fauna and flora.[29] While all of these items previously have been the subject of efforts to remove, control and assimilate, the 'new' attacks are aimed at what remains of the indigenous estate and are a very sharp reminder of how control over the agenda, the terms of reference, and the processes for settling the unsettled business of indigenous matters is still held and determined by the colonizing majority. Indigenous peoples who have actively resisted moves to create regional free trade areas as part of the global market place are viewed as a major barrier to free trade. Trading the Other is big business. For indigenous peoples trading ourselves is not on the agenda.

Defining the Indigenous 'Problem'

It might seem curious to link travellers and traders with the more serious endeavours of amateur researchers and scientists. From indigenous perspectives the finer distinctions between categories of colonizers were not made along the lines of science and the rest. It was more likely to be a distinction between those who were 'friends' and those who were not. One of the sites where different knowledges about indigenous peoples intersect is in discussions on 'The … (*insert name of indigenous group*) problem'. This was sometimes expressed as 'The … question'. The 'indigenous problem' is a recurrent theme in all imperial and colonial attempts to deal with indigenous peoples. It originates within the wider discourses of racism, sexism and other forms of positioning the Other. Its neatness and simplicity gives the term its power and durability. Framing 'the … problem', mapping it, describing it in all its different manifestations, trying to get rid of it, laying blame for it, talking about it, writing newspaper columns about it, drawing cartoons about it, teaching about it, *researching* it, over and over ... how many occasions, polite dinner parties and academic conferences would be bereft of conversation if 'the indigenous problem' had not been so problematized?

Concern about 'the indigenous problem' began as an explicitly militaristic or policing concern. The problem was articulated in terms of 'putting down rebellions' or 'getting rid of' recalcitrant rebels. Individual chiefs or leaders who resisted various attempts to control them were labelled as rebels and the 'real problems' and media accounts helped whip up a frenzied hatred of these individuals by white settlers. The level of hatred legitimated attempts to 'hunt them down' or to 'protect the people' from their own leadership. The systematic undermining of the legitimacy of indigenous leaders was part of the wider strategy for colonization. This strategy has not gone away as contemporary indigenous activists are also represented in the same ways. Even when leaders used passive resistance and simply withdrew from any participation in white society their actions were regarded as provocative and likely to encourage rebellious thinking. In New Zealand one example of the use of passive resistance in Taranaki in the 1870s by a leader called Te Whiti was interpreted by the government as a challenge to European sovereignty and civilization and a sustained war was waged in which Te Whiti and his people did not retaliate. Te Whiti and other leaders were labelled as fanatics and their followers as disillusioned and unthinking followers whose minds had been taken over. Eventually Te Whiti's community at Parihaka was invaded, the leaders were arrested and the community destroyed.[30]

Once indigenous peoples had been rounded up and put on reserves the 'indigenous problem' became embedded as a policy discourse which reached out across all aspects of a government's attempt to control the natives. Both 'friends of the natives' and those hostile to indigenous peoples conceptualized the issues of colonization and European encroachment on indigenous territories in terms of a problem of the natives. The natives were, according to this view, to blame for not accepting the terms of their colonization. In time social policies – for example, in health and education – were also viewed as remedies for the 'indigenous problem'. By the 1960s this approach had been theorized repeatedly around notions of cultural deprivation or cultural deficit which laid the blame for indigenous poverty and marginalization even more securely on the people themselves. The 'indigenous problem' had by then also become an academic discourse in which research played a crucial role. Many Maori people who grew up in New Zealand in that era believed that we were to blame. Other indigenous peoples shared the same belief. Problematizing the indigenous is a Western obsession. The discourse has shifted away from cultural deficit views to cultural diversity views. Even within these views the indigenous can be perceived as a problem because many are considered 'inauthentic' and too ungrateful. The belief in the 'indigenous problem' is still present in the Western psyche. It has been portrayed by some writers as a deeply held fear and hatred of the Other.[31]

A continuing legacy of what has come to be taken for granted as a natural link between the term 'indigenous' (or its substitutes) and 'problem' is that many researchers, even those with the best of intentions, frame their research in ways that assume that the locus of a particular research problem lies with the indigenous individual or community rather than with other social or structural issues. For example, researchers investigating poor health or educational under-achievement among indigenous communities often focus on the community as the sole source of the problem and, because this is their focus, obviously fail to analyse or make sense of the wider social, economic and policy contexts in which communities exist. Often their research simply affirms their own beliefs. For indigenous communities the issue is not just that they are blamed for their own failures but that it is also communicated to them, explicitly or implicitly, that they them-selves have no solutions to their own problems. This view is exacerbated by media and politician rhetoric about the general hopelessness or corruption of indigenous communities and indigenous peoples. This environment provides an absolutely no-win position and sets up the conditions for nurturing deep resentment and radical resistance from indigenous groups. In the research context the terms 'research' and 'problem' are also closely linked. It becomes somewhat complicated for indigenous researchers to discuss 'research', 'problem' and 'indigenous' without individuals or communities 'switching off' because of the history of defining indigenous peoples as … the problem. For many indigenous communities research itself is taken to mean 'problem'; the word research is believed to mean, quite literally, the continued construction of indigenous peoples as the problem.

Notes

1 For example, Clifford, J. and Gregory, D. (1994), *Geographical Imaginations*, Blackwell, Cambridge.
2 hooks, b. (1992), *Black Looks, Race and Representation*, Boston, South End Press, pp. 165–78.
3 Stocking refers to some travellers as 'gentlemen travellers' who had a 'scientific inclination'. Stocking, G. Jr (1987), *Victorian Anthropology*, The Free Press, p. 92.
4 Salmond, A. (1991), *Two Worlds, First Meetings Between Maori and Europeans 1642–1772*, Viking, Auckland.

5 *Ibid.*, p. 82.

6 *Ibid.*, p. 84.

7 This claim is made, for example, by Syd Jackson in an article for the magazine *Metro*, 1987, Vol. 7, No. 73, pp. 190–1, but the claim has been around much longer. I have heard the same claim made in Australia by Aborigine people, by a Sami woman while in New Zealand, in the United States and in Canada by Indian and First Nations people.

8 Beaglehole, J. C. (1962), *The Endeavour Journal of Joseph Banks 1768–1771*, Angus and Robertson, Sydney, p. 3.

9 *Ibid.*, p. 4.

10 Freire, P. (1987), *Literacy: Reading the Word and the World*, Routledge and Kegan Paul, London.

11 Salmond, *Two Worlds*, p. 12.

12 Rowse, A. L. (1989), *The Controversial Colensos*, Dyllansow Truran Cornish Publishing, Cornwall.

13 Captain Gilbert Mair and Major William Mair are two such examples. Both brothers were active in the Land Wars. William was involved in campaigns against Ngati Awa and then acted as an interpreter for Ngati Awa men who were put on trial. Gilbert was an interpreter during the Land Wars and was then made a captain during a campaign against Te Kooti. Gilbert Mair later became very influential in matters relating to Maori land.

14 Thompson, A. S. (1859), *The Story of New Zealand. Past and Present – Savage and Civilized,* John Murray, London, p. 81.

15 Gould, Stephen Jay (1981), *The Mismeasure of Man*, Penguin Books, London.

16 Stocking, *Victorian Anthropology*, p. 81.

17 *Ibid.*, p. 81.

18 Craig, E. (1964), *Man of the Mist: A Biography of Elsdon Best*, Reed, Wellington.

19 See also Sisson, J. (1991), *Te Waimana. The Spring of Mana,* University of Otago Press, Dunedin.

20 McClellan, J. E. (1985), *Science Reorganized: Scientific Societies in the Eighteenth Century,* Columbia Press, New York.

21 See Salmond, *Two Worlds*, pp. 97–100, for a discussion of the Royal Society.

22 McClellan, *Science Reorganized.*

23 *Ibid.,* p. 29.

24 Sorrenson, M. P. K. (1992), *Manifest Destiny, The Polynesian Society over 100 Years*, The Polynesian Society, Auckland.

25 *Ibid.*, p. 24.

26 *Sunday News*, Independent News Auckland, Ltd., 2 February 1997, p. 11. 'No Clouds but Big Storm Blows, Maori Should be Paid in Blankets Fumes Act Leader Richard Prebble', columnist Barry Soper.

27 The word 'stolen' is used quite literally when indigenous peoples talk about land. Margo Thunderbird: 'They came for our land, for what grew or could be grown on it, for the resources in it, and for our clean air and pure water. They stole these things from us, and in taking they also stole our free ways and the best of our leaders, killed in battle or assassinated.' Cited in W. Rose (1992), 'The Great Pretenders. Further Reflections on Whiteshamanism', in *The State of Native America; Genocide, Colonization, and Resistance*, ed. M. A. Jaimes, pp. 403–22.

28 hooks, p. 21.

29 Smith, G. H. (1995), 'New Formations of Colonization', in *The Fiscal Enveloped.*

Economics, Politics and Colonization, Moko Productions and The Research Unit for Maori Education, Auckland, pp. 33–9.

30 Riseborough, H. (1989), *Days of Darkness: Taranaki 1878–1884*, Allen and Unwin, Wellington.

31 See Mander, J. (1991), *In the Absence of the Sacred: the Failure of Technology and the Survival of the Indian Nations*, Sierra Book Club, San Francisco.

CHAPTER 5

Notes from Down Under

The End of One Part the Beginning of Another

For many people European imperialism is a thing of the past. Many would argue further that the lessons of the past have been learned and that the world is now a different place, one which is much more sympathetic to indigenous peoples and to other cultures. These notes from 'down under' draw a close to the first part of the book and introduce the second part. They are notes on imperialism at the dawning of the twenty-first century. As this chapter is being written several companies and communities in New Zealand and the South Pacific are vying for the world-wide television rights to celebrate the ending of one century and the beginning of another. While the northern hemisphere is asleep champagne and finger foods will flow in blue and white striped marquees, television cameras will record the activities of celebrities. To show some diversity the cameras may zoom in on less glamorous scenes, a barbecue on a beach perhaps, 'kiwis having a good time'. To show political stability selected leaders will make suitably authoritative pronouncements on the future. And to show that the event has some ritualistic symbolic significance some Maori will be shown chanting traditional incantations, probably on top of a mountain. These images will be beamed across the world and show New Zealand as a successful and happy nation.

One of my *iwi* is nestled in the valleys and along the coasts of the mountain range which is the focus of some of this millennial activity. The communities which make up the *iwi* live in small, rural settlements or isolated valleys. If the members who live outside the tribal boundaries are included, the *iwi* population numbers over 54,000 people. The beaches are beautiful and uncluttered by tourists. The sea is a source of food. Lands once covered in native bush, then cleared for sheep farming, have now been planted in pine forests while native bush clings to the sharp edges of the ranges. Dotted within each settlement are *marae*, the wooden, carved meeting houses and community venues built by extended families. Some of these are over a hundred years old, others more recent. Beside each *marae* is a neatly maintained cemetery which almost always has the signs of a recent burial, of newly piled earth and dying wreaths. The people of this *iwi* have a reputation for being fiercely independent, proud and nationalistic; the women of the *iwi* are seen as being especially assertive and confident, strident according to some accounts. It is an image which is consciously fostered in the way we are socialized. Culturally, in terms of our language, songs and customs, the *iwi* has always been strong. It is an *iwi* of many leaders, of many orators. Many of whom die young.

Unemployment, ill health and poverty underpin what on the surface look like idyllic conditions. Young people are sent away to seek further education and employment. Many people live on welfare benefits. Once in a while, someone dies violently; others simply die of heart disease, cancer, respiratory disease, diabetes, rheumatic fever, suicide, accidents. Many of those who die do so away in the cities and are brought home for burial. In the mid-1980s a cyclone inflicted huge devastation on the region: flood damage, stock damage, land washed out to sea. The cyclone brought a temporary respite in unemployment as work schemes were developed to repair the damage. In the mid-1980s also, a government economic restructuring programme began which took away farm subsidies, privatized state industries and instituted a raft of 'user-pays' policies. This signalled New Zealand's neo-liberal economic experiment, one that resulted in huge redundancies and tore the heart out of the Maori labour force. From time to time police helicopters scan the hillsides for crops of cannabis. In the township that I come from there is a church for every *marae*. In fact, there are more churches than would seem possible in such a small community. While the churches on the *marae* are usually Anglican, the religion brought to Maori by early missionaries, the churches which are on the main street are the churches of the Latter Day Saints, the Seventh Day Adventists, the Assembly of God. For a while there was an underground campaign which resulted in the burning down of several churches. Disillusioned young people try and make sense of their lives while being put through training programmes to prepare for work in communities where no one is employing. Television imports American culture and educates the tastes of the young for labelled clothes and African American rap.

In the town is the local tribal radio station which beams out the news and local music in the tribal dialect of both English and Maori languages. Local *iwi* politics are discussed regularly along with the finer details of the most recent rugby games. The *marae* have all been renovated and new ones are being built or contemplated. When gatherings are held, providing food for the visitors is still a major mark of tribal hospitality and wealth. In summer this region is famous for the provision of crayfish and sea eggs and other foods from the sea. Despite unemployment people still work hard, the young are expected to contribute to the collective needs of their extended families. People are still expected to care for the sick and the elderly. Children's laughter and mischief are still highly valued. The Runanga, or tribal council, has been grappling with the issues of economic development. Forestry, fishing, aquaculture, and ecotourism raise new hopes. Multinational companies talk business with tribal leaders. New missionaries and traders make their way into the region. Some tribal leaders talk economic development, others talk self-determination. Other tribes have vigorously pursued a corporate ethos and have attempted to turn collective knowledges and resources into corporate asset bases and financial wealth. Most tribes are struggling to take care of themselves. People are still trying to survive.

Is this imperialism? No, we are told, this is post-colonialism. This is globalization. This is economic independence. This is tribal development. This is progress. Others tell us that this is the end of modernism, and therefore the end of imperialism as we have known it. That business is now over, and so are all its associated projects such as decolonization. People now live in a world which is fragmented with multiple and shifting identities, that the oppressed and the colonized are so deeply implicated in their own oppressions that they are no more nor less authentic than anyone else.

While the West might be experiencing fragmentation, the process of fragmentation known under its older guise as colonization is well known to indigenous peoples. We can talk about the fragmentation of lands and cultures. We know what it is like to have our identities regulated by laws and our languages and customs removed from our lives. Fragmentation is not an indigenous project, it is something we are recovering from. While shifts are occurring in the ways in which indigenous peoples put ourselves back together again, the greater project is about recentring indigenous identities on a larger scale.

The New Language of Imperialism

While not exactly the generic indigenous tribe, the tribe I have described above shares many of the conditions which beset other indigenous communities as we begin the twenty-first century. The economic, cultural and scientific forms of imperialism associated with the nineteenth and early twentieth centuries have been reformulated. The geography of empire has been redrawn. The North–South divide has become a more meaningful way of distinguishing between what were once referred to as First, Second, Third and Fourth worlds. Territories are called markets, interesting little backwaters are untapped potentials and tribal variations of culture and language are examples of diversity. Evangelicals and traders still roam its landscape, as fundamentalists and entrepreneurs. Adventurers now hunt the sources of viral diseases, prospectors mine for genetic diversity and pirates raid ecological systems for new wealth, capturing virgin plants and pillaging the odd jungle here and there. Food is packaged up and sold as a Mc-something, ready to go. Television beams in live from America with the latest world news, world murder trials, world icons, world music, world sports, world weather and world shopping. The imperial armies assemble under the authority of the United Nations defending the principles of freedom, democracy and the rights of capital. Dispatches from the war zones are instantly sent across the Internet. Two Russian cosmonauts hurtle around space along with a growing pile of technological space junk. Companies are trying to ship toxic waste into the Pacific, defined in their eyes as 'empty land', unused by the natives who populate its islands.

Some of the categories through which we have understood the world with some certainty have been challenged by the so-called new realities, new social identities, new power alliances with which we are now confronted. New analyses and a new language mark, and mask, the 'something' that is no longer called imperialism. For indigenous peoples, one term that has signalled the striking shift in discourse is 'post-colonial'. Naming the world as 'post-colonial' is, from indigenous perspectives, to name colonialism as finished business. In Bobby Sykes's cryptic comment post-colonial can only mean one thing: the colonizers have left. There is rather compelling evidence that in fact this has not occurred. And, even when they have left formally, the institutions and legacy of colonialism have remained. Decolonization, once viewed as the formal process of handing over the instruments of government, is now recognized as a long-term process involving the bureaucratic, cultural, linguistic and psychological divesting of colonial power.

Indigenous peoples too have changed, however: they have regrouped, learned from past experiences, and mobilized strategically around new alliances. The elders, the women and various dissenting voices within indigenous communities maintain a collective memory and critical conscience of past experiences. Many indigenous communities are spaces of hope and possibilities, despite the enormous odds aligned against them. Some indigenous peoples use a new language. Sovereignty and self-determination still dominate the talk but there are terms like 'negotiate', 'reconcile', and 'settle'. Many indigenous communities, tribes and nations are in dialogue with the states which once attempted by all means possible to get rid of them. Serious intellectual thought is going into the considering the possibilities of new arrangements between states and indigenous peoples. The terms 'indigenous rights' or 'indigenous peoples and self-determination' appear from time to time in academic conferences, in the talk of major political figures and business leaders. I read novels written by indigenous writers and can talk with colleagues from other nations who share similar interests. Perhaps it is not all entirely depressing. Then again, perhaps it is.

A new generation of indigenous elites also walk across the landscape with their cell phones, briefcases and assets. Corporate chiefs and corporate warriors attempt to make deals with the new brokers of power and money. In developing countries these elites still protect the interests of the big Western power blocs. Many such leaders, though totally corrupted and evil, are kept in power by the very states which espouse democracy and human rights. Other indigenous leaders have become separated from their own indigenous value system and have been swept up into the games and machinations of a world they only partly understand. Divide and rule still operates as a basic strategy for dealing with indigenous peoples. It still operates because unfortunately it still works.

Ten Ways to be Researched (Colonized)

Scientific and technological advances this century place indigenous peoples and other marginalized and oppressed groups at extreme risk in the next century. The search is still on for the elixir of life, no longer gold this time but DNA, cures for Western diseases, and the other ways of finding enlightenment and meaning. The mix of science, cultural arrogance and political power continues to present a serious threat to indigenous peoples. As Jerry Mander has argued, the unrelenting imperative of corporations and governments to promote technology as a solution to our lives is the same imperative which suppresses and destroys indigenous alternatives.[1] The most fundamental clash between Western and indigenous belief systems, in Mander's view, stems from a belief held by indigenous peoples that the earth is a living entity, Mother Earth.[2] From this belief indigenous values and practices, social structures and relations are derived, which place indigenous views in direct opposition to Western values.

The colonizing projects listed below are not new. The projects are all under way in one form or another. Indigenous knowledges, cultures and languages, and the remnants of indigenous territories, remain as sites of struggle. Attempts by governments and companies to flood territories in order to build hydroelectric dams, to destroy rain forests in order to mine the lands beneath, to poison the land, the waterways and the air bring indigenous groups into direct confrontation with a wide range of Western power blocs which include scientific communities, environmental organizations, local and national governments and their bureaucracies, rich country alliances, multinational corporations and the media.

Embedded within each of these sectional interests are views about knowledge, more specifically about the inherent dominance of Western knowledge. Local or indigenous knowledges are even more at risk now than ever before. According to Vandana Shiva, 'Over and above rendering local knowledge invisible by declaring it non-existent or illegitimate, the dominant system also makes alternatives disappear by erasing and destroying the reality which they attempt to represent.'[3] According to Aroha Mead, the 'misappropriation of indigenous knowledge' is escalating and is particularly virulent in key areas of research such as the environmental sciences and medicine.[4]

The language of imperialism may have changed, the specific targets of colonization may have shifted and indigenous groups may be better informed, but imperialism still exists.

1 Having your genealogy and identity (cell-lines) stolen, patented, copied
The 'vampire' project or The Human Genome Diversity Project (HUGO) is the largest and best-known attempt to map the genetic diversity of isolated and threatened indigenous communities. It is not, however, the only project in town as there are other examples of companies or countries attempting to patent human genetic materials.[5] The US government had also attempted, through its National Institute of Health, to patent an individual of the Hagahai people of Papua New Guinea. For indigenous peoples the dehumanizing of the theft so that it is classified as 'scientific' knowledge is part of a process which has a long history. Aroha Mead suggests that the scientific community goes to great lengths to 'de-humanise the human-ness of genes' through the process of copying and reproducing synthetic varieties.[6]

2 Having the umbilical cord blood of aborted babies 'farmed'
Most indigenous peoples regard blood, the placenta and afterbirth as something 'special'. For Maori people it is regarded as 'still active' and highly *tapu*. The afterbirth used to be buried in the land. The Maori term for land and afterbirth are the same word, *whenua*. Hospitals until very recently refused to recognize Maori requests to take the afterbirth away and have it buried. Now that the blood from the cord and the afterbirth have been shown to be useful for treating certain sorts of diseases, there has been a request from some medical professionals in New Zealand to

'farm' (their word) the cord blood from aborted foetuses. While non-indigenous people will also find that difficult, they are more likely to be persuaded by arguments that the cord blood is useful, and that 'farming' it will not harm anyone as long as the mother gives consent, because they have no other cultural grounds on which to object. Maori do object culturally.

3 Having your cultural institutions and their rituals patented either by a non-indigenous person or by another indigenous individual
Strange as this may seem, apparently an attempt was made by a non-indigenous New Age male to patent the North American Indian sweat lodge ceremony because the Indians were not 'performing it correctly'.[7] The current fashion of patenting anything likely to be desired by others in order to both control and profit from it is placing great pressure on indigenous communities to protect themselves. Profiting from art and designs is already common, as art can be marketed through the Internet with very limited controls and by mass reproduction on T-shirts, tea towels and other tourist items. It is possible also to buy bottled *kava* 'tea' used in Pacific *kava* or *ava* ceremonies and to purchase various beauty products invented and used by indigenous peoples.

4 Scientific and political reconstruction of a previously extinct indigenous people
With new advances in science and the knowledge being extracted by projects such as the Human Genome Diversity Project, it is now possible to replicate the genetic structure of peoples who no longer exist as long as some tissue sample is available, for example in a corpse or mummified remains. Science can theoretically do that already; politics can ensure that the newly created indigenous people are socially constructed as well. New indigenous peoples can be recreated as experimental pure populations to be farmed and exploited much like laboratory rats. Or, they can be invented as land claimants with much more ancient claims to territories. If Western scientists are left to determine such an outcome it is sure to be utterly devastating. As Aroha Mead argued, 'If they die through racism then bring them back in 25 years. The racism will still be there but then science can do anything!'[8]

5. Dying and then coming back to life as a flock of sheep or variety of tomatoes
This is not about spiritual reincarnation but about the capabilities of science and genetic engineering to change or create new species of life.[9] Unlikely, one may think, but already in New Zealand a Scottish company has attempted to breed sheep which have human genetic material in their make-up. The purpose is to produce milk that contains a gene resistant to emphysema. The consequences for humans and animals of eating

genetically engineered food have yet to unfold. The immediate benefits for treating illnesses or prolonging human life or growing bigger and redder tomatoes that are resistant to disease are considered adequate as justifications for actions that will have long-term consequences for people.

6. Commodifying indigenous spirituality

This is not so new – but the spirituality industry will continue to expand as people, particularly those in First World nations, become more uncertain about their identities, rights, privileges and very existence. New Age groups currently appropriate indigenous spiritual beliefs at will; some claim to be inhabited by indigenous spirit guides while others merely interpret their 'own' (individualized) dreams as an indigenous spiritual experience. Writers and poets have also created a mystique around their work which, as Wendy Rose has argued, 'aspires to "embody the Indian", in effect "becoming" the "real" Indian'.[10] Despite protestations that spirituality is an experience through which non-indigenous people aim to help people, it is clearly a profitable experience.

7 Creating virtual culture as authentic culture

For those who can afford it, virtual reality can already substitute for exotic travel and armchair voyeurism. Art collections from museums can now be viewed from anywhere in the world and ancient ruins can be reconstructed and entered by a tourist who never needs to leave home. According to Tasmanian Aborigine Jimmy Everett, 'White people actually "farm" Aboriginal culture ... moulding it into static stereotyped images of what is accepted by white Australians as being Aboriginal. Anything that doesn't fit the white criteria is rejected on the presumption that it is not wholly Aboriginal.'[11] 'Scientific' knowledge of peoples can be created for virtual experience and conversations can be designed between ancient warriors and modern day observers. Cultural differences can be controlled by selecting and pushing buttons. Dehumanization of the Other continues.

8 Feeding consumption, tuberculosis of the marketplace

Whereas the tastes of indigenous peoples for commodities of trade were once developed literally as tastes for alcohol and sugar, television now provides the medium through which the tastes for American culture are fed in a constant barrage of advertising. Indigenous communities notice it most in the young, whose new heroes have become American sports or rap stars, whose language is peppered with American expressions and whose interactions with adults have become tainted with the social relations of middle-class white America. Consumption and the constant need to possess more and more 'things' become more important for many young people than the collective value systems of their own communities. The danger is that consumption masks economic and political inequalities and numbs people into believing that they are autonomous 'choosers' in a culturally neutral marketplace.

9 Creating sovereign reservations for the elite

Indigenous peoples have argued strenuously for the right to self-determination and the right to establish sovereign nations within their tribal territories. These arguments have been mounting against a backdrop of social fragmentation in the West. The city is the dominating metaphor for the apparent breakdown of Western social values, systems and practices. Although now quite established as a term, the idea of the 'urban jungle', evil and pervasive, crime-laden and populated by savages, presents the middle classes with new challenges to what counts as their domain. The very wealthy have always been able to escape, while the middle classes have been able to move out to suburbia or go on holiday from time to time. The middle classes, however, are also shifting more permanently into their own security zones with privatized police forces and self-contained social services. The possibility of disengaging themselves from the Other through the establishment of sovereign reserves is not too far-fetched.

10 Denial of global citizenship

Indigenous peoples have already experienced the denial of their humanity and many indigenous peoples have struggled for recognition of their citizenship within the states which colonized them. The new global political entities being established under such arrangements as GATT and other regional free market zones make participation within these zones dependent on certain sorts of compliances such as doing away with any protections of local economies and cultures. It costs to belong. To refuse to pay or to pull out will effectively deny nation states and their members citizenship status within the global world order.

The New Millennium

For Maori, the end of night and the beginning of day is an important spiritual time. The first breath of life in a new-born baby, the beginning of a season, the opening of a new meeting house, the start of a new project – all are imbued with both a sense of optimism and a sense of unease. Rituals are performed and people are brought together to make the transition from one state of being to another a peaceful and settled process. If things do not go well it is thought that maybe the rituals were not carried out properly or that important issues were not addressed before the assumption of a new beginning. It is after all very arrogant of humans to assume a beginning, to name it and set its date, when we are such minor beings in the universe, really only the earth's caretakers and not its dictators.

For indigenous peoples the beginning of a new century is really a continuation of a struggle that began five centuries ago. The optimism that prevails is based on the belief that now more than ever before in the last 500 years indigenous peoples are better able to respond. The following chapter will discuss some of the attempts made by indigenous peoples to re-position strategically around international alliances in ways which have reinforced a sense of movement towards a positive future. But that is an optimistic view. The pessimistic view is that we are dying and that the legacy of the presence of indigenous peoples on earth will be obliterated. Indigenous peoples are positioned along both ends of that continuum. It is not surprising that in New Zealand the renewed focus on warrior traditions has come at a time when Maori people sense a turning point which could go either forward or backward. For Maori that tradition is to be found in the often quoted saying of the chief Rewi Maniapoto, *Ka whawhai tonu matou, ake tonu ake*, 'we will fight on for ever and ever'. The context of change, instability and uncertainty faced by post-industrial societies positions indigenous peoples and indigenous issues in different sorts of spaces with different possibilities. For many indigenous leaders these possibilities are hopeful, the spaces are spaces to be claimed. In the process of global changes indigenous peoples are socially interested activists rather than passive bystanders. Perhaps it is this positioning that offers greater possibility for the survival of indigenous peoples.

While the language of imperialism and colonialism has changed, the sites of struggle remain. The struggle for the validity of indigenous knowledges may no longer be over the *recognition* that indigenous peoples have ways of viewing the world which are unique, but over proving the authenticity of, and control over, our own forms of knowledge. The debates about intellectual and cultural property rights cast the contestation of knowledge in a new frame. The commodification of knowledge as intellectual property, of collective knowledge as public knowledge, and of knowledge as value-added takes the struggle into another set of cultural interpretations. Now indigenous peoples have to prove that what was used for centuries to heal an illness was something which was 'discovered' and then had a value added to that discovery through some sort of scientific process. The notion of authenticity is critical in this arena because it is often crucial to the arguments mounted by indigenous peoples in relation to knowledge and culture. Even if the grounds of the debate have shifted, the clash between science and indigenous knowledge remains constructed around the interests of science. In the new century indigenous peoples will continue to have to defend and seek to protect indigenous knowledges and cultures.

At the same time indigenous peoples offer genuine alternatives to the current dominant form of development. Indigenous peoples have philosophies which connect humans to the environment and to each other and which generate principles for living a life which is sustainable, respectful and possible. Jerry Mander's chart of distinctive differences between technological and natives peoples poses starkly contrasting world views which have generated starkly different ways of organizing social, political, economic and spiritual life.[12] In quite small but effective projects many of these indigenous alternatives have been incorporated into such diverse spheres as restorative justice programmes using healing circles, community health initiatives using holistic indigenous interventions, government consultation models for dealing with communities, group conferencing models for resolving young people's care and protection, hospital practices incorporating native healers, museum practices involving indigenous owners of artefacts, and indigenous pedagogical styles in the classroom. Many such initiatives involved huge political debates and resistance from agencies and powerful interests, but once established they have been discussed at international conferences and inter-government meetings as if the whole idea came about through the generosity of non-indigenous people.

What is more important than what alternatives indigenous peoples offer the world is what alternatives indigenous peoples offer each other. The strategies that work for one community may well work for another. The gains made in one context may well be applied usefully in another. The sharing of resources and information may assist groups and communities to collaborate with each other and to protect each other. The development of international protocols and strategic alliances can provide a more sustained critique of the practices of states and corporations. The survival of one community can be celebrated by another. The spiritual, creative and political resources that indigenous peoples can draw on from each other provide alternatives for each other. Sharing is a good thing to do, it is a very human quality. To be able to share, to have something worth sharing gives dignity to the giver. To accept a gift and to reciprocate gives dignity to the receiver. To create something new through that process of sharing is to recreate the old, to reconnect relationships and to recreate our humanness.

Notes

1 Mander, J. (1991), *In the Absence of the Sacred: the Failure of Technology and the Survival of the Indian Nations*, Sierra Club Books, San Francisco.
2 *Ibid.*, pp. 212–24.
3 Shiva, V. (1993), *Monocultures of the Mind*, Zed Books, London, Third World Network, Malaysia, p. 12.
4 Mead, A. (1994), 'Misappropriation of Indigenous Knowledge: the Next Wave of Colonization', in *Nga Tikanga, Nga Taonga. Cultural and Intellectual Property Rights – The Rights of Indigenous Peoples,* Research Unit for Maori Education, Monograph 23, University of Auckland.
5 See, for example, *Third World Resurgence*, 1995, No. 63, pp. 9–30.
6 Mead, A. (1995), 'The Integrity of the Human Gene: Genes and Whakapapa', paper presented to the New Zealand Health Research Council Consensus Development Workshop, Health Research Council, Auckland, New Zealand.
7 Whitt, L. (1995), 'Indigenous Peoples and the Cultural Politics of Knowledge', in *Issues in Native American Cultural Identity*, Peter Lang Publishing, New York, pp. 223–72.
8 Mead, A. (1993), 'Cultural and Intellectual Property Rights of Tangata Whenua', paper presented to Women in Science Conference, Wellington, September 1993, reprinted in *Nga Tikanga Nga Taonga. Cultural and Intellectual Property Rights of Indigenous Peoples*, Research Unit for Maori Education, Monograph 23, University of Auckland.
9 See Mander, J. (1991), pp. 161–77.
10 Rose, W. (1992), 'The Great Pretenders: Further Reflections on Whiteshamanism', in *The State of Native America: Genocide, Colonization and Resistance*, ed. M. Annette Jaimes, South End Press, Boston, pp. 403–21.
11 Everett, J. (1994), 'Australian Museums: a Role to Play in a Changing Indigenous Environment', in *Issues in the Control of Aboriginal Knowledge,* Research Unit for Maori Education, Monograph 21, University of Auckland.
12 Mander, J. (1991), pp. 215–19.

CHAPTER 6

The Indigenous Peoples' Project:
Setting a New Agenda

While the previous chapters have attempted to explain why indigenous peoples have an abhorrence and distrust of research, the following chapters shift the focus towards the developments that have occurred in the field of research that have been conceptualized and carried out by indigenous people working as researchers in indigenous communities. Often because of the reasons outlined in the previous chapters, the burden of history makes the positioning of an indigenous person as a researcher highly problematic. And yet the indigenous context has changed dramatically and in some areas there is a huge interest being shown by indigenous peoples in research, more specifically in particular kinds of research. It is out of these contexts that a field of indigenous research is being formed. It is a field which privileges indigenous concerns, indigenous practices and indigenous participation as researchers and researched. The following chapters discuss different aspects of indigenous research.

This chapter sets out the framework of the modern indigenous peoples' project. This is a project which many of its participants would argue has been defined by over 500 years of contact with the West. In this sense it might also be described as a modernist resistance struggle. For most of the past 500 years the indigenous peoples' project has had one major priority: *survival*. This has entailed survival from the effects of a sustained war with the colonizers, from the devastation of diseases, from the dislocation from lands and territories, from the oppressions of living under unjust regimes; survival at a sheer basic physical level and as peoples with our own distinctive languages and cultures. Whilst for many indigenous peoples across the world survival at a basic human level is still the priority concern, the indigenous peoples' project was reformulated around a much wider platform of concerns following the Second World War and more particularly from the 1960s. Some of these concerns were struggled for through violent revolution or armed resistance, others have been born out of the 'decolonization of the mind' strategies and still others have been nurtured and sustained within the cultural systems of every indigenous community. The significance of the period and the reformulation of the indigenous peoples' project that unfolded during this era is that a new agenda for indigenous activity has been framed that goes beyond the decolonization aspirations of a particular indigenous community towards the development of global indigenous strategic alliances. The chapter will discuss two aspects of the indigenous peoples' project: the social movement of indigenous peoples which occurred from the 1960s and the development of an agenda or platform of action which has influenced indigenous research activities.

The Social Movement of Indigenous Peoples

The activities of indigenous peoples can be understood at one level simply as an indigenous social movement which started as a movement of people and became a movement of peoples. The movement developed simultaneously out of the survival strategies and cultural systems which have nurtured people, their values and their beliefs within their own communities, reserves, tribes and nations for over 500 years. It is often referred to as cultural revitalization but that term tends to imply that cultures needed rescuing. While that is an element it is not the only one. Depending on the context, different indigenous writers have explained the movement as one born out of the frustrations of urbanization, out of traditional revivalism, out of the grassroots, or out of the reserves.[1] What is agreed is that generally the movement began out of sight (of the dominant society) before bursting on to the national and international stages. According to Franke Wilmer,

> indigenous peoples use all of the strategies typically associated with social movements and interest groups. Where possible, they participate directly in the political process of national government. Where this is not possible or effective, they have mobilised resistance efforts, engaging in protest and other kinds of direct, 'extraordinary' politics'.[2]

In explaining the emergence in New Zealand of radical Maori organizations, Ranginui Walker writes that they 'were an underground expression of rising political consciousness'.[3]

In New Zealand the movement for Maori has been contested, debated, developed, refined, prioritized and shaped by radical action. The journey towards a wider movement by Maori has been fraught with political strife and social conflict. It has witnessed the challenges of a younger generation of Maori to the dominant hegemony held by Maori in the 1960s and 1970s, and the challenges of Maori across the multiple sites of education, health, development, government policy and of the non-indigenous society generally. Some of the signposts which have marked this journey include such activities as the Land March of 1974, Waitangi Day protests from 1971, the occupation of Bastion Point (1978) and of Raglan Golf Course (1978), the disruption of the Springbok Rugby Tour (1981), Te Kohanga Reo (1982), the Maori Education Development Conference (1984), the Maori Economic Development Conference (1985) and Kura Kaupapa Maori (1986). While political protests are still a feature of Maori action, what needs to be seen alongside the protests are the range of initiatives and cultural revitalization projects which have been advanced. For Maori a purposeful dream has been conceptualized partially around key cultural concepts such as *tino rangatiratanga* (sovereignty), *whanau, hapu, iwi* (extended family, sub-tribal groupings and tribe), *te reo* (Maori language) and *tikanga Maori* (Maori cultural customs). These concepts, which are embedded in the Maori language and world view, provided a way of coming together on Maori terms. What is better known is that the Treaty of Waitangi provided an organizing framework for dialogue with the dominant interests of New Zealand society and of government while education, health, justice and Maori development have provided more defined sites of struggle.

In Australia Aborigines across all states had had a long struggle for recognition as citizens of Australia and for land rights. Resistance is traced back prior to the Second World War. The 1960s saw the taking of direct action across several different states and the Northern Territories. Challenges were made by Aborigine groups for title to lands which were consistently refused by the courts and the state governments. One petition over land rights was made by the Yirrkala people on bark and written in their own language.[4] Substantive citizenship rights at a federal level for all Aborigines, including the right to be counted in the census, were not won until after a national referendum was held in 1967 to change the Australian constitution. Although the referendum was overwhelmingly supportive, it is ironic that white Australians were asked to vote on whether indigenous Australians could have rights in their own land. The change in the constitution did not in itself radically transform the lives of Aboriginal people.[5] The struggle over land rights after 1967 is similarly signposted with direct action, petitions, a tent embassy in 1972, silent protests during white Australia's celebration of two hundred years of settlement in 1988, challenges both through the courts and state governments. The Mabo court decision which overturned the doctrine of *terra nullius* has resulted in political retrenchment by a conservative Commonwealth government aimed at containing native title and appeasing the powerful non-indigenous interests of groups such as the pastoralists and mining companies.

Similar protest actions over land rights, language and cultural rights, human rights and civil rights were taking place literally across the globe, from the very northern reaches of the Sami people in Norway, to Welsh language actions, Basque protests in Spain, to different indigenous peoples in the Middle East, Africa, North, Central and South America, the Philippines, India, Asia and the Pacific. All these national struggles have their own independent histories but the rising profile of political activities occurring on a world-wide scale did give a renewed impetus to other indigenous groups. The social movement contains many features which reflect both a huge diversity of interests and objectives, of approaches and ways of working, and a unity of spirit and purpose. While rhetorically the indigenous movement may be encapsulated within the politics of self-determination it is a much more dynamic and complex movement which incorporates many dimensions, some of which are still unfolding. It involves a revitalization and reformulation of culture and tradition, an increased participation in and articulate rejection of Western institutions, a focus on strategic relations and alliances with non-indigenous groups. The movement has developed a shared international language or discourse which enables indigenous activists to talk to each other across their cultural differences while maintaining and taking their directions from their own communities or nations.

The international social movement of indigenous peoples is at all levels highly political. It intersects in complex and often contradictory ways with the internal politics of many indigenous nations. According to Gerald Alfred, 'It has been said that being born Indian is being born into politics. I believe this to be true; because being born a Mohawk of Kahnawake, I do not remember a time free from the impact of political conflict'.[6] For Maori people it was often the Treaty of Waitangi which framed the political talk. Both the cultural institutions which encouraged oral debate and the sense of injustice which fuelled the debates made politics the basis of everyday life. The pressure internally is frequently manifested through struggles over leadership, over what counts as 'traditional', and over which interests within the community are being privileged by particular deals and settlements.

The strength of the movement is to be found in the examples of how communities have mobilised locally, the grassroots development. It is at the local level that indigenous cultures and the cultures of resistance have been born and nurtured over generations. Successful initiatives have been developed by communities themselves using their own ideas and cultural practices. Considerable reserves of confidence and creativity within many communities have generated a wide range of social, educational, health, and artistic initiatives. The cultural and linguistic revitalization movements have tapped into a set of cultural resources that have recentred the roles of indigenous women, of elders and of groups who had been marginalized through various colonial practices. These groups in the community were often the groups who had retained 'traditional' practices, had been taught by elders, were fluent in the language and had specialized knowledges pertaining to the land, the spiritual belief systems and the customary lore of the community.

While some communities focused primarily on cultural revitalization, others, either as separate organizations or as small groups of individuals, became much more intent on engaging in reorganizing political relations with the state. Challenges have been made by indigenous communities with varying degrees of success both through the courts and through the legislature. The constitutional challenges made by indigenous nations have deeply disturbed the colonial comfort of some states. In the case of Canada, for example, such challenges by First Nations peoples to the constitutional crisis in relation to Quebec forced the issue of indigenous rights on to the agenda. There have been wide-ranging claims which have challenged the legitimacy of the doctrines upon which colonial states have built their foundations. Australian Aborigines have consistently challenged the doctrine of *terra nullius* or 'empty land' which has been used to deny the advancement of any claims to territory. Other indigenous peoples have asserted claims based on treaties. Still others have simply asked for an apology. Many of the claims made on the state have been based on the legitimacy, from the perspective of indigenous peoples, of being the first peoples of the land. To Wilmer, 'The indigenous voice speaks critically to the narrative (some would say myth) of the nation-state – the hierarchical, incorporative, coercive state that exists, in part, to facilitate the process of creating economic surplus on an international scale'.[7]

It can be argued that indigenous claims on the state were part of a much greater crisis of legitimacy faced by modern nation states in the face of widespread cultural and economic shifts. Indigenous activism assembled around, or was part of, some often uneasy alliances with other marginalized groups in society – white feminists, socialists, communists, anti-racists, church activists and labour unions. In New Zealand protest against the rugby tours to or from South Africa mobilized widespread actions involving anti-racist groups, middle-class organizations and Maori groups. In Australia the Aboriginal land rights and anti-racism struggles were often conflated, although this did not necessarily gain the support of other ethnic minorities for the Aboriginal cause. Alliances with non-indigenous groups were a significant part in some places of the general politics. These alliances were always regarded by indigenous groups as problematic, however; in New Zealand, for example, Donna Awatere argued that 'These alliances are necessary because changes cannot occur with the Maori on our own. White people have cut across class barriers to unite on the basis of white hegemony; that is, white domination of the Maori. To overcome this requires a restructuring of the white alliance'.[8] Others argued a more fundamental position that alliances with non-indigenous organizations and individuals were totally unnecessary. Certainly many indigenous people whose contacts with whites had been overwhelmingly negative had no trust whatsoever in the activities or intentions of non-indigenous groups or individuals.

International Mobilization

Frustrations at working within the nation state led some indigenous communities towards establishing or reestablishing, in some cases, international linkages or relations with other indigenous communities. Michael Dodson, an Aboriginal and Torres Strait Islander Social Justice Commissioner, suggests that for indigenous peoples 'It is in our disadvantage and our struggle for the recognition of our rights that we are united.'[9] The process however took time as communities rediscovered themselves and connected nationally, regionally, linguistically and then internationally. Wilmer lists a chronology of the formation of indigenous organizations which shows a development over 20 years which brought together the different indigenous groups from the North, the Amazon and Latin America, Canada, the United States, Australia and New Zealand. Subsequent indigenous world conferences have had delegates from all parts of the globe. The international mobilization of indigenous peoples has occurred in alliances with many supportive non-indigenous organizations working in the field of human rights. Publishing networks based in the North have assisted in the distribution of information and funding assistance has been provided to facilitate indigenous participation at important events.

For indigenous peoples both international relations (relations between nations) and resistance movements have a history going back both prior to, and after, contact with the West.[10] Under European imperialism indigenous peoples were positioned within new political formations which ruptured previous relations, strategic alliances, trade routes and ways of communicating with other indigenous nations. The assertion of European sovereignty over indigenous peoples effectively shifted the focus of indigenous international relations to a colonizer/ colonized relationship. Hence, in the New Zealand example, efforts by Maori to redress grievances were directed at the Queen of England and there are several examples in the nineteenth century and this century of petitions and delegations to London being sent specifically to the Queen. Similar delegations were sent from Australia, Canada and other colonies of the British Empire. In the United States trips by the representatives and chiefs of various Native American nations, including the delegations from the sovereigns of the Kingdom of Hawai'i, were made to Washington DC to see the President. In the French colonies it was to Paris. The international relations established by indigenous peoples in this context existed within the boundaries of empire, defined within these boundaries more as domestic matters than as 'international' relations.[11] The close and often intimate relationship that indigenous peoples presumed to have with sovereigns or heads of state because they had been represented as protectors and 'great fathers and mothers of the natives' was always disappointing. Indigenous peoples invested huge amounts of energy and belief in the notion that appeals to the centre of power would work. Many indigenous groups developed or had in place already quite sophisticated ways of conducting encounters between themselves and the heads of state or high-ranking dignitaries. The protocols involved were enormously respectful of colonial officials, even those whose status and powers were low. The lack of respect and the ridicule which was often displayed to indigenous delegations by imperial and colonial powers has never been forgotten by those communities.

   The development of international indigenous relations which began after the Second World War needs to be seen within the context of indigenous struggles for self-determination which were occurring at the grassroots level. In New Zealand, Australia and Canada as in the United States, the rise of indigenous activism paralleled the activism surrounding the civil rights movement, women's liberation, student uprisings and the anti-Vietnam War movement. Rebecca Robins links the 'upsurge of Indian activism' in the United States 'to a more generalized breakdown – manifested in the civil rights and Black liberation movements, student power and anti-war movements, and incipient Chicano rights and women's liberation movements'.[12] In many ways indigenous protests have been written out of the way this period has been characterized as a significant historical moment for modernity. Indigenous strategies for action were pursued vigorously, however, and international links were made through protest actions and the mounting of various stands and events. Tent embassies were established by Aborigines in Australia 1972 and by Maori in New Zealand. Land and building occupations were also effective strategies for gaining the attention of the world's media and of the authorities. Many of the 'leaders' of protest events were targeted by the police and other surveillance authorities as the 'enemies within'. In New Zealand, policemen who were Maori were used in the front lines to break up the Bastion Point occupation, similar state strategies were used elsewhere. In the United States the case of Leonard Peltier is one used to illustrate the involvement of the Federal Bureau of Investigation in the targeting for 'neutralization' of an indigenous activist.[13]

One of the first post-war initiatives by indigenous groups in the international arena was mounted by an organization called the North American Indian Brotherhood (NAIB) which originated in British Columbia in the 1950s under the leadership of Andrew Paull. NAIB sent a delegation to the United Nations.[14] Ties between First Nations communities in Canada and Native American communities in the United States were already closely bound by traditional relationships. Later visits were made by different indigenous communities from Canada to New Zealand through the efforts of George Manuel who headed the National Indian Brotherhood of Canada between 1970 and 1976.[15] These small-scale initiatives were followed by the American Indian Movement (AIM), which facilitated a major international meeting involving a wide range of international indigenous delegations. From this meeting and under the strong leadership of individuals like Russell Means and Jimmy Durham emerged the International Indian Treaty Council in 1974.[16] Almost simultaneously across the border in Canada the National Indian Brotherhood established the World Council of Indigenous Peoples in 1975. Both these organizations sought status as non-government representatives to the Economic and Social Council (ECOSOC) of the United Nations.[17]

Whilst new forms of resistance were being nurtured quietly within indigenous communities in the 1950s, international moves were being undertaken, often involving the support of human rights and other non-government and non-indigenous organizations. In 1957 the International Labour Organization (ILO) adopted Convention 107, 'The Convention of Indigenous Populations' which was one of the first international instruments to recognize indigenous issues.[18] This convention did not contain all that indigenous people wanted but was significant in its recognition and use of the term 'indigenous'. A later initiative in the 1970s was undertaken through the commissioning of a report known now as the Cobo Report after its chairperson, Martinez Cobo, by the United Nations Sub-Commission on the Prevention of Discrimination and Protection of Minorities. As the decade of the 1970s unfolded various initiatives at the international level were being advanced, often by sympathetic officials and with the support of non-indigenous groups and non-government organizations already attached to the United Nations.

A key issue in the international debates has focused on the term 'peoples'. It is regarded as crucial by indigenous activists because it is peoples who are recognized in international law as having the right to self-determination. As argued by Thornberry,

The legal discourse on the indigenous has moved through consideration of the rights of infidels, native sovereignty, the doctrine of terra nullius, 'Christian right', the empty lands doctrine, the paternalistic doctrine of guardianship, and all the incidents of the civilising mission of the Powers. Indigenous groups entered the twentieth century with hardly a remnant of any former 'subject' status in international law.[19]

So within indigenous discourses the term 'peoples' has become an important linguistic symbol of our identification as self-determining peoples. According to Michael Dodson, 'By any reasonable definition, indigenous peoples are unambiguously "peoples". We are united by common territories, cultures, traditions, histories, languages, institutions and beliefs. We share a sense of kinship and identity, a consciousness as distinct peoples and a political will to exist as distinct peoples.'[20] The struggle to be accorded this definition and status is continuing through the drafting process of the Draft Declaration for the Protection of Indigenous Peoples' Rights which was developed by the United Nations Working Group on Indigenous Peoples. As the member states of the United Nations in the end will be the forum who approve the Declaration, its progress through the drafting and consultations is not only highly educative but extremely political, with member states positioning themselves in ways which advance their own image at one level while protecting their own sovereignty at another.

An Agenda for Indigenous Research

The social movement of indigenous peoples unleashed a whole array of activities and bursts of energy. Looking backwards it is possible now to identify themes and sub-projects which have come to engage different groups of indigenous peoples. It is also possible to discuss the ways in which many of the themes which emerged in the late 1960s have been developed or shaped in the intervening years. These themes constitute an agenda for action. The agenda connects local, regional and global efforts which are moving towards the ideal of a self-determining indigenous world. It is not clear yet how this world might sit alongside the current situation of nation states. It is not assumed even that nation states will necessarily remain as effective political ways of organizing polities. The rise in influence of different sorts of power blocs which cut across the nation state, such as multinational corporations, regional economic alliances and globally based interest groups suggests a possible space for indigenous peoples.

The research agenda is conceptualized here as constituting a pro-gramme and set of approaches that are situated within the decoloniza-tion politics of the indigenous peoples' movement. The agenda is focused strategically on the goal of self-determination of indigenous peoples. Self-determination in a research agenda becomes something more than a political goal. It becomes a goal of social justice which is expressed through and across a wide range of psychological, social, cultural and economic terrains. It necessarily involves the processes of transformation, of decolonization, of healing and of mobilization as peoples. The processes, approaches and methodologies – while dynamic and open to different influences and possibilities – are critical elements of a strategic research agenda.

Figure 6.1 is a simple representation of an indigenous research agenda. The chart uses the metaphor of ocean tides. From a Pacific peoples' perspective the sea is a giver of life, it sets time and conveys movement. Within the greater ebb and flow of the ocean are smaller localised environments which have enabled Pacific peoples to develop enduring relationships to the sea. For Polynesian peoples the significant deity of the sea is Tangaroa. Although there are many directions that can be named, the chart takes the Maori equivalent of the four directions: the northern, the eastern, the southern and the western. The tides represent movement, change, process, life, inward and outward flows of ideas, reflections and actions. The four directions named here – decolonization, healing, transformation and mobilization – represent processes. They are not goals or ends in themselves. They are processes which connect, inform and clarify the tensions between the local, the regional and the global. They are processes which can be incorporated into practices and methodologies.

Four major tides are represented in the chart as: survival, recovery, development, self-determination. They are the conditions and states of being through which indigenous communities are moving. It is not sequential development – the survival of peoples as physical beings, of languages, of social and spiritual practices, of social relations, and of the arts are all subject to some basic prioritizing. Similarly, the recovery of territories, of indigenous rights, and histories are also subject to prioritizing and to recognition that indigenous cultures have changed inexorably. Recovery is a selective process, often responding to immediate crises rather than a planned approach. This is related to the reality that indigenous peoples are not in control and are subject to a continuing set of external conditions. In reality this means that specific lands and designated areas become a priority because the bulldozers are due to start destruction any day now.

Figure 6.1 The Indigenous Research Agenda

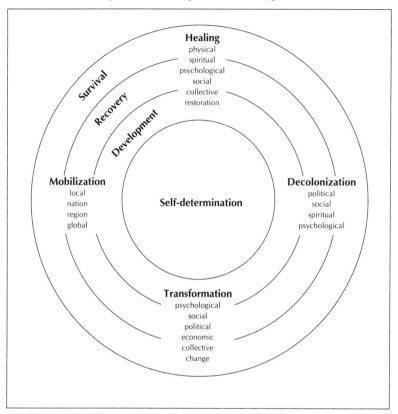

The indigenous research agenda is broad in its scope and ambitious in its intent. There are some things which make this agenda very different from the research agenda of large scientific organizations or of various national science research programmes. There are other elements, however, which are similar to any research programme which connects research to the 'good' of society. The elements that are different can be found in key words such as healing, decolonization, spiritual, recovery. These terms seem at odds with the research terminology of Western science, much too politically interested rather than neutral and objective. The intentions conveyed by these terms, however, are embedded in various social science research methodologies. The belief, for example, that research will 'benefit mankind' conveys a strong sense of social responsibility. The problem with that particular term, as outlined in previous chapters, is that indigenous peoples are deeply cynical about the capacity, motives or methodologies of Western research to deliver any benefits to indigenous peoples whom science has long regarded, indeed has classified, as being 'not human'. Because of such deep cynicism there are expectations by indigenous communities that researchers will actually 'spell out' in detail the likely benefits of any research.

Ethical Research Protocols

The huge credibility problem the research community faces with indigenous peoples has also been addressed within an indigenous agenda. Initially the problem was framed entirely in the negative, with indigenous individuals, communities and organizations reacting to research as something done only by white researchers to indigenous peoples. These reactions positioned indigenous communities as powerless and research as disempowering. There seemed little space for changing that perception. The nexus of debates rising out of the indigenous movement, discussions raised by other interested groups in relation to ethical research and shifts in some social science paradigms (to be discussed in Chapter 9) have created space for negotiating better research relationships. Some scholarly communities of scientists may have well-established ethical guidelines, many have not. Even if such communities have guidelines, the problem to be reiterated again is that it has been taken for granted that indigenous peoples are the 'natural objects' of research. It is difficult to convey to the non-indigenous world how deeply this perception of research is held by indigenous peoples.

Many of the ethical issues have been raised by interested groups in relation to the rapid advances of science and technology and the rapid disappearance of diversity. In the debate about ethics distinctions are drawn between legal requirements and ethical codes of conduct. Indigenous groups argue that legal definitions of ethics are framed in ways which contain the Western sense of the individual and of individualized property – for example, the right of an individual to give his or her own knowledge, or the right to give informed consent. The social 'good' against which ethical standards are determined is based on the same beliefs about the individual and individualized property. Community and indigenous rights or views in this area are generally not recognized and not respected. Indigenous peoples have attempted through the development of instruments such as treaties, charters and declarations to send clear signals to the world's scientific and research communities that open-cast mining approaches to research (see, take and destroy) are absolutely unacceptable. Debates within the indigenous world about intellectual and cultural property rights are taking place against the background of rampant prospecting in the biodiversity and pharmaceutical fields. Cultural ethics or indigenous codes of conduct are being promulgated by different organizations often as a sheer act of survival.

The charter of the Indigenous Tribal Peoples of the Tropical Forests signed in Penang (1993) includes statements referring to the collective rights of peoples to intellectual and cultural property, participation by indigenous peoples in the management of projects, promotion of health systems, control over own knowledges, and an insistence that 'all investigations in our territories should be carried out with our consent and under joint control and guidance (Article 45)'. The Mataatua Declaration on Cultural and Intellectual Property Rights of Indigenous Peoples signed in Whakatane, New Zealand (1993) addresses these issues by declaring that 'indigenous peoples of the world have the right to self-determination and in exercising that right must be recognized as the exclusive owners of their cultural and intellectual property. It insists that the first beneficiaries of indigenous knowledge must be direct indigenous descendants of that knowledge.' The Declaration calls on governments and states 'to develop policies and practices which recognise indigenous peoples as the guardians of their customary knowledge and have the right to protect and control dissemination of that knowledge and that indigenous peoples have the right to create new knowledge based on cultural traditions'. The Declaration is one of several indigenous peoples' declarations. Other international indigenous statements and declarations which aim to protect indigenous rights and enforce ethical standards include: the Amazon Basin Declaration, the Kari Oca Declaration 1993, the Pan American Health Organization, the Native Pan-American Draft Declaration, the Blue Mountain Declaration, the International Alliance of the Indigenous Tribal Peoples of the Tropical Forests Charter 1993, and the Coolangatta Statement on Indigenous Rights in Education, 1993. There are many other such statements being prepared at local community level.

In the New Zealand context research ethics for Maori communities extend far beyond issues of individual consent and confidentiality. In a discussion of what may constitute sound ethical principles for research in Maori communities, Ngahuia Te Awekotuku has identified a set of responsibilities which researchers have to Maori people.[21] Her framework is based on the code of conduct for the New Zealand Association of Social Anthropologists, which in turn is based on the American Anthropological Association's guidelines.[22] Te Awekotuku sets out fairly basic guidelines aimed at respect for and protection of the 'rights, interests and sensitivities' of the people being studied. There are, however, some culturally specific ideas which are part of what is referred to as Kaupapa Maori practices.[23] These are not prescribed in codes of conduct for researchers, but tend to be prescribed for Maori researchers in cultural terms:

1 Aroha ki te tangata (a respect for people).
2 Kanohi kitea (the seen face, that is present yourself to people face to face).
3 Titiro, whakarongo ... korero (look, listen ... speak).
4 Manaaki ki te tangata (share and host people, be generous).
5 Kia tupato (be cautious).
6 Kaua e takahia te mana o te tangata (do not trample over the *mana* of people).
7 kaua e mahaki (don't flaunt your knowledge).[24]

These sayings reflect just some of the values that are placed on the way we behave. They are very different from the 'public' image of Maori society as a forum for ritual, oratory and chiefly leaders, but they are the kinds of comments which are used to determine if someone has 'good' qualities as a person. There are several other proverbs and sayings which contain the ideals and aspirations which are worth seeking, as well as the moral messages for those who decide not to conform to the rules of practice.

From indigenous perspectives ethical codes of conduct serve partly the same purpose as the protocols which govern our relationships with each other and with the environment. The term 'respect' is consistently used by indigenous peoples to underscore the significance of our relationships and humanity. Through respect the place of everyone and everything in the universe is kept in balance and harmony. Respect is a reciprocal, shared, constantly interchanging principle which is expressed through all aspects of social conduct. Haig-Brown and Archibald write that, 'to be in harmony with oneself, other members of the animal kingdom, and other elements of nature requires that First Nations people respect the gift of each entity and establish and maintain respectful, reciprocal relations with each'.[25] The denial by the West of humanity to indigenous peoples, the denial of citizenship and human rights, the denial of the right to self-determination – all these demonstrate palpably the enormous lack of respect which has marked the relations of indigenous and non-indigenous peoples.

Notes

1 See, for example, Alfred, G. R. (1995), *Heeding the Voices of our Ancestors. Kahnawake Mohawk Politics and the Rise of Nationalism*, Oxford University Press, Toronto; Awatere, D. (1984), *Maori Sovereignty*, Broadsheet, Auckland; Jaimes, M. A., ed.

(1992), *The State of Native America: Genocide, Colonization and Resistance,* South End Press, Boston; Walker, R. (1990), *Ka Whawhai Tonu Matou: Struggle Without End,* Penguin, Auckland; Wilmer, F. (1993), *The Indigenous Voice in World Politics,* Sage, Newbury Park.

2 Wilmer, *The Indigenous Voice,* p. 135.

3 Walker, *Ka Whawhai,* p. 210.

4 Lippman, L. (1981), *Generations of Resistance. The Aboriginal Struggle for Justice,* Longman Cheshire, Melbourne, p. 49

5 See, for example, Sykes, R. (1989), *Black Majority,* Hudson Hawthorn, Victoria. Roberta (Bobbi) Sykes was herself an activist during the 1970s and her book is an analysis of the conditions of Aborigines in the 21 years since the changes to the constitution were made. It paints a stark picture across the fields of justice, housing, health, education, employment and human rights.

6 Alfred, *Heeding the Voices,* p. 1.

7 Wilmer, *The Indigenous Voice,* p. 194.

8 Awatere, *Maori Sovreignty,* p. 34.

9 Dodson, M. (1996), *Fourth Report of the Human Rights and Equal Opportunity Commission,* Australian Government, Commonwealth of Australia, p. i.

10 Radha Jhappan, C. (1992), 'Global Community? Supranationational Strategies of Canada's Aboriginal Peoples', in *Journal of Indigenous Studies,* Vol. 3, No. 1, pp. 59–97.

11 Morris, G. T. (1993), 'International Structures and Indigenous Peoples', in *Indigenous Peoples Politics: An Introduction,* eds Marc Sills and G. T. Morris, Fourth World Centre, University of Colorado, pp. 22–45.

12 Robbins, R. (1992), 'Self-Determination and Subordination: the Past, Present and Future of American Indian Government', in *The State of Native America,* ed. Jaimes, p. 101.

13 Van der Wall, J. (1992), 'A Warrior Caged; the Continuing Struggle of Leonard Peltier', in *The State of Native America,* ed. Jaimes, Boston, pp. 291–310.

14 Sanders, D. E. (1977), *The Formation of the World Council for Indigenous Peoples,* International Work Group for Indigenous Affairs Document 29, Copenhagen, pp. 10–12.

15 *Ibid.,* p. 11.

16 Morris, G. T. (1992), 'International Law and Politics: Towards a Right to Self-Determination for Indigenous Peoples', in *The State of Native America,* ed. Jaimes, p. 76.

17 The International Indian Treaty Council was granted consultative status to ECOSOC in 1977 and the World Council for Indigenous Peoples was granted status in 1979. For further information see Aga Khan, Sadruddin and Hassan bin Talal (1987), *Indigenous Peoples: A Global Quest for Justice, a Report for the Independent Commission on International Humanitarian Issues,* Zed Books, London.

18 Morris, 'International Law and Politics', in *The State of Native America,* ed. Jaimes, pp. 55–86.

19 Thornberry, P. (1991), *International Law and the Rights of Minorities,* Clarendon Press, Oxford, p. 332.

20 Dodson, M. (1994), 'Voices of the Peoples – Voices of the Earth; Indigenous Peoples – Subjugation or Self-determination?', in *Voices of the Earth,* ed. Leo van der Vlist, International Books, NCIP, Netherlands, pp. 24–5.

21 Te Awekotuku, N. and Manatu Maori (1991), *He Tikanga Whakaaro. Research Ethics*

in the Maori Community, Manatu Maori, Wellington.

22 New Zealand Association of Social Anthropologists Principles of Professional Responsibility and Ethical Conduct (adopted in 1987 and amended in 1990).

23 See Chapter 9.

24 I have selected these sayings, having heard them used on several occasions as evaluative comments on people. The saying 'Titiro, whakarongo, korero' comes from Te Atarangi, the Maori language programme for adults. It seems to be a basic code of conduct in a number of situations for researchers. Actually these sorts of sayings are often spoken by the *kuia*, or older women, on a *marae* as they watch, very keenly, what people are doing.

25 Haig-Brown C. and Archibald, J. (1996), 'Transforming First Nations Research with Respect and Power', in *Qualitative Studies in Education*, Vol. 9, No. 3, pp. 245–67.

CHAPTER 7

Articulating an
Indigenous Research Agenda

Diary notes

1991 Ottawa. [Husband] Graham and I invited as guest delegates to attend the All Chiefs Special Conference on Education, hosted by the Assembly of First Nations, sat with friends from the Squamish delegation, the Pacific links are very strong.

1991 Published journal of Maori women's writings *Te Pua.*

1992 [Sister] Aroha in official delegation to Rio de Janeiro for Earth Summit.

1993 January 1st attended gathering of Ngati Porou for celebration of the International Year for Indigenous Peoples, convened women's meeting.

1993 Whakatane, Mataatua. Gathering of indigenous delegates to discuss cultural and intellectual property rights, organized by Aroha, conference produced the Mataatua Declaration on Cultural and Intellectual Property Rights of Indigenous Peoples.

1993 Wollongong, New South Wales, World Indigenous Peoples Conference on Education. Attended along with several thousand others, including about two thousand Maori. Conference issued the Coolangatta Statement.

1994 Aroha away overseas involved in discussions on the Convention on Biological Diversity.

1994 Wellington, meeting of Maori health researchers, developed draft declaration on Maori health research.

1994 Academic adviser for Te Wananga o Awanuiarangi, tribal university.

1995 Prepared submission on behalf of Ngati Awa for the Waitangi Tribunal.

1995 Began research project on Maori truancy.

1996 Saskatechewan, invited workshop on indigenous issues, opportunity to spend time with indigenous people working across fields of education, law, health, community.

1996 Graham attended indigenous workshop in New South Wales, worked on indigenous research ethics document.

1996 Developed proposal for research institute.

1996 Research project on community diversion.

1997 Invited to speak about research to indigenous programme in Western Australia.

1997 Panel speaker at a conference on educational research.

• • •

As previous chapters have indicated, research is highly institutionalized through disciplines and fields of knowledge, through communities and interest groups of scholars, and through the academy. Research is also an integral part of political structures: governments fund research directly and indirectly through tertiary education, national science organizations, development programmes and policies. Rich nations spend vast amounts of money on research across every dimension possible to imagine. Poor nations also spend huge amounts of money on research. Corporations and industries fund their own research and are sometimes funded by governments to carry out research. Their research programmes can involve large amounts of money and resources, and their activities take place across several parts of the globe. Non-government organizations and local community groups also carry out research and involve themselves in the analysis and critique of research. All of these research activities are carried out by people who in some form or another have been trained and socialized into ways of thinking, of defining and of making sense of the known and unknown. It seems rather difficult to conceive of an articulation of an indigenous research agenda on such a scale. To imagine self-determination, however, is also to imagine a world in which indigenous peoples become active participants, and to prepare for the possibilities and challenges that lie ahead.

This chapter reports on the development of indigenous initiatives in research and discusses some of the ways in which an indigenous research agenda is currently being articulated. It is striking that for indigenous peoples there are distinctly different ways of thinking about and naming research. Often projects are not referred to as research despite having research as a central core of the project activity. In addition to reasons outlined in earlier chapters about the general regard for research by indigenous peoples, there is another reason for a reticence in naming an activity or project as research. Research is also regarded as being the domain of experts who have advanced educational qualifications and have access to highly specialized language and skills. Communities carrying out what they may regard as a very humble little project are reluctant to name it as research in case it provokes the scorn and outrage of 'real' researchers. Furthermore, indigenous communities as part of the self-determination agenda do engage quite deliberately in naming the world according to an indigenous world view. What researchers may call methodology, for example, Maori researchers in New Zealand call Kaupapa Maori research or Maori-centred research. This form of naming is about bringing to the centre and privileging indigenous values, attitudes and practices rather than disguising them within Westernized labels such as 'collaborative research'. Institutions such as the academy and major funding agencies maintain and reinforce the idea that research is a highly specialized skill which by definition 'has to be' developed and supported at a distance from the community.

There are two distinct pathways through which an indigenous research agenda is being advanced. The first one is through community action projects, local initiatives and nation or tribal research based around claims. The second pathway is through the spaces gained within institutions by indigenous research centres and studies programmes. Although the community-based approach is often said to have greater community control and ownership than it is possible to achieve through the academy, that is not always or necessarily the case. Community-based projects are often conceptualized, funded and directed by researchers who have been trained within a discipline or paradigm and are often employed by a research organization. Also, university researchers who work within the protection of such notions as academic freedom and academic research can legitimate innovative, cutting-edge approaches which can privilege community-based projects. In other words, the two pathways are not at odds with each other but simply reflect two distinct developments. They intersect and inform each other at a number of different levels.

Community Research

The idea of community is defined or imagined in multiple ways, as physical, political, social, psychological, historical, linguistic, economic, cultural, and spiritual spaces. For colonized peoples many local communities have been made through deliberate policies aimed at putting people on reserves which are often out of sight, on the margins. Legislation and other coercive state practices have ensured that people stay within their own community boundaries. Communities have also made themselves, however, despite policies aimed at fragmenting family bonds and separating people from their traditional territories. Indigenous communities have made even their most isolated and marginal spaces a home place imbued with spiritual significance and indigenous identity. In North America, the term 'Indian Country' defines one sense of community, a named nation such as the Navaho Nation defines another sense of community, a named reserve defines yet another sense. In Australia the term 'mob' is used to identify and distinguish different levels and organizations of community.

Some writers refer to these multiple layers of belonging as 'nested identities'. Gerald Alfred, for example, conceptualizes Kahnawake identity as including 'localised Kahnawake, national Mohawk, broader Iroquois, and pan-Native'.[1] He says, 'Thus people of Mohawk descent who live in Kahnawake have a multi-layered identity which incorporates each one of the "communities" he or she has inherited, and which also includes the broader Native – or the more common "Indian" – identity flowing from their racial affiliation and identification as the indigenous peoples of North America.'[2] In describing Chicano communities in the United States, Irene Blea argues that,

> By entering into a discussion of the factors comprising the Chicano community, as a physical, social-historical, and spiritual setting, a clearer definition of the Chicano community emerges. It is futile to attempt to categorise these aspects of the community for they frequently overlap. For example, the spiritual element of Aztlan crosses over into its social-historical aspect because Aztlan is not only a physical region but is also a state of mind, a spiritual belief.[3]

When visiting New Zealand in 1996, African American historian Bernice Reagon Johnson visited a Maori community and, in response to discussions about the significance of land to Maori identity, described her own community as one held together by song rather than by territory. An Aborigine friend also made the comment that 'we sing the land into existence'. For Maori there are several ways of identifying one's indigenous 'community'. One commonly used way is to introduce yourself by naming the mountain, the river, the tribal ancestor, the tribe and the family. Through this form of introduction you locate yourself in a set of identities which have been framed geographically, politically and genealogically.

Defining community research is as complex as defining community. For example, 'the community' is regarded as being a rather different space, in a research sense, to 'the field'. 'Community' conveys a much more intimate, human and self-defined space, whereas 'field' assumes a space 'out there' where people may or may not be present. What community research relies upon and validates is that the community itself makes its own definitions. There are many examples of research projects carried out at a local community level. Some projects have been initiated and carried out by local people working in local settings, generating local solutions to local problems. Other projects, which have been supported by development agencies, focus on developing self-help initiatives and building skilled communities. Social research at community level is often referred to as community action research, or emancipatory research. Both approaches are models which seek to make a positive difference in the conditions or lives of people. Community action research, according to Stringer, 'is a collaborative approach to inquiry or investigation that provides people with the means to take systematic action to resolve specific problems'.[4] These approaches not only enable communities but also enable indigenous researchers to work as researchers within their own communities. Community action approaches assume that people know and can reflect on their own lives, have questions and priorities of their own, have skills and sensitivities which can enhance (or undermine) any community-based projects.

There are also communities of interest that do not necessarily occupy the same geographical space in which local community research occurs. Indigenous women are such a community, as are indigenous rights workers, indigenous artists and writers, indigenous health workers and indigenous researchers. Indigenous communities of interest have formed quite extensive networking and collaborative relationships. They are talking circles of people with similar interests. The community has its own borders and negotiating entry can be every bit as complex as entering a local village. Communities of interest have formed around their own priorities and particularities; they often have their own language or codes; they have their own analysis of self-determination; they may have a strong suspicion of the outsider; some may have formal membership, others may recognize each other through various language and dress codes. For many indigenous women, for example, their analyses have emerged from the intersections formed through the politics of Western feminism and the politics of their own indigenous communities. Writing and talking about the experiences of women within these spaces has developed into a major research priority for indigenous women. This priority connects and grounds a wide range of indigenous women's concerns at local, nation and global level. There is a burgeoning of a distinctive indigenous women's literature which actively works against Western literary categories. In all community approaches *process* – that is, methodology and method – is highly important. In many projects the process is far more important than the outcome. Processes are expected to be respectful, to enable people, to heal and to educate. They are expected to lead one small step further towards self-determination.

Tribal Research

Despite the negative connotations of 'tribe', it is used here generically to describe one form of indigenous organization. Tribe encompasses many different communities. For Maori it is the larger political entity of several smaller groups linked closely by genealogy and shared customary practices. Tribal research is currently being conducted in New Zealand across a wide range of areas. Apart from claims being put forward to the Waitangi Tribunal in respect of lands and resources taken unjustly by the government since the signing of the Treaty of Waitangi in 1840, tribal research is being conducted in the area of resource management, economic development, health, education, justice, family and children, flora and fauna, traditional knowledges. In the case of one tribe, Ngati Awa, a Ngati Awa Research Centre has been working since about 1989. The centre has carried out research which has resulted in the return or repatriation of the carved meeting house Mataatua; it has undertaken archival and historical research, social impact analysis, oral histories and local development. The research centre is one activity managed by the tribal *runanga* or council. It has two offices, one in New Zealand's capital Wellington, where the major national archives and libraries are located, and the other in Whakatane, the main town centre of the Ngati Awa. It has employed several young people with academic qualifications as researchers. Ngati Awa has also established a tribal university, Whare Wananga o Awanuiarangi, which offers degrees in education, Maori studies and indigenous studies. The vision is that the tribe will develop and educate its own members and other people who live in the area.

Another tribe, Tainui, is in the process of establishing a very large research centre in association with their local university. The tribe has invested large amounts of resources into graduate scholarships to assist Tainui students to complete both their studies and a relevant piece of research. In addition, this tribe have their own centre where specific research is being conducted by a team of mostly young researchers. This centre is led by a highly respected non-indigenous researcher and the expectation is that he will train the researchers as well as manage the range of different projects being undertaken. Other tribes have relied on the very small pool of Maori with tertiary-level qualifications to conduct the extensive research required to sustain a claim. Research through the claims process has fostered a demand for expertise across diverse fields of knowledge. This has radically invigorated Maori demands for advanced educational qualifications and put the role of institutions under scrutiny.

The process of mounting a treaty claim and preparing it for an eventual 'hearing' requires the collective knowledge, effort and commitment of the people in the various sections of the tribe. There is a great deal at stake in such research and failure to take into account the views and feelings of different tribal interests can have huge negative ramifications for the tribe once the claim has been heard and a settlement awarded. Any sign that secret deals have been made, or that traditional processes have been overridden, can result in a halt to further work and a schism in the tribe itself. Outsiders often view such contest-ability as proof that tribal 'infighting' is rampant. Those within tend to interpret such politics as a consequence of being driven by the govern-ment agenda for settlement at any cost rather than a reflection of traditional practices. The processes of consultation, collective meetings, open debate and shared decision making are crucial aspects of tribal research practices.

The Case Study of an Indigenous Research Initiative Inside the Academy

Research is a distinguishing characteristic of universities. Universities are committed to the creation of knowledge through research, reflection, scholarship and academic freedom. It is a role, historians of the university have argued, which has been hard won over centuries of development. The curriculum of a university shapes the way knowledge is reproduced as a curriculum for schools and for society. Intellectuals provide leadership for society in relation to knowledge. For indigenous peoples universities are regarded as rather elite institutions which reproduce themselves through various systems of privilege. Even those universities which are state-funded are considered major bastions of Western elitism. It is not surprising, then, that many indigenous students find little space for indigenous perspectives in most academic disciplines and most research approaches. In many examples indigenous and ethnic studies programmes have struggled to survive in rather hostile environments. Indigenous staff and students, too, have found the institution to be toxic. Haunani Kay Trask describes some turbulent experiences as a Hawai'ian academic attempting to work *as* a Hawai'ian academic in the University of Hawai'i.[5] Unfortunately, her experiences are not unique. The university represents a special sort of struggle and the following small case study outlines one initiative which has managed to survive and actually get stronger.

Research activities are mostly organized around the interests of like-minded people. The development of research groups tends to occur organically within universities. It is part of what is referred to as a research culture, embedded in the day-to-day practices and values of academic life. Most research activities which operate at a group level share either topics of interest or methodologies of interest. When some research groups develop more formalized arrangements, however, specialized research organizations develop inside the university. In the university system they tend to fall into three types: research units which are situated inside teaching departments; research centres which are situated within schools or faculties; and research institutes which cross faculty and teaching boundaries. The task of becoming any one of these entities is a highly political process.

In the New Zealand university context indigenous Maori developments have occurred as academic developments, initially through the study of Maori within the discipline of anthropology and in more recent times through the development of Maori academic centres within faculties and departments such as education, medicine, law, commerce, art history and literature. This is somewhat different from other contexts where indigenous programmes exist more as student services subject to administration constraints and outside the academic domain. There are distinct advantages in being located in the academic structures which relate very directly to knowledge and to the issue of who can teach and carry out research. Maori peoples are comparatively speaking a significant minority indigenous population, representing about 15 per cent of the total population of New Zealand. Although participation rates by Maori in universities have been extremely low, where Maori have participated they have been extremely successful as academics. Sir Apirana Ngata, for example, trained at Canterbury University in the 1890s and as a member of parliament was one of the better educated members, Maori or non-Maori. Sir Peter Buck trained as a medical anthropologist, taught at Yale University and was a foremost scholar of Pacific Anthropology. Later generations of Maori academics gained their doctoral degrees in Britain or the United States. The academic focus for Maori, then, is small in numbers but strong in a tradition.

The Research Unit for Maori Education was formed shortly after two Maori academics were appointed to a shared senior lecturer's position in the Education Department of the University of Auckland in 1988. The decision to form a research unit was seen as a way of promoting indigenous research which could make a difference for Maori (communities and researchers) and developing some strategic alliances with sympathetic non-indigenous academics The aims of the unit were:

- to promote Maori research which was going to make a positive difference;
- to develop strategies for influencing Maori educational policy,
- to develop and train Maori researchers;
- to disseminate research to Maori audiences through publications and through regular contact with communities; and
- to create an environment for change within the institution.

Gaining support and approval for the research unit was a long and tedious process drawing on the goodwill of senior academics. The first step was to get the proposal accepted by the host department, education. The conditions of this support were discussed around the issue of resources; the research unit had to be self-sustaining and by implication the unit's activities were not to impinge on or limit in any way the activities of other colleagues. Then the proposal went around the university committee system, from committee to committee, from chairperson to head of department. This happened more than once. The issues at this level were about the validity of the activity: for example, was it worthwhile? Were the aims appropriate? Were the people involved appropriate? In most institutions support for indigenous issues is not overt and the ability of academic colleagues to assess on an informed basis what might count as appropriate and worthwhile in the indigenous arena is questionable. A standard institutional response is to bury matters regarded as potentially controversial 'in committee' and in informal consultative processes. Where no indigenous academics exist in an institution, the consultation processes depend on the institutional indigenous experts (non-indigenous academics whose research may be on an indigenous topic). Where an indigenous academic is available, then that person is expected by colleagues to be the all-encompassing resident indigenous expert whose role is to mediate but maintain the *status quo*, often referred to as academic standards. For such a person to say no to indigenous initiatives is interpreted by conservative academics as a strength; to say yes is seen as giving in to self-interest. In the case of this research unit, the head of the Maori Studies Department was consulted and after discussion a slight change of title was required and the Research Unit for Maori Education was formally approved. Research units report through the research committee structures and through the academic departmental structures.

The strengths of the Research Unit for Maori Education over the years 1989–96 can best be summarized as follows:

- the development and promotion of appropriate methodologies for research with Maori, including a theorized approach now referred to as Kaupapa Maori Research;

- the support through undergraduate curriculum development of Maori educational perspectives;
- the mentoring and supervision of Maori graduate students through their course work and thesis work;
- the provision of opportunities for graduate students to become involved as research assistants in research carried out by staff;
- the attention given to participation in conferences and research discussions by staff and graduate students;
- the hosting of indigenous scholars;
- the networking by members of the Research Unit with other indigenous units and centres;
- the dissemination of research to Maori people; and
- the strong interface between empirical and theoretical approaches to research.

Members of the research unit have gained major research contracts and grants, including one from the Marsden foundation, which is New Zealand's only blue skies fund for 'pure' research. Graduate students have been supported to attend international conferences and have been mentored through the development of their academic careers, going on to gain positions in universities and polytechnics. Non-indigenous colleagues have also been supported through conference programmes and research collaboration.

It became increasingly difficult, however, to achieve as a research unit all the things that members of the unit wanted to achieve. This was due in large part to the success of the unit. Contracts were being offered which could not be taken because of the lack of administrative support. The unit had no staff at all. Research work was carried out by academic staff and students on small limited contracts. The host department worked on a grace and favour basis in terms of support, and this tended to be uneven and unreliable. Students who had become more skilled as researchers were seeking more challenging research tasks which could also provide employment. The Maori academic staff had increased, enabling each Maori academic to develop more specialized research interests. The demands on staff time had also grown with the success of the graduate studies programme, which had become the most popular in New Zealand for Maori graduate studies. The university was very proud of this level of success and included the research unit in its annual research reports and international publicity. The unit's achievement – academically and in terms of making space for indigenous developments within a university – had also attracted attention and invitations from other indigenous centres across the world. The two original appointments, both full-time and tenured by 1991, were able to build relations and networks with indigenous groups and communities, especially in Australia, Canada, the United States, Wales, Scotland and Ireland. By 1995, however, the Research Unit for Maori Education had outgrown itself.

In 1995 an external review was conducted of the host department, education. The Research Unit for Maori Education took this opportunity to rethink and reposition its aims and activities. This process involved several meetings and other smaller work groups to develop a new vision and new aims. The proposal was written for the university audience in the same way as the earlier research unit proposal. The support for the transition from a research unit to a research institute was much stronger at all levels of the system than was the original proposal for a unit. The research unit had a proven success record which the university had promoted proudly. The new proposal's journey through the committee structures was nevertheless a highly political process. While the academic case was strongly supported, the resource implications were as strongly resisted. This was despite the fact that the institute had already attracted corporate funding for a visiting professorship. The proposal limped from committee to committee, eventually to senate and to council. Minor matters of detail still had to be attended to, including the title. (Specifically, the use of the word 'indigenous', the use of the word 'international' and the use of the word 'the' came under debate!) A supplementary letter of explanation had to be provided before approval of the title could be gained. The International Research Institute for Maori and Indigenous Education finally passed through council at the end of 1996.

It is possible to see many of the barriers and glitches which occurred as examples of institutional racism. The form that racism takes inside a university is related to the ways in which academic knowledge is structured as well as to the organizational structures which govern a university. The insulation of disciplines, the culture of the institution which supports disciplines, and the systems of management and governance all work in ways which protect the privileges already in place. The infant institute's rough passage can be viewed also as part of the contestable nature of knowledge which has similarly impeded the development of other ways of organizing or thinking about knowledge in the academy: women's studies, cultural studies and other ethnic studies have all had similar rough passage through the system. For indigenous development, however, those are barriers which are taken on simply as a challenge to be met, as there are much greater issues at stake. In New Zealand the political and legislative support for this struggle has been gained through the acknowledgement of the Treaty of Waitangi in the charter statements of all state-funded educational institutions, and through the moral arguments mounted in relation to the university's role in the community. Maori people are clearly a significant group within the New Zealand community. Universities have not served those communities well in the past. They have few avenues into Maori communities in the present. Indigenous developments within an institution such as a university can mediate and structure new relations between institution and community, between indigenous people and non-indigenous people, between communities of the 'researched' and communities of 'researchers'. At the same time indigenous centres which exist inside institutions such as universities continue to struggle for legitimacy. Seeking the international interface in the research field with other indigenous peoples serves two purposes: it supports and strengthens indigenous approaches globally; and it strengthens and supports indigenous developments locally. The mission of the new institute summarizes some of the points made earlier: 'To conduct and disseminate research, scholarship and debate which will make a positive difference to the lives of Maori and other indigenous peoples by drawing together a group of highly skilled and respected scholars who are dedicated to quality outcomes in Maori and indigenous education.'

Training Indigenous Researchers

What large research institutions and research cultures offer are the programmes, resources, facilities and structures which can, if the conditions are appropriate, support and train indigenous researchers. Although communities have a critical perspective of universities and what they represent, at the same time these same communities want their members to gain Western educations and high-level qualifications. But they do not want this to be achieved at the cost of destroying people's indigenous identities, their languages, values and practices. What indigenous students have experienced in universities has been shared by women and other minority group students. For many students it can be an alienating and destructive experience. This is well described by Janice Acoose, who writes about her experiences as a returning student to the University of Saskatchewan,

> Once inside the classroom, even though I had been away from educational institutions for many years, I realized that not much had changed in terms of the ideological character of the teachings or pedagogical strategies. Indeed there were many professors in various disciplines (albeit perhaps unconsciously ignorant or naïve) who attempted both implicitly and explicitly to reinforce notions of white cultural supremacy.[6]

Surviving the experience while gaining the qualification produces a range of strategies which are employed to varying degrees by indigenous students. These strategies range from becoming as invisible as possible to becoming as visible as possible. Surviving undergraduate work is the first hurdle for potential research students as the more systematic mentoring and training of researchers does not normally occur until either graduate level or when employed as a researcher.

Most indigenous researchers who work with indigenous communities or on indigenous issues are self-taught, having received little curriculum support for areas related to indigenous concerns. There are, however, a number of academic programmes being established which are directed specifically towards developing research skills. The Centre for Aboriginal Studies at Curtin University in Western Australia offers a masters programme designed for the needs of indigenous students working with indigenous communities. Emphasis is placed on developing action research skills through specific research tasks. At the University of Auckland, the training of Maori researchers occurs across several faculties including arts, education, law, health sciences, management and science. In education, Auckland's Maori programme has been the forerunner of many of the developments both within this university and across other sites. The programme has developed through a coordinated approach to course work, family and student support, thesis mentoring, role modelling by senior students, and employment on research projects. Students are expected to develop sophisticated theoretical skills alongside their research speciality interests. While the training of researchers is much more focused than standard course work, the programme is also located in a context in which Maori academic staff and researchers are conducting research on an ongoing basis. The creation of a Maori research culture has been deliberate and students are involved in the discussions and debates around research problems from the time they begin their graduate programme. Training tends to be project-specific, with some students employed part-time or on scholarships as research assistants carrying out literature reviews, data entry, transcribing, data analysis and conducting interviews, gradually building up towards taking primary responsibility for a small project. Many students have their own topics which they are encouraged to think through and prepare as proposals, while others arrive with a community project already in mind. Those students with strong family or community support networks are encouraged to involve their communities in their own projects. Those students who may have grown up in bicultural families are encouraged to use the skills gained in their own contexts. The programme assumes that students bring considerable knowledge and skills with them. By sharing with other students from diverse backgrounds, including other indigenous students from the Pacific, and participating in a structured programme, they are expected to gain enough additional skills to be very useful when they return to their own communities.

For some indigenous students one of the first issues to be confronted is their own identities as indigenous and their connected identities to other indigenous peers. While this may seem unusual, given that they appeared to select an indigenous programme, it is often more likely that their participation in the programme is related to needs which are not necessarily educational – for example, emotional support or reassurance. Some may need assistance to reconnect with their own communities or to feel safe. Gender and age are two quite critical factors in some indigenous contexts. For younger students there is a very real constraint on access to knowledge when working with elders. There are also protocols of respect and practices of reciprocity. The relatively simple task of gaining informed consent can take anything from a moment to months and years. Some indigenous students have had to travel back and forth during the course of a year to gain the trust of an individual elder, and have been surprised that without realizing it they gained all the things they were seeking with much more insight, and that in the process they gained a grandparent or a friend. Asking directly for consent to interview can also be interpreted as quite rude behaviour in some cultures. Consent is not so much given for a project or specific set of questions, but for a person, for their credibility. Consent indicates trust and the assumption is that the trust will not only be reciprocated but constantly negotiated – a dynamic relationship rather than a static decision. Similarly, indigenous elders can do wonderful things with an interview. They tell stories, tease, question, think, observe, tell riddles, test and give trick answers. Conversely, they can also expect that an indigenous researcher will do the same back to them. The quality of the interaction is more important than ticking boxes or answering closed questions. Then again, they can simply reply passively to questions, playing the game required of non-indigenous research. Usually young indigenous researchers are used to building and having relationships with elders: the issues tend to be related to the way some research methodologies exclude such extended conversations, especially as they are initiated by the person being interviewed.

Negotiating entry to a community or a home can also be daunting for indigenous researchers. Formal approaches can require several meetings in which the whole ugly history of research on indigenous peoples is reiterated, followed by open and frank discussions of the merit and desirability of a project intersected by other unrelated debates and commentaries, and a conclusion which is highly ambivalent or inconclusive, meaning that the process has to repeated again. Informal approaches can be just as fraught, with one elder consulting others on one matter, and then the consultation process repeated again on another matter. It is common practice in many indigenous contexts for elders to be approached as the first point of contact and as a long-term mentor for an indigenous researcher. Some elders are more appropriate and helpful than others. Some elders can pursue their own agenda while others can be quietly in the background providing assurance, support and critical and insightful feedback. The dynamics of relationships are by nature hugely complicated. For researchers the skills and reflexivities required to mediate and work with these dynamics are quite sophisticated. Indigenous researchers have to be clear about their intentions. They need to have thought about the larger picture of research and have a critical analysis of their own processes.

Insider/Outsider Research

Many of the issues raised by indigenous researchers are addressed in the research literature in relation to both insider and outsider research. Most research methodologies assume that the researcher is an outsider able to observe without being implicated in the scene. This is related to positivism and notions of objectivity and neutrality. Feminist research and other more critical approaches have made the insider methodology much more acceptable in qualitative research. Indigenous research approaches problematize the insider model in different ways because there are multiple ways of both being an insider and an outsider in indigenous contexts. The critical issue with insider research is the constant need for reflexivity. At a general level insider researchers have to have ways of thinking critically about their processes, their relationships and the quality and richness of their data and analysis. So too do outsiders, but the major difference is that insiders have to live with the consequences of their processes on a day-to-day basis for ever more, and so do their families and communities. For this reason insider researchers need to build particular sorts of research-based support systems and relationships with their communities. They have to be skilled at defining clear research goals and 'lines of relating' which are specific to the project and somewhat different from their own family networks. Insider researchers also need to define closure and have the skills to say 'no' and the skills to say 'continue'.

How does this work in practice? One of my very first experiences as a researcher was with a community of Maori mothers and children who had formed a Maori 'language nest'. I was part of the same group. I was an insider as a Maori mother and an advocate of the language revitalization movement, and I shared in the activities of fund raising and organizing. Through my different tribal relationships I had close links to some of the mothers and to the woman who was the main organizer. With other women I shared a background in another way as I had taught some of their older children at the local school. To my academic supervisors I was well and truly an insider in this project. When I began the discussions and negotiations over my research, however, I became much more aware of the things which made me an outsider. I was attending university as a graduate student; I had worked for several years as a teacher and had a professional income; I had a husband; and we owned a car which was second-hand but actually registered. As I became more involved in the project, interviewing the women about their own education stories, and as I visited them in their own homes, these differences became much more marked. What really struck me when I visited the women in their homes as a researcher, having done so on many previous occasions as a mother, were the formal cultural practices which the women observed. An interview with a researcher is formal. I could see immediately that homes were extra spotless and I knew from my own background that when visitors are expected considerable energy goes into cleaning and dusting the house. There was also food which I knew had been prepared for my visit. The children were in their pyjamas (the top matching the bottom) all bathed and ready for bed at 7.30 pm. I knew and the mothers knew that as a group we were all quite casual about bedtime rituals but on the night of the interview everything was in the kind of order which is organized solely for the benefit of the outsider. Other signs and comments made during the interview reinforced the formalities in which my interview participants were engaging. These were signs of respect, the sorts of things I have seen members of my communities do for strangers and the practices I had been taught to observe myself. They were also barriers constructed to keep the outsider at bay, to prevent the outsider becoming the intruder. I had not understood that before, that there were some practices which the communities had control over as a way of resisting the prying eyes of researchers. Both during the research and at the end I was asked to discuss general matters at our regular meetings, but there were many confidences some of which I was asked to protect and others I decided to keep silent on. After the project was completed and I had reported back to them on the finished piece of work, our former relations were restored and have continued as our children have gone on to elementary and secondary schools. I learned many things about research in my own community through those women. I never really did justice to them in the report I eventually wrote as an assignment; I never quite knew how, never possessed the skills or confidence at that time to encapsulate the intricacies of the researcher/ researched relations or my own journey as a beginning researcher. But I remember learning more about research and about being a researcher from that small project than I did from any research course, any lecture or any book.

Insider research has to be as ethical and respectful, as reflexive and critical, as outsider research. It also needs to be humble. It needs to be humble because the researcher belongs to the community as a member with a different set of roles and relationships, status and position. The outside 'expert' role has been and continues to be problematic for indigenous communities. As non-indigenous experts have claimed considerable acceptability amongst their own colleagues and peers, government officials and society on the basis of their research, indigenous voices have been silenced or 'Othered' in the process. The role of an 'official insider voice' is also problematic. The comment, 'She or he lives in it therefore they know' certainly validates experience but for a researcher to assume that their own experience is all that is required is arrogant. One of the difficult risks insider researchers take is to 'test' their own taken-for-granted views about their community. It is a risk because it can unsettle beliefs, values, relationships and the knowledge of different histories. Family-based research for example, can reveal stories of grave injustice, perpetrated by one section of a family and suffered by another. Research can also lead to discoveries which contradict the image that some idealistic younger researchers hold of elders.

The complexities of an insider research approach can be mediated by building support structures. One of the following chapters gives an example of *whanau* structures used by Maori researchers to ensure that relationships and issues, problems and strategies can be discussed and resolved. Whilst most indigenous communities have some form of governance organization, it is more useful to work with such an existing governing body to establish a purpose-developed support group which brings together any outside academic or organizational people involved, the community and the researcher/s. In some contexts an elder has been selected or self-selected to act as a guardian of the researcher, mediating their journeys through the community and through the research. Before either of these supports can be established, in most cases, the community representatives have had to be convinced that the research project is worthwhile and in their interests. Some research models do not allow for change – for example, many questionnaires and other 'measures' have already been developed and tested for reliability long before a project has begun. The 'norms', or the groups with which the measures were developed, are nearly always non-indigenous people. Convincing an indigenous community to participate in such a study requires a thorough knowledge of the research paradigm and an ability to mount a sophisticated and honest justification. Not all indigenous communities are averse to such projects; they tend to be persuaded not by the technical design, however, but by the open and 'good' intentions of the researchers. They also expect and appreciate honesty. Spelling out the limitations of a project, the things that are not addressed, is most important. Many community projects require intensive community input. The implications of such input for impoverished communities or communities under stress can be enormous. Every meeting, every activity, every visit to a home requires energy, commitment and protocols of respect. In my own community there are some very descriptive terms which suggest how bothersome and tiring this activity can be! Idealistic ideas about community collaboration and active participation need to be tempered with realistic assessments of a community's resources and capabilities, even if there is enthusiasm and goodwill. Similarly, the involvement of community resource people also needs to be considered before putting an additional responsibility on individuals already carrying heavy burdens of duty.

Indigenous research focuses and situates the broader indigenous agenda in the research domain. This domain is dominated by a history, by institutional practices and by particular paradigms and approaches to research held by communities of like-minded scholars. The spaces within the research domain through which indigenous research can operate are small spaces on a shifting ground. Negotiating and transforming institutional practices and research frameworks is as significant as the carrying out of actual research programmes. This makes indigenous research a highly political activity and while that is understood by very experienced non-indigenous researchers and organizations it can also be perceived as a threatening activity. The research community has a number of terms which are used to good effect as exclusionary devices to dismiss the challenges made from outside the fold. Research can be judged as 'not rigorous', 'not robust', 'not real', 'not theorized', 'not valid', 'not reliable'. Sound conceptual understandings can falter when the research design is considered flawed. While researchers are trained to conform to the models provided for them, indigenous researchers have to meet these criteria as well as indigenous criteria which can judge research 'not useful', 'not indigenous', 'not friendly', 'not just'. Reconciling such views can be difficult. The indigenous agenda challenges indigenous researchers to work across these boundaries. It is a challenge which provides a focus and direction which helps in thinking through the complexities of indigenous research. At the same time the process is evolving as researchers working in this field dialogue and collaborate on shared concerns.

Notes

1 Alfred, G. R. (1996), *Heeding the Voices of our Ancestors*, Oxford University Press, Toronto, p. 18.

2 *Ibid.*, p. 19.

3 Blea, I. I. (1995), *Researching Chicano Communities*, Praeger, Westport, p. 2.

4 Stringer, E. T. (1996), *Action Research. A Handbook for Practitioners*, Sage Books, California, p. 15.

5 Trask, H. (1993), *From a Native Daughter*, Common Courage Press, Maine.

6 Acoose, J. (1995), *Iskwewak- Kah' Ki Yaw Ni Wahkomakanak. Neither Indian Princesses nor Easy Squaws*, Women's Press, Toronto, p. 30. See also Garrod, A. and C. Larimore, eds (1997), *First Person, First Peoples. Native American College Graduates Tell Their Life Stories*, Cornell University Press, Ithaca.

CHAPTER 8

Twenty-Five Indigenous Projects

The implications for indigenous research which have been derived from the imperatives inside the struggles of the 1970s seem to be clear and straightforward: the survival of peoples, cultures and languages; the struggle to become self-determining, the need to take back control of our destinies. These imperatives have demanded more than rhetoric and acts of defiance. The acts of reclaiming, reformulating and reconstituting indigenous cultures and languages have required the mounting of an ambitious research programme, one that is very strategic in its purpose and activities and relentless in its pursuit of social justice. Within the programme are a number of very distinct projects. Themes such as cultural survival, self-determination, healing, restoration and social justice are engaging indigenous researchers and indigenous communities in a diverse array of projects. The projects intersect with each other in various ways. They have multiple goals and involve different indigenous communities of interest. Some projects, for example, have been driven by indigenous lawyers and constitutional experts, others by indigenous women and health workers, or by social workers and policy analysts. This chapter sets out 25 different projects currently being pursued by indigenous communities. The projects constitute a very complex research programme. Each one intersects with the agenda for indigenous research discussed in Chapter 6 in two or three different ways, that is by site/s and by processes. Each project is outlined to give a bare indication of the parameters offered within it and how these may link in with some of the others.

The projects are not claimed to be entirely indigenous or to have been created by indigenous researchers. Some approaches have arisen out of social science methodologies, which in turn have arisen out of methodological issues raised by research with various oppressed groups. Some projects invite multidisciplinary research approaches. Others have arisen more directly out of indigenous practices. There are two technical points to make here. First, while most projects fall well within what will be recognized as empirical research, not all do. Some important work is related to theorizing indigenous issues at the level of ideas, policy analysis and critical debate, and to setting out in writing indigenous spiritual beliefs and world views. Second, the focus is primarily on social science research projects rather than what may be happening in the natural or physical sciences or technology. There is one technical distinction to clarify. In the chapter I draw on Sandra Harding's very simple distinction between methodology and method, that is, 'A research methodology is a theory and analysis of how research does or should proceed ...' and, 'A research method is a technique for (or way of proceeding in) gathering evidence.'[1] Methodology is important because it frames the questions being asked, determines the set of instruments and methods to be employed and shapes the analyses. Within an indigenous framework, methodological debates are ones concerned with the broader politics and strategic goals of indigenous research. It is at this level that researchers have to clarify and justify their intentions. Methods become the means and procedures through which the central problems of the research are addressed. Indigenous methodologies are often a mix of existing methodological approaches and indigenous practices. The mix reflects the training of indigenous researchers which continues to be within the academy, and the parameters and common sense understandings of research which govern how indigenous communities and researchers define their activities.

The Projects

The following projects are not ranked or listed in any particular order.

1 Claiming

In a sense colonialism has reduced indigenous peoples to making claims and assertions about our rights and dues. It is an approach that has a certain noisiness to it. Indigenous peoples, however, have transformed claiming into an interesting and dynamic process. Considerable work and energy has gone into developing the methodologies which relate to 'claiming' and 'reclaiming'. For some indigenous groups the formal claims process demanded by tribunals, courts and governments has required the conducting of intensive research projects resulting in the writing of nation, tribe and family histories. These 'histories' have a focus and purpose, that is, to establish the legitimacy of the claims being asserted for the rest of time. Because they have been written to support claims to territories and resources or about past injustices, they have been constructed around selected stories. These claiming histories have

also been written for different audiences. One audience is the formal
court or tribunal audience, who are generally non-indigenous, another the
general non-indigenous population, and a third the people themselves.
For this last audience the histories are also important teaching histories.
They teach both the non-indigenous audience and the new generations
of indigenous peoples an official account of their collective story. But,
importantly, it is a history which has no ending because it assumes that
once justice has been done the people will continue their journey. It may
be that in time the histories have to be rewritten around other priorities.

2 Testimonies

'My Name is Rigoberta Menchu, I am twenty-three years old, and this is
my testimony.'[2]

Testimonies intersect with claiming because they are a means through
which oral evidence is presented to a particular type of audience. There
is a formality to testimonies and a notion that truth is being revealed
'under oath'. Indigenous testimonies are a way of talking about an
extremely painful event or series of events.[3] The formality of testimony
provides a structure within which events can be related and feelings
expressed.[4] A testimony is also a form through which the voice of a
'witness' is accorded space and protection. It can be constructed as a
monologue and as a public performance. The structure of testimony –
its formality, context and sense of immediacy – appeals to many
indigenous participants, particularly elders. It is an approach that
translates well to a formal written document. While the listener may ask
questions, testimonies structure the responses, silencing certain types of
questions and formalizing others.

3 Story telling

Story telling, oral histories, the perspectives of elders and of women have
become an integral part of all indigenous research. Each individual story
is powerful. But the point about the stories is not that they simply tell
a story, or tell a story simply. These new stories contribute to a collective
story in which every indigenous person has a place. In a book called *The
Wailing: A National Black Oral History*, Stuart Rintoul has called the oral
histories he gathered 'stories handed down in the homes of Black
Australians, told to new generations, taught in explanation of racism and
mistreatment, recited with rage and dignity and sorrow'.[5] Rintoul writes
further that the stories are also 'memories of injustice ... an avalanche
of voices crying out in hundreds of countries across innumerable
Dreamings'.[6] For many indigenous writers stories are ways of passing
down the beliefs and values of a culture in the hope that the new

generations will treasure them and pass the story down further. The story and the story teller both serve to connect the past with the future, one generation with the other, the land with the people and the people with the story. As a research tool, Russell Bishop suggests, story telling is a useful and culturally appropriate way of representing the 'diversities of truth' within which the story teller rather than the researcher retains control.[7] Bishop also suggests that 'the indigenous community becomes a story that is a collection of individual stories, ever unfolding through the lives of the people who share the life of that community'.[8]

Intrinsic in story telling is a focus on dialogue and conversations amongst ourselves as indigenous peoples, to ourselves and for ourselves. Such approaches fit well with the oral traditions which are still a reality in day-to-day indigenous lives. Importantly, story telling is also about humour and gossip and creativity. Stories tell of love and sexual encounters, of war and revenge. Their themes tell us about our cultures. Stories employ familiar characters and motifs which can reassure as well as challenge. Familiar characters can be invested with the qualities of an individual or can be used to invoke a set of shared understandings and histories.

4 Celebrating survival

Celebrating survival is a particular sort of approach. While non-indigenous research has been intent on documenting the demise and cultural assimilation of indigenous peoples, celebrating survival accentuates not so much our demise but the degree to which indigenous peoples and communities have successfully retained cultural and spiritual values and authenticity. The approach is reflected sometimes in story form, sometimes in popular music and sometimes as an event in which artists and story tellers come together to celebrate collectively a sense of life and diversity and connectedness. Events and accounts which focus on the positive are important not just because they speak to our survival, but because they celebrate our resistances at an ordinary human level and they affirm our identities as indigenous women and men. Celebrating survival as an approach is also a theme running through the collections of elders' stories. In one such collection told to Sandy Johnson she writes of the way in which '[the elders] speak openly of their personal struggles to stay on the path against impossible odds. Their stories of what they have lost and what they have fought to save are both tragic and heroic.'[9] Gregory Cajete writes that 'celebrating is a natural outcome of spiritual sharing and it too can take a diversity of forms. It is an individual and communal process that celebrates the mystery of life and the journey that each of us takes. Celebration is a way of spreading the lights around.'[10]

5 Remembering

The remembering of a people relates not so much to an idealized remembering of a golden past but more specifically to the remembering of a painful past and, importantly, people's responses to that pain. While collectively indigenous communities can talk through the history of painful events, there are frequent silences and intervals in the stories about what happened after the event. Often there is no collective remembering as communities were systematically ripped apart, children were removed for adoption, extended families separated across different reserves and national boundaries. The aftermath of such pain was borne by individuals or smaller family units, sometimes unconsciously or consciously obliterated through alcohol, violence and self-destruction. Communities often turned inward and let their suffering give way to a desire to be dead. Violence and family abuse became entrenched in communities which had no hope. White society did not see and did not care. This form of remembering is painful because it involves remembering not just what colonization was about but what being de-humanized meant for our own cultural practices. Both healing and transformation become crucial strategies in any approach which asks a community to remember what they may have decided unconsciously or consciously to forget.

6 Indigenizing

This project has two dimensions. The first one is similar to that which has occurred in literature with a centring of the landscapes, images, languages, themes, metaphors and stories in the indigenous world and the disconnecting of many of the cultural ties between the settler society and its metropolitan homeland. This project involves non-indigenous activists and intellectuals. The second aspect is more of an indigenous project. The term is used more frequently in South and Central America. The concept of indigenist, says Ward Churchill, means 'that I am one who not only takes the rights of indigenous peoples as the highest priority of my political life, but who draws upon the traditions – the bodies of knowledge and corresponding codes of values – evolved over many thousands of years by native peoples the world over'.[11] The term centres a politics of indigenous identity and indigenous cultural action. M. Annette Jaimes refers to indigenism as being grounded in the alternative conceptions of world view and value systems, 'These differences provide a basis for a conceptualisation of Indigenism that counters the negative connotations of its meanings in third world countries, where it has become synonymous with the "primitive", or with backwardness among superstitious peoples.'[12] Lester Rigney, an Aborigine researcher in New South Wales, names the approach he takes as indigenist research, an approach which borrows freely from feminist research and critical approaches to research, but privileges indigenous voices.

7 *Intervening*

Intervening takes action research to mean literally the process of being proactive and of becoming involved as an interested worker for change. Intervention-based projects are usually designed around making structural and cultural changes. Graham Smith describes this approach as a necessary approach when faced with crisis conditions. Smith argues

> firstly, that Maori educational crises continue – this points to a failure of educational policy reforms, research and researchers. Secondly, educational researchers have continued to fail to intervene because of the lack of responsibility and accountability placed on researchers and policy makers. Thirdly much of research has been counter productive to Maori interests, and has merely served the dominant Pakeha group interests, by maintaining the status quo of unequal power distribution.[13]

It is not ethical to walk away, or simply to carry out projects which describe what is already known. State policies for indigenous peoples were also interventionist in profoundly destructive ways. The indigenous intervening project carries with it some working principles. For example, the community itself invites the project in and sets out its parameters. The various departments and agencies involved in such a project are also expected to be willing to change themselves in some way, redirect policy, design new programmes or train staff differently. Intervening is directed then at changing institutions which deal with indigenous peoples and not at changing indigenous peoples to fit the structures.

8 *Revitalizing*

Indigenous languages, their arts and their cultural practices are in various states of crisis. Many indigenous languages are officially 'dead' with fewer than a hundred speakers. Others are in the last stages before what is described by linguists as 'language death'. Revitalization initiatives in languages encompass education, broadcasting, publishing and community-based programmes. While the Welsh people are not formally part of the indigenous peoples' movements as described in Chapter 6, their programmes are often studied as examples of indigenous achievement. The Welsh language programme is promoted as a model for language revitalization. Welsh schools, from kindergarten to secondary schools, offer teaching through the medium of Welsh. This is supported officially through government funding. Television and newspapers in the medium of Welsh – which include children's programming, drama, documentaries, news, and sports – provide a comprehensive approach to language revitalization. The European Bureau of Lesser Languages has a role of supporting the diverse minority languages of Europe. Maori language development has followed a similar pattern to the Welsh language example, with an official Language Act and associated educational programmes. In the case of Maori and Welsh language, there is a clear singular language. Many places have to battle for the survival of several languages spoken by small populations. In Canada, for example, most of the indigenous languages could be categorized as being on the verge of extinction. British Columbia has a diverse range of indigenous languages, all of which require support. The Squamish language, for example, has few native speakers. The Squamish Nation helped co-host a conference on indigenous languages in 1989 in order to stimulate discussions and seek solutions to the language crisis. Their Nation's Band Office has an education centre whose staff develop resources for schools and encourage the use of the language by their remaining native speakers. For much of the indigenous world there is little proactive coordination or support. Literacy campaigns tend to frame language survival programmes. Such campaigns are designed around either official languages or one or two dominant languages. The indigenous language is often regarded as being subversive to national interests and national literacy campaigns.

9 Connecting

The importance of making connections and affirming connectedness has been noted also by other minority group researchers. Connectedness positions individuals in sets of relationships with other people and with the environment. Many indigenous creation stories link people through genealogy to the land, to stars and other places in the universe, to birds and fish, animals, insects and plants. To be connected is to be whole. The project of connecting is pursued in New South Wales in one form as literally connecting members of families with each other. A link programme has been designed to restore the descendants of 'stolen children', ones forcibly taken from their families and adopted, to their family connections. Forced adoption and dehumanizing child welfare practices were carried out in many indigenous contexts. Being reconnected to their families and their culture has been a painful journey for many of these children, now adults. Connecting also involves connecting people to their traditional lands through the restoration of specific rituals and practices. In New Zealand one example of this is the practice of burying the afterbirth in the land. The word for afterbirth is the same as the word for land, *whenua*. The practice was prohibited as Maori mothers were forced to have their babies in hospitals rather than at home. The policies and hospital practices have now changed and Maori parents have reinstituted the practice of taking the afterbirth and burying it in traditional territory. Connecting children to their land and their genealogies through this process is also part of a larger health project designed to encourage young Maori mothers to take better care of themselves and their babies through stronger cultural supports. Connecting is related to issues of identity and place, to spiritual relationships and community wellbeing.

There are other challenges in relation to the project of connecting. Researchers, policy makers, educators, and social service providers who work with or whose work impacts on indigenous communities need to have a critical conscience about ensuring that their activities connect in humanizing ways with indigenous communities. It is a very common experience to hear indigenous communities outline the multiple ways in which agencies and individuals treat them with disrespect and disregard. Connecting is about establishing good relations.

10 Reading

Critical rereading of Western history and the indigenous presence in the making of that history has taken on a different impetus from what was once a school curriculum designed to assimilate indigenous children. The new reading programme is motivated partly by a research drive to establish and support claims, but also by a need to understand what has informed both internal colonialism and new forms of colonization. The genealogy of colonialism is being mapped and used as a way to locate a different sort of origin story, the origins of imperial policies and practices, the origins of the imperial visions, the origins of ideas and values. These origin stories are deconstructed accounts of the West, its history through the eyes of indigenous and colonized peoples. The rereading of imperial history by post-colonial and cultural studies scholars provides a different, much more critical approach to history than was previously acceptable. It is no longer the single narrative story of important white imperial figures, adventurers and heroes who fought their way through undiscovered lands to establish imperial rule and bring civilization and salvation to 'barbaric savages' who lived in 'utter degradation'.

11 Writing

Indigenous people are writing. In Chapter 1 the writing project was named as 'the empire writes back' project. In a localized context, however, writing is employed in a variety of imaginative, critical, and also quite functional ways. Maori author Witi Ihimaera has assembled a five-volume anthology of Maori literature which he argues represents the 'crossroads … of a literature of a past and a literature of a present and future'.[14] The title of an anthology of Native Women's writings of North America, *Reinventing the Enemy's Language*, gives a sense of the issues being explored through writing.[15] Similar anthologies and works of indigenous literature are being published around the world by indigenous writers for indigenous reading audiences.[16] The boundaries of poetry, plays, song writing, fiction and non-fiction are blurred as indigenous writers seek to use language in ways which capture the messages, nuances and flavour of indigenous lives. The activity of writing has produced the related activity of publishing. Maori newspapers, which were quite common in the nineteenth century, have been revived as different organizations and tribes seek to provide better information than is available in the mainstream media. Language revitalization initiatives have created a demand for multi-media language resources for children. In the Western Isles of Scotland, a Stornaway publishing house called Acair has produced children's comic books in Scottish Gaelic and cookbooks and other material which supports the Gaelic language. Similar small publishing groups are operating across the indigenous world. Writing workshops and writing courses offered by indigenous writers for indigenous people who want to write are held in many places. The work of authors such as Patricia Grace, Paula Gunn Allen, Louise Erdrich, Witi Ihimaera and Sally Morgan is read by both indigenous and non-indigenous audiences. Biographies and autobiographies including those which are accounts 'told to a non-indigenous person', are sought after by a new reading audience of indigenous people.

12 Representing

Indigenous communities have struggled since colonization to be able to exercise what is viewed as a fundamental right, that is to represent ourselves. The representing project spans both the notion of representation as a political concept and representation as a form of voice and expression. In the political sense colonialism specifically excluded indigenous peoples from any form of decision making. States and governments have long made decisions hostile to the interests of indigenous communities but justified by a paternalistic view that indigenous peoples were like children who needed others to protect them and decide what was in their best interests. Paternalism is still present in many forms in the way governments, local bodies and non-government agencies decide on issues which have an impact on indigenous communities. Being able as a minimum right to voice the views and opinions of indigenous communities in various decision-making bodies is still being struggled over. Even at the minimal level of representation indigenous communities are often 'thrown in' with all other minorities as one voice amongst many. The politics of sovereignty and self-determination have been about resisting being thrown in with every other minority group by making claims on the basis of prior rights.

Representation is also a project of indigenous artists, writers, poets, film makers and others who attempt to express an indigenous spirit, experience or world view. Representation of indigenous peoples by indigenous people is about countering the dominant society's image of indigenous peoples, their lifestyles and belief systems. It is also about proposing solutions to the real-life dilemmas that indigenous communities confront and trying to capture the complexities of being indigenous. Many of the dilemmas are internalized stress factors in community life which are never named or voiced because they are either taken for granted or hidden by a community. There is an element of the raw, tough and unsympathetic representation of indigenous life by a writer such as Allen Duff who wrote the novel *Once Were Warriors*. And there is the humour of Alexie Sherman who wrote *Reservation Blues*. Film makers such as Merata Mita have a very clear purpose in their work which locates it firmly within a decolonization framework. She says that,

> Not surprisingly, when my obsessive struggle with filmmaking began, it was with the issues that most concerned us as Maori women that I became pre-occupied – the issues of injustice, land, te reo Maori [Maori language], the Treaty, and racism. Add to that women and gender issues, and for those who don't know, these are the things that consume us, consume our energy, beset us every moment of our daily lives, they are brutalising, violent, and some of us die because of them.[17]

13 Gendering

Gendering indigenous debates, whether they are related to the politics of self-determination or the politics of the family, is concerned with issues related to the relations between indigenous men and women. Colonization is recognized as having had a destructive effect on indigenous gender relations which reached out across all spheres of indigenous society. Family organization, child rearing, political and spiritual life, work and social activities were all disordered by a colonial system which positioned its own women as the property of men with roles which were primarily domestic. Indigenous women across many different indigenous societies claim an entirely different relationship, one embedded in beliefs about the land and the universe, about the spiritual significance of women and about the collective endeavours that were required in the organization of society. Indigenous women would argue that their traditional roles included full participation in many aspects of political decision making and marked gender separations which were complementary in order to maintain harmony and stability. Gendering contemporary indigenous debates occurs inside indigenous communities and while it is debated in other contexts, such as in Western feminist debates, indigenous women hold an analysis of colonialism as a central tenet of an indigenous feminism. A key issue for indigenous women in any challenge of contemporary indigenous politics is the restoration to women of what are seen as their traditional roles, rights and responsibilities. Aroha Mead gives an account of a statement delivered by two Maori women to the Twelfth Session (1994), of the United Nations Working Group on Indigenous Peoples which addressed the way colonialism has influenced indigenous men and had a detrimental affect on indigenous gender relations. She says that

> never before have I witnessed what occurred while the full statement was being read out. Indigenous women sitting within their delegations were visibly moved – some looked around to see who was talking about their pain – some gave victory signals and physical signs of agreement, and many, perhaps even the majority, sat stoically, with tears swelling in their eyes. The words broke through the barriers of language and regionalism. A raw wound was clearly touched.[18]

14 Envisioning

One of the strategies which indigenous peoples have employed effectively to bind people together politically is a strategy which asks that people imagine a future, that they rise above present day situations which are generally depressing, dream a new dream and set a new vision. The confidence of knowing that we have survived and can only go forward provides some impetus to a process of envisioning. In New Zealand, for example, tribes which began their grievance claims against the Crown last century have not only had their claims heard but are negotiating a settlement. For the people who began the process these settlements were simply dreams. If they had listened to politicians, taken the mainstream media seriously, taken heed of scholars and commentators, they would not have begun. Similarly, communities who have worked to revitalise their language or build a new economic base or renegotiate arrangements with governments have worked on the basis of a shared vision. The power of indigenous peoples to change their own lives and set new directions despite their impoverished and oppressed conditions speaks to the politics of resistance.

Sometimes the visions which bind people were set a long time ago and have been passed down the generations as poems, songs, stories, proverbs or sayings. Every indigenous community probably has special sayings, predictions, riddles and proverbs which are debated frequently and raised both informally and formally. Children are socialized into these sayings and pass them down to their own children. The profound statements of indigenous leaders from the last century and the centuries before are often written in diaries and notebooks, carved into stone, distributed by T-shirt and poster. Often the original source of the comment has been forgotten but the power of the words remain. They make our spirits soar and give us hope. Indigenous people have borrowed freely from each other and it is not uncommon to find the saying of an Indian chief stuck to the kitchen wall in a Maori home, or the saying of a Maori chief embroidered into a wall hanging in an Aborigine home. These sayings have acted like resistance codes which can be passed down by word of mouth to the next person, to the next generation.

15 Reframing

Reframing is about taking much greater control over the ways in which indigenous issues and social problems are discussed and handled. One of the reasons why so many of the social problems which beset indigenous communities are never solved is that the issues have been framed in a particular way. For example, governments and social agencies have failed to see many indigenous social problems as being related to any sort of history. They have framed indigenous issues in 'the indigenous problem' basket, to be handled in the usual cynical and paternalistic manner. The framing of an issue is about making decisions about its parameters, about what is in the foreground, what is in the background, and what shadings or complexities exist within the frame. The project of reframing is related to defining the problem or issue and determining how best to solve that problem. Many indigenous activists have argued that such things as mental illness, alcoholism and suicide, for example, are not about psychological and individualized failure but about colonization or lack of collective self-determination. Many community health initiatives address the whole community, its history and its wider context as part of the problem and part of the solution.

Reframing occurs in other contexts where indigenous people resist being boxed and labelled according to categories which do not fit. This is particularly pertinent in relation to various development programmes, government and non-government. In the case of Maori, for example, a Maori language initiative for young children from birth to school age – known as Te Kohanga Reo, or Maori language nests – constantly has to explain why it is not a child-care centre but a language and culture initiative for young children. The problem of definition is important in this case because it affects funding, but the constant need to justify difference is experienced by many other communities whose initiatives are about changing things on a holistic basis rather than endorsing the individualized programme emphasis of government models. The need to reframe is about retaining the strengths of a vision and the participation of a whole community.

Reframing occurs also within the way indigenous people write or engage with theories and accounts of what it means to be indigenous. In the politics of indigenous women, for example, there is continuing resistance to the way Western feminists have attempted to define the issues for indigenous women and categorize the positions in which indigenous women should be located. Moves to discuss patriarchy without addressing imperialism and racism are always reframed by indigenous women, and of course other minority women, as inadequate analyses. Similarly moves to attack indigenous culture or indigenous men 'as a group' are also resisted because for indigenous women the issues are far more complex and the objective of analysis is always focused on solving problems. In the end indigenous men and women have to live together in a world in which both genders are under attack.

16 Restoring

Indigenous peoples across the world have disproportionately high rates of imprisonment, suicide and alcoholism. Some indigenous activists regard these rates as the continuation of a war. Says Bobbi Sykes, 'The main question, which has not been addressed by government, is the legitimacy or otherwise of the assumption that white domination of Aboriginal people is in itself a concept of justice.'[19] For Aborigines the high rates of black deaths in custody eventually provoked the establishment of a Royal Commission of Inquiry in 1987 into a problem which had been hidden for many years. The Aborigine rates of death in custody was said to be higher than the rate in South Africa. Inside the incarceration rates for indigenous peoples are similar rates for youth offending and for indigenous women. In the health arena indigenous people have high rates of morbidity and mortality. Maori women have one of the highest rates of lung cancer in the world. Maori suicide rates, both male and female, have risen sharply over the last decade, with New Zealand rates amongst the highest in OECD countries. Aborigine rates of illness have frequently been cited as examples of the Fourth World, rates, which are worse than the rates in developing Third World states, and are made more horrific by the fact that these communities live in nations that have the highest standards of living. At a recent gathering of Pacific leaders, for example, the Australian Prime Minister John Howard was reported to have been reluctant to agree on helping to counter the effects of global warming, citing his duty to put the standard of living of Australians first. He was not talking about indigenous Australians.

The restoring of wellbeing spiritually, emotionally, physically and materially has involved social workers and health workers in a range of initiatives, some of which have been incorporated into mainstream programmes. Restorative justice in Canada, for example, applies concepts of the 'healing circle' and victim restoration which are based on indigenous processes. These systems have been discussed widely and used to motivate other societies to develop better ways of dealing with offenders and victims. In New Zealand adoption policies and programmes for dealing with children have similarly coopted indigenous practices. Restoring is a project which is conceived as a holistic approach to problem solving. It is holistic in terms of the emotional, spiritual and physical nexus, and also in terms of the individual and the collective, the political and the cultural. Restorative programmes are based on a model of healing rather than of punishing. They sometimes employ concepts such as public shaming as a way of provoking individual accountability and collective problem solving. Health programmes addressing basic health issues have begun to seek ways to connect with indigenous communities through appropriate public health policy and practice models. The failure of public health programmes to improve the health of indigenous communities significantly has motivated a self-help approach by communities. It is especially infuriating when projects such as the Human Genome Project are justified on the grounds that knowledge about genetic resistances to various diseases will 'benefit mankind' when Western health has failed to benefit indigenous human beings.

17 Returning

This project intersects with that of claiming. It involves the returning of lands, rivers and mountains to their indigenous owners. It involves the repatriation of artefacts, remains and other cultural materials stolen or removed and taken overseas. Sykes lists the following examples: 'pickled heads, human gloves, scrotum tobacco pouches, dried scalps, pickled foetus, cicatured skins, complete stuffed, mummified children's bodies and women with child'.[20] In New Zealand the current Minister of Maori Affairs, who is a Maori, has set out a plan to return all tattooed Maori heads which are housed in museums and other collections across the world. They apparently number in the hundreds. In a previous chapter I discussed the house Mataatua which has now been returned to Ngati Awa.

Returning also involves the living. One major tribe in New Zealand has negotiated the return of traditional food gathering sites which will be marked out for their exclusive use by tribal members. Other programmes have been initiated to repatriate people either through ensuring their membership in official tribal registers or by physically reclaiming them. Adopted children, for example, are encouraged to seek their birth families and return to their original communities.

18 Democratizing

Although indigenous communities claim a model of democracy in their traditional ways of decision making, many contemporary indigenous organizations were formed through the direct involvement of states and governments. Legislation was used to establish and regulate indigenous councils and committees, indigenous forms of representation and indigenous titles to lands. They are colonial constructions that have been taken for granted as authentic indigenous formations. Furthermore many such councils, because they were established through colonialism, have privileged particular families and elite groups over other indigenous families from the same communities. Needless to say, many councils were created as exclusively male domains while the health and welfare programmes were assigned to the women. Maori lawyer Annette Sykes argues, for example, in relation to a claim being made by Maori women to the Waitangi Tribunal, that

> The essence of the claim is to bring to the forefront of the current Treaty jurisprudence, the need to look at notions of governance in Aotearoa and the exclusionary practices that exist, which inhibit and prevent participation by Maori women in the tribal models for self-determination, that have been erected under New Zealand legislation, and the erosion that this in itself has had on Te Mana Wahine in Te Ao Maori [the *mana* of women in the Maori World].[21]

Democratizing in indigenous terms is a process of extending participation outwards through reinstating indigenous principles of collectivity and public debate.

19 Networking

Networking has become an efficient medium for stimulating information flows, educating people quickly about issues and creating extensive international talking circles. Building networks is about building knowledge and data bases which are based on the principles of relationships and connections. Relationships are initiated on a face to face basis and then maintained over many years often without any direct contact. People's names are passed on and introductions are used to bring new members into the network. The face to face encounter is about checking out an individual's credentials, not just their political credentials but their personalities and spirit. Networking by indigenous peoples is a form of resistance. People are expected to position themselves clearly and state their purposes. Establishing trust is an important feature. In many states police surveillance of indigenous activists and their families is common practice. In some states, such as Guatemala, the disappearance of indigenous peoples has also been common practice. In these contexts networking is dangerous.

Networking is a way of making contacts between marginalized communities. By definition their marginalization excludes them from participation in the activities of the dominant non-indigenous society, which controls most forms of communication. Issues such as the Conventions on Biodiversity or GATT, for example, which have a direct impact on indigenous communities, are not addressed by mainstream media for an indigenous audience. Indigenous peoples would not know of such agreements and their impact on indigenous cultural knowledge if it were not for the power of networking. The project of networking is about process. Networking is a process which indigenous peoples have used effectively to build relationships and disseminate knowledge and information.

20 Naming

This project takes its name from Brazilian educator Paulo Freire whose saying, 'name the word, name the world' (which was about literacy programmes), has been applied in the indigenous context to literally rename the landscape. This means renaming the world using the original indigenous names. Naming as a project of Maori people can be seen in the struggles over the geographical names of some of New Zealand's mountains and significant sites which were renamed randomly after British people and places. Many of the Maori names have now been restored. Naming can also be seen in the naming of children. Indigenous names carried histories of people, places and events. As a result of Christian baptism practices, which introduced Christian names and family names, and schooling practices, where teachers shortened names or introduced either generic names or nicknames, many indigenous communities hid their indigenous names either by using them only in indigenous ceremonies or by positioning them as second names. A more recent assertion in Maori naming practices has been to name children again with long ancestral names and to take on new names through life, both of which were once traditional practices. Children quite literally wear their history in their names.

Naming applies to other things as well. It is about retaining as much control over meanings as possible. By 'naming the world' people name their realities. For communities there are realities which can only be found in the indigenous language; the concepts which are self-evident in the indigenous language can never be captured by another language.

21 Protecting

This project is multifaceted. It is concerned with protecting peoples, communities, languages, customs and beliefs, art and ideas, natural resources and the things indigenous peoples produce. The scale of protecting can be as enormous as the Pacific Ocean and the Amazon rainforest or as small as an infant. It can be as real as land and as abstract as a belief about the spiritual essence of the land. Every indigenous community is attempting to protect several different things simultaneously. In some areas alliances with non-indigenous organizations have been beneficial in terms of rallying international support. In other areas a community is trying to protect itself by staying alive or staying off alcohol.

Some countries have identified sacred sites and have designated protected areas. Many of these, unfortunately, become tourist spots. Issues about the protection of indigenous knowledge have been discussed at various indigenous conferences which have produced charters and conventions aimed at signalling to the world at large that indigenous knowledges ought to be protected. History seems to suggest that many of these calls for international adherence to such charters will be at best highly selective. The need to protect a way of life, a language and the right to make our own history is a deep need linked to the survival of indigenous peoples.

22 Creating

The project of creating is about transcending the basic survival mode through using a resource or capability which every indigenous community has retained throughout colonization – the ability to create and be creative. The project of creating is not just about the artistic endeavours of individuals but about the spirit of creating which indigenous communities have exercised over thousands of years. Imagination enables people to rise above their own circumstances, to dream new visions and to hold on to old ones. It fosters inventions and discoveries, facilitates simple improvements to people's lives and uplifts our spirits. Creating is not the exclusive domain of the rich nor of the technologically superior, but of the imaginative. Creating is about channelling collective creativity in order to produce solutions to indigenous problems. Every indigenous community has considered and come up with various innovative solutions to problems. That was before colonialism. Throughout the period of colonization indigenous peoples survived because of their imaginative spirit, their ability to adapt and to think around a problem.

Indigenous communities also have something to offer the non-indigenous world. There are many programmes incorporating indigenous elements, which on that account are viewed on the international scene as 'innovative' and unique. Indigenous peoples' ideas and beliefs about the origins of the world, their explanations of the environment, often embedded in complicated metaphors and mythic tales, are now being sought as the basis for thinking more laterally about current theories about the environment, the earth and the universe.

Communities are the ones who know the answers to their own problems, although their ideas tend to be dismissed when suggested to various agencies and governments. Visits to communities which have developed their own programmes demonstrate both the creativity alive and well at the community level and the strength of commitment shown when the programme is owned by the community.

23 Negotiating

Negotiating is about thinking and acting strategically. It is about recognizing and working towards long-term goals. Patience is a quality which indigenous communities have possessed in abundance. Patience and negotiation are linked to a very long view of our survival. When one reads of the decisions made by various indigenous leaders to accept the terms and conditions of colonization, what emerges from those stories is the concern shown by leaders for the long-term survival chances of the collective, of their own people. That was the basis of their courage and, despite the outrage younger generations of indigenous people might feel about the deal which some leaders accepted, the broader picture across several indigenous contexts is one of dignity and acceptance of a specific reality. Their negotiations were undertaken quite literally with guns held at their heads, with their people starving and with death around them.

In today's environment negotiation is still about deal making and it is still about concepts of leadership. Negotiations are also about respect, self-respect and respect for the opposition. Indigenous rules of negotiation usually contain both rituals of respect and protocols for discussion. The protocols and procedures are integral to the actual negotiation and neglect or failure to acknowledge or take seriously such protocols can be read as a lack of commitment to both the process and the outcome. Many indigenous societies are socialized into some forms of negotiation because they are part of trading practices or basic communication styles. The contemporary negotiation project is related to self-determination, in that indigenous nations are negotiating terms for settlements which often mean semi-autonomous government or statutory representation or control over key resources, such as natural resources within their own territories. Negotiation also occurs where small gains are at stake, however, such as when local communities have worked out an agreement with a local government or agency or another local community. The formality of negotiation is important in protecting the sanctity of the agreement which emerges from a negotiation. Indigenous peoples know and understand what it means for agreements to be dishonoured. The continued faith in the process of negotiating is about retaining a faith in the humanity of indigenous beliefs, values and customary practices.

24 Discovering

This project is about discovering Western science and technology and making science work for indigenous development. There are very few indigenous scientists who remain closely connected to their own indigenous communities. Indigenous students across many contexts have struggled with Western science as it has been taught to them in schools. Science has been traditionally hostile to indigenous ways of knowing. Science teaching in schools has also been fraught with hostile attitudes towards indigenous cultures, and the way indigenous students learn. There are huge debates within the scientific community about the nature of science and how it ought to be taught. This debate is over the notion of constructivism, and concerns the extent to which knowledge is socially constructed or exists 'out there' as a body of knowledge which students simply learn. The development of ethno-science and the application of science to matters which interest indigenous peoples such as environmental and resource management or biodiversity offer some new possibilities for indigenous people to engage with the sciences which they decide are most relevant.

25 Sharing

The final project discussed here is about sharing knowledge between indigenous peoples, around networks and across the world of indigenous peoples. Sharing contains views about knowledge being a collective benefit and knowledge being a form of resistance. Like networking, sharing is a process which is responsive to the marginalized contexts in which indigenous communities exist. Even in the context of New Zealand – a small country, relatively well-off in terms of televisions and communications – Maori people learn more about the issues which affect them at one of the many community gatherings which are held on *marae* then they do from the mainstream media. These gatherings may be for weddings or funerals but they are also used as opportunities to keep the community informed about a wide range of things. The face-to-face nature of sharing is supplemented with local newspapers which focus on indigenous issues and local radio stations which specialize in indigenous news and music. Sharing is also related to the failure of education systems to educate indigenous people adequately or appropriately. It is important for keeping people informed about issues and events which will impact on them. It is a form of oral literacy, which connects with the story telling and formal occasions that feature in indigenous life.

Sharing is a responsibility of research. The technical term for this is the dissemination of results, usually very boring to non-researchers, very technical and very cold. For indigenous researchers sharing is about demystifying knowledge and information and speaking in plain terms to the community. Community gatherings provide a very daunting forum in which to speak about research. Oral presentations conform to cultural protocols and expectations. Often the audience may need to be involved emotionally with laughter, deep reflection, sadness, anger, challenges and debate. It is a very skilled speaker who can share openly at this level within the rules of the community.

Summary

The projects touched on in this chapter are not offered as the definitive list of activities in which indigenous communities are engaged. There are numerous collaborative projects being undertaken with non-indigenous researchers and organizations. Many of these research partnerships help to develop a trained workforce through the mentoring and guidance provided by the non-indigenous researchers. There are also the more standard types of research projects and methodologies in the social sciences that have not been mentioned here. Some of these approaches, for example those in critical ethnography, have been written about and theorized by scholars working in those disciplines. The naming of the projects listed in this chapter was deliberate. I hope the message it gives to communities is that they have issues that matter and processes and methodologies which can work for them.

Notes

1 Harding, S. (1987), *Feminism and Methodology*, Indiana University Press, Bloomington, pp. 2–3.
2 Menchu, R. (1984), *I, Rigoberta Menchu. An Indian Woman in Guatamala*, trans. A. Wright, Verso, London.
3 See, for example, Jonas, S., E. McCaughan and E. Martinez (1984), *Guatemala: Tyranny on Trial, Synthesis Publications*, San Francisco; and Beverley, J. (1992), 'The Margin at the Centre: on Testimonies', in *De/ Colonizing the Subject: The Politics of*

Gender in Women's Autobiography, eds S. Smith and J. Watson, University of Minneapolis Press, Minneapolis; and Yudice, G. (1991), 'Testimonies and Post Modernism', in *Latin American Perspectives: a Journal on Capitalism and Socialism*, Vol. 18, Nos 3–4, pp. 15–31.

4 See also Nabokov, P. (1992), *Native American Testimony*, Penguin Books, New York.

5 Rintoul, S. (1993), *The Wailing: a National Black Oral History*, Heinemann, Australia, p. 8.

6 *Ibid.*, p. 8.

7 Bishop, R. (1996), *Collaborative Research Stories,* Dunmore Press, Palmerston North, p. 24.

8 *Ibid.*, p. 169.

9 Johnson, S. and D. Budnik (1994), *The Book of Elders*, Harper, San Francisco, p. 7.

10 Cajete, G. (1994), *Look to the Mountain. An Ecology of Indigenous Education*, Kivaki Press, Colorado, p. 73.

11 Churchill, W. (1993), 'I Am Indigenist', in *Struggle for the Land*, ed. Ward Churchill, Common Courage Press, Maine, pp. 403–51.

12 Jaimes, M.A. (1995), 'Native American Identity and Survival: Indigenism and Environmental Ethics', in *Issues in Native American Cultural Identity*, ed. M. K. Green, Peter Lang Publishers, New York.

13 Smith, G. H. (1990), 'Research Issues Related to Maori', *The Issue of Research and Maori*, ed. G. H. Smith and M. Hohepa, Research Unit for Maori Education, Monograph 9, University of Auckland, pp. 14–22.

14 Ihimaera, W. (1990), *Te Ao Marama*, Reed Books, Auckland, Vol. 1.

15 Harjo, J. and G. Bird, eds (1997), *Reinventing the Enemy's Language. Contemporary Native Women's Writings of North America*, W. W. Norton and Company, New York.

16 See, for example, Moses, D. D. and T. Goldie (1992), *An Anthology of Canadian Native Literature in English*, Oxford University Press, Toronto.

17 Mita, M. (1994), 'Trick or Treat. Issues of Feminism and Post-colonialism in Relation to the Arts', in *Te Pua Journal of Maori Women's Writing*, Research Unit for Maori Education, University of Auckland, Vol. 3, No. 1, pp. 37–41.

18 Mead, A. (1994) 'Maori Leadership', in *Te Pua Journal of Maori Women's Writing*, Research Unit for Maori Education, Vol. 3, No. 1, pp. 11–20.

19 Sykes, R. B. (1989), *Black Majority*, Hudson Hawthorn, Melbourne, p. 146.

20 *Ibid.*, p. 226.

21 Sykes, A. (1994), 'Constitutional Reform and Mana Wahine', in *Te Pua Journal of Maori Women's Writing*, Research Unit for Maori Education, University of Auckland, Vol. 3, No. 2, pp. 15–20.

CHAPTER 9

Responding to the Imperatives of an Indigenous Agenda: A Case Study of Maori

The following two chapters represent a case study of one indigenous development, which demonstrates how many of the issues raised in the previous chapters come together. This chapter discusses the beginnings of a different type of involvement in research by Maori. Rather than accept the position either of 'victim' or of 'object,' Maori people voiced resistance to research from the late 1960s and began to pose their own research questions. There were three incentives for this shift in approach to research: (1) the establishment of the Waitangi Tribunal;[1] (2) the development of a language revitalization movement known as Te Kohanga Reo; and (3) the spaces opened up in the social sciences by more critical and reflexive approaches to research. This chapter tracks the transition from Maori as the researched to Maori as the researcher. Although this transition has occurred in the last 20 years, it would be wrong to claim either an overall change in attitudes by Maori to research or a steady progression of changes made. The intersecting spaces opened up by the development of research for the Waitangi Tribunal, the new enthusiasm shown for Te Kohanga Reo, and the critique of positivist research by feminist and critical theorists created a set of conditions from which culturally sensitive approaches to research were developed, and from which a more sympathetic Maori approach started to emerge.

There are three distinct parts to this chapter. The first part examines the creation of a set of more favourable conditions for research involving Maori. There is a brief discussion of the spaces opened up through feminist and critical critiques of positivism, followed by a consideration of the impact of the Waitangi Tribunal and Te Kohanga Reo on setting the scene for establishing Maori research priorities. The second part of the chapter picks up on issues related to research of Maori and to the ways in which research has been employed and/or represented as 'truth'. Also in the second part of the chapter there is a very brief discussion of alternative Maori claims about knowledge and research which intersect with the assumption that research extends knowledge. The question which begins the second part asks, 'Whose knowledge has been extended by research?' This then leads into some general issues that relate to Maori views about knowing. The third part of the chapter examines the parameters of 'culturally sensitive research' which is still an essentially Western research model. It ends with a brief discussion of the limits of this model in relation to non-indigenous research of Maori.

Western Critiques of Western Research

As discussed in the previous chapter, the Western cultural archive contained within it several traditions of knowledge and rules of practice for engaging in debates over knowledge. These rules enabled systems or methods of self-critique. The notion of research as an objective, value-free and scientific process for observing and making sense of human realities is taken for granted by many social scientists. Philosophers of science refer to this attitude as 'positivism'. Differences in approach to research, however, have been the subject of continuous debate, as those engaged in attempts to understand human society grapple with the problematic nature of social science inquiry. Within the social sciences there have been a number of disputes over method, meanings and what constitutes 'good' research. Method is important because it is regarded as the way in which knowledge is acquired or discovered and as a way in which we can 'know' what is real. Each academic discipline is attached not just to a set of ideas about knowledge, but also to methodologies. Disputes over method occur both within disciplines and across disciplines. This is not surprising, considering that all academic disciplines, as defined by the West, are derived from shared philosophical foundations. Some disputes, however, have 'raged' within the scientific world and have contributed to major schisms in theoretical positions.[2] At one level, this debate has been concerned primarily with issues related to methodology and method. These issues focus upon the appropriateness of research design and analysis. Definitions of validity and reliability are of critical importance here as researchers attempt to construct and perfect scientific instruments for observing and explaining human behaviour and the human condition. At a broader level, however, the debate has been concerned with the wider aims and role of research. Social science fields of inquiry are dependent on the way society is viewed, and the body of knowledge which legitimates that viewpoint. The dispute at this level is over the validity of scientific methods within the positivist paradigm, and whether this is an appropriate paradigm for understanding human society.

It was not really until the 1960s that critical theory took hold as a theory for research, although the death camps of Nazi Germany were seen by critics of positivism as demonstrating the ultimate irrationality of science and of modernity.[3] By the 1960s fundamental questions about knowledge and power were being articulated not just through academic discourse but through social movements such as the civil rights movement, the Anti-Vietnam War movement, the second wave of feminism and widespread student unrest culminating for many observers in the student riots in Paris in 1968. In the 1960s and 1970s other social events also took place for indigenous peoples. Protests over the Treaty of Waitangi, Bastion Point, land marches, tent embassies, sit-ins and petitions were the key events for Maori.[4] These events were reflected in other parts of the indigenous world. It is at this point that the questions asked by critical theory were also being asked by people on the ground. These people were indigenous activists rather than Marxists, but were asking similar sorts of questions about the connections between power and research. Such questions were based on a sense of outrage and injustice about the failure of education, democracy and research to deliver social change for people who were oppressed. These questions related to the relationship between knowledge and power, between research and emancipation, and between lived reality and imposed ideals about the Other.

During this period social theory shifted, and in the global arena of scholarship, Marxist theorists challenged the liberal theories of modernization and development which had determined how the imperial world dealt with its former colonies. Gunder Frank and others working in the South American and African contexts reexamined ideas of development and suggested that there was a causal relationship between First World economic policies and Third World underdevelopment. In education, Marxist researchers also drew attention to the structural relationship between society and schooling, with schools viewed as agencies which systematically reproduce social inequalities.[5] The links between imperialism, education and development were drawn by theorists such as Martin Carnoy.[6] These views have been criticized for their heavy emphasis on deterministic models of analysis and denial of culture as a mediating force. The central question of power and emancipation which was raised by Marxist theorists did connect, however, with the radical aspirations of a number of indigenous communities and former colonies which were struggling for self-determination.

The Challenges of Feminist Analyses

The debate over positivism which emerged from European academic tradition has been continued in the Anglo-American world by feminist and other radical critiques of the positivist position. While Marxism provided a powerful counter to liberal thought in the first part of the twentieth century,[7] in the latter part of this century, the second wave of feminism may have been far more important in its challenge to the epistemological foundations of Western philosophy, academic practice and research. 'Old' philosophical themes about human nature, patriarchal accounts of the past, and rules of practice taken for granted within the academy have been rigorously scrutinized and reformed by feminist theorists working across a wide range of disciplines and from a wide spectrum of philosophical orientations. Each field of study has been subject to a critique from feminist theorists.[8]

One of the more significant challenges to white feminism has come from women variously described as 'women of colour', 'Third World women', 'black women' and 'indigenous women'. These groups of women challenged the assumptions of the Western/white women's movement that all women shared some universal characteristics and suffered from universal oppressions which could be understood and described by a group of predominantly white, Western-trained women academics. The problems of 'voice' and 'visibility', 'silence' and 'invisibility', became important concerns at a concrete level, as women attended international conferences and attempted to develop international policies related to women's rights, population control, development and justice. For women interested in research and the emancipatory potential of research, there was considerable work to be done in terms of undoing or deconstructing the dominant paradigms by which most scientific research was bounded, and connecting the research enterprise to feminism and to a social reality with which feminism connects.[9] This has involved critique, the development of new methodologies, and the possibility of alternative ways of knowing or epistemologies.[10]

Part of the feminist critique has also occurred within the field of critical theory. This critique has two aspects to it. One is in terms of the failure of critical theory to deliver emancipation for oppressed groups.[11] The second aspect is in terms of the failure of critical theorists who belonged to the academy of scientists to recognize their own patriarchal practices which continued to marginalize and silence women academics. This challenge has focused on the notion of reflexivity in research, a process of critical self awareness, reflexivity and openness to challenge. Feminist scholarship has slowly moved into the academy and, in the area of research in particular, feminist methodologies are widely accepted as having legitimacy as method and as breaking new ground in terms of research and scholarship.

Patti Lather has referred to this new ground research as post-positivism, a term which comes out of poststructuralist and postmodern approaches to knowledge.[12] Lather outlines some of these approaches in Table 9.1, with categories drawn partly from Habermas's categories of prediction, understanding and emancipation, and her own addition of deconstruction.[13] This chart is useful because it sets out the different names by which various critiques of positivist science are known. These 'labels' are frequently used to describe different approaches to non-positivist research. What is significantly absent are the organic and indigenous approaches to research, which have led to the development of a world indigenous movement and to major constitutional claims on Western states by indigenous peoples. Such approaches to research are often regarded as deriving from Freirian approaches, which are seen to be 'Western'. As will be argued later, the possibility that approaches can be generated from very different value systems and world views are denied even within the emancipatory paradigm of 'postpositivism'.

Table 9.1 Postpositivist Inquiry			
Predict	Understand	Emancipate	Deconstruct
postivism	interpretative	critical	poststructural
	naturalistic	neoMarxist	postmodern
	constructivist	feminist	post-paradigm
	phenomenological	praxis-oriented	diaspora
	hermeneutic	educative	
		Freirian participatory	
		action research	
P Lather 1991			

The work being carried out by Western feminists has been countered by the work of black women and other 'women with labels'. In fact, the very labelling of women demonstrates the pluralism within the feminist world, and the multiple directions from which feminist theory has emerged and to which it may be heading. These Other/ed women have argued that oppression takes different forms, and that there are interlocking relationships between race, gender and class which makes oppression a complex sociological and psychological condition. Many have argued that this condition cannot be understood or analysed by outsiders or people who have not experienced, and who have not been born into, this way of life. Patricia Hill Collins has argued that 'while Black feminist thought may be recorded by others, it is produced by Black women'.[14] Further, she argues that 'Black women possess a unique standpoint on, or perspective of, their experiences … [and] … while living life as Black women may produce certain commonalities of outlook, the diversity of class, region, age, and sexual orientation shaping Black women's lives has resulted in different expressions of these common themes.'[15] This position intersects with Maori attitudes to research, and the writings of African American women in particular have been useful for Maori women in legitimating, with literature, what Maori women have experienced.

The Waitangi Tribunal and Te Kohanga Reo

The significance of the establishment of the Waitangi Tribunal in New Zealand in 1975, in relation to research, was that it gave a very concrete focus for recovering and/or representing Maori versions of colonial history, and for situating the impact of colonialism in Maori world views and value systems. Struggles over land issues had been ongoing since the Treaty of Waitangi was signed between Maori chiefs and representatives of the British Crown in 1840 and land alienation was facilitated efficiently through the establishment of the Native Land Court in 1865.[16] Successive governments and local authorities had imposed a series of laws and regulations, which were designed to alienate Maori land from Maori people.[17] This approach continued throughout the 1950s and 1960s with what has been called a 'use it or lose it' philosophy.[18] The 1975 Treaty of Waitangi Act gave limited powers to the Tribunal, which could not hear land claims that went back to 1840. Although most of the land subject to Maori discontent had been taken prior to 1975, a forum through which Maori could legitimately voice concerns was regarded positively.

The Treaty of Waitangi Amendment Act 1985 broadened the scope of the Tribunal, and it is from this period that *iwi*/tribes started quite seriously to develop their own research programmes.[19] The research priorities were determined by the nature of the claim being made and driven by the sense of injustice felt by the *iwi* concerned. There were few Maori people skilled in research and many of those available to do the work were unemployed or retired. Other tribal research programmes were reliant on one skilled researcher and many young and enthusiastic trainees, some of whom had been unemployed or on job skills training programmes. Very few had university qualifications. In general these early programmes were carried out with limited funding and with few skilled researchers. This often told when the evidence was finally presented and a number of claims required further substantiation. The first level of research which needed to be done required archival research, familiarity with Land Court records, and oral histories. This was followed by another level of interpretative research, especially over contestable issues such as establishing prior ownership of lands or resources also being claimed by other *iwi* or contested by the Crown. In this process the Crown was not and is not neutral. After 1985 the state moved rapidly into economic reforms and the privatization of state assets. It was the contention of *iwi* that most of the state's assets had been built upon Maori lands. Privatization activities have continued unabated and the Crown's activities in relationship to the Tribunal are to subsume its importance and deal with what is politically acceptable.

Although at one level there was an impetus in terms of bringing cases against the Crown, there was a much broader desire by Maori communities to regain or hold on to Maori language and cultural knowledge. This desire and mood is what Te Kohanga Reo captured and for which it provided a new and positive focus. While the claims to the Tribunal were being made on the basis of tribal interests, and even these were contested within tribes, the Te Kohanga Reo was built on the more fundamental unit of *whanau* or extended family. Te Kohanga Reo was represented and represented itself as 'the future'. As a national phenomenon, it did not depend on *iwi* structures for its credibility or financial support. Although some Te Kohanga Reo are clearly situated within tribes, their administrative centre is the National Te Kohanga Reo Trust, based in the capital city of Wellington. The two developments, therefore, the Waitangi Tribunal process and Te Kohanga Reo, were operating quite independently of each other and having an impact on communities in very different ways. Te Kohanga Reo, furthermore, discouraged research but encouraged autonomy amongst its individual units. A consequence of such autonomy is that there was space for *whanau* to solve problems for themselves and this process generated a wide range of activities, one of which was information gathering. It was also a process which committed parents to thinking far more seriously about education and the relationship between schooling and society.

Research as an Extension of Knowledge – Whose Knowledge?

The critique of positivism by feminist theorists, ethnic minorities and indigenous peoples has emerged from the experience of people who have been studied, researched, written about, and defined by social scientists. It is from the position of being the researched that Maori, too, have resisted and then challenged social science research. This challenge has confronted both methodological issues and epistemological concerns: that is, both the techniques of research and the presuppositions about knowledge which underlie research. The criticisms raised by Maori people locate the theoretical debates of the wider world within a local New Zealand context.

Research is about satisfying a need to know, and a need to extend the boundaries of existing knowledge through a process of systematic inquiry. Rationality in the Western tradition enabled knowledge to be produced and articulated in a scientific and 'superior' way. As Europeans began to explore and colonize other parts of the world, notions of rationality and conceptualizations of knowledge became the 'convenient tool for dismissing from serious comparison with Western forms of thought those forms of "primitive" thought which were being encountered'.[20] As Salmond has argued, this view has led to 'European evaluations of Maori knowledge ... [which] have characteristically been ideological'.[21] For Maori people, European conceptions of knowledge and of research have meant that, while being considered 'primitive', Maori society has provided fertile ground for research. The question of whose knowledge was being extended by research was of little conse- quence, as early ethnographers, educational researchers and occasional 'travellers' described, explained and recorded their accounts of various aspects of Maori society. Distortions of Maori social reality by ethno- centric researchers overly given to generalizations were initially apparent only to Maori people.[22] While this type of research was validated by 'scientific method' and 'colonial affirmation', it did little to extend the knowledge of Maori people. Instead, it left a foundation of ideologically laden data about Maori society, which has distorted notions of what it means to be Maori.

This in turn has entrapped Maori people within a cultural definition which does not connect with either our oral traditions or our lived reality. Maori women, for example, are caught between the written accounts of white male writers and the assertions of the few Maori women who are contesting those early accounts. For example, Elsdon Best says of his research among the Tuhoe tribe, 'As in most other barbaric lands, we find that women were looked upon here as being inferior to man.'[23] Compare that with what Rangimarie Rose Pere, herself a descendant of Tuhoe Potiki, has to say: 'As a female, I have been exposed to very positive female role models from both my natural parents' descent lines. The most senior men and women ... made it quite clear from the legacy they left that men and women, adults and children, work alongside each other and together'.[24] The problem is not simply about redressing the past. Much of what was written about Maori people in the last century and in this century has become part of a body of common knowledge that is taken for granted. Hence the uphill task for Maori women seeking to reconstruct traditional roles is that they are having to challenge existing 'knowledge' which is primarily ideological or false. Consider the following three examples:

1 Culturally, the role of women was made clear in the account of their creation. The first woman was formed out of a mound of earth and impregnated by her male creator with a life spirit. From this, woman was regarded as being a passive receptacle for the dominant male spirit.[25]

There are three points which can be made in relation to this account. Firstly, Maori would claim that we were created by a *tipuna*, of 'god-like' status, who also impregnated most other living things on earth with 'life spirits'. The problem lies in the reduction of our creation myths to a story of 'man' and 'woman', like a Judaeo-Christian account of 'Adam and Eve'. The second problem with this interpretation lies with the concept of male and female 'spirits'. Humans as well as plants, animals, stones, carvings and other animate and inanimate objects (according to Western classifications) have a 'life force' or *mauri*. In many oral accounts both male and female 'essences' reside in that life force. While the life force in people and animals may be manifested in physically 'male' or 'female' characteristics, *mauri* is not itself gendered. The third problematic aspect of this quote is the concept of a 'passive receptacle'. There are enough examples in oral histories to demonstrate that women were always considered more than 'passive receptacles'.

2 In Maori attitudes towards a woman's place, there was, on the surface, little conflict with the Victorian espousal of a limited domestic sphere.[26]

The difficulties with this quote are its comparative appeal to Victorian attitudes and the concept of a 'limited domestic sphere'. The comparison is a dangerous one in two respects: it reduces and decontextualizes Maori values and practices on one hand (in order to make the comparison), and, secondly, it poses unproblematically the normative 'reality' of notions such as 'woman's place' and 'domestic spheres'.

3 [Maori] women suffered a social oppression typical of all societies that reject the fatherhood of God.[27]

The third quotation uses a single almighty generalization to justify a new form of colonialism (fundamentalist Christianity). No sources are acknowledged for this information and, in a sense, none are required, because it is posited as 'common sense'. This has been the danger of ethnocentric research paradigms.

The extracts above were not written by Maori but by people who were informed by the research and material which has been written and recorded by other non-Maori about Maori society. The effect of a process which tends to give greater legitimacy to written sources is that the most accessible material was not written by Maori. Therefore, the potential to reproduce colonizing ideologies and colonizing perspectives is always present. As argued by Merata Mita, however, 'paternalism doesn't work and as soon as we reject it we're the ones seen to be causing the "problem" when in fact the problem is created by whoever is looking through the microscope'.[28]

The Validity of Maori Knowledge

The reassertion of Maori aspirations and cultural practice which came about through Te Kohanga Reo, the Waitangi Tribunal and other forms of Maori activism has demonstrated a will by Maori people to make explicit claims about the validity and legitimacy of Maori knowledge. This will has been expressed through various educational and community programmes. Government policies on devolution and the retraction of state assets have also stimulated *iwi* to carry out research on their own behalf.[29] In many cases Maori organizations have been reluctant to allow research to be carried out until they have developed a sufficiently strong base.

When Cook arrived here in the eighteenth century, he found a thriving and complex society. Later voyagers and travellers, including Christian missionaries, were fascinated and heartened that Maori concepts relating to cosmology and spirituality were so sophisticated. Missionaries, for example, were reported to have had little difficulty in talking about spiritual concepts with Maori people.[30] Although later settlers saw little that was civilizing in Maori beliefs or practice, earlier visitors, including many missionaries, were appreciative of the breadth and sophistication of Maori epistemology. Because of the way Maori society was structured, because of its unique world view, and because of its strong oral tradition, knowledge itself was never held to be universally available. Maori society valued knowledge highly, to such an extent that certain types of knowledge were entrusted to only a few members of the *whanau*. Some knowledge was considered to be *tapu* and there were sanctions that ensured that it was protected, used appropriately, and transmitted with accuracy.

Maori have a highly developed story of how knowledge was gained. In one of our first 'research projects' Tane-nui-a-rangi, one of the children of the first parents, (the sky father and the earth mother) journeyed to the twelfth 'universe' to gain knowledge.[31] Two points to emphasize in this story are that Tane-nui-a-rangi sought knowledge on behalf of everyone else, and, secondly, the knowledge he gained was differentiated into three separate baskets.[32] These baskets contained different types of knowledge. Knowledge was perceived as being highly specialized, but each aspect was essential to collective wellbeing. It was also perceived as being hierarchical. There was knowledge that all people needed to carry out their daily activities. It was acquired through observation, practice, and the guidance of *kaumatua*. Stories and proverbs show that sloppiness, laziness and the non-completion of tasks were not tolerated and earned retribution.

The whole process of colonization can be viewed as a stripping away of *mana* (our standing in our own eyes), and an undermining of *rangatiratanga* (our ability and right to determine our destinies). Research is an important part of the colonization process because it is concerned with defining legitimate knowledge. In Maori communities today, there is a deep distrust and suspicion of research. This suspicion is not just of non-indigenous researchers, but of the whole philosophy of research and the different sets of beliefs which underlie the research process. Even in very recent studies, this hostility or negative attitude to research in general has been noted.[33] Research methodology is based on the skill of matching the problem with an 'appropriate' set of investigative strategies. It is concerned with ensuring that information is accessed in such a way as to guarantee validity and reliability. This requires having a theoretical understanding, either explicitly or implicitly, of the world, the problem, and the method. When studying how to go about doing research, it is very easy to overlook the realm of common sense, the basic beliefs that not only help people identify research problems that are relevant and worthy, but also accompany them throughout the research process. Researchers must go further than simply recognizing personal beliefs and assumptions, and the effect they have when interacting with people.[34] In a cross-cultural context, the questions that need to be asked are ones such as:

Who defined the research problem?
For whom is this study worthy and relevant? Who says so?
What knowledge will the community gain from this study?
What knowledge will the researcher gain from this study?
What are some likely positive outcomes from this study?
What are some possible negative outcomes?
How can the negative outcomes be eliminated?
To whom is the researcher accountable?
What processes are in place to support the research, the researched and the researcher?

Moreover, it is also important to question that most fundamental belief of all, that individual researchers have an inherent right to knowledge and truth. We should not assume that they have been trained well enough to pursue it rigorously, nor to recognize it when they have 'discovered' it. An analysis of research into the lives of Maori people, from a Maori perspective, would seem to indicate that many researchers have not only not found 'truth' or new knowledge; rather, they have missed the point entirely, and, in some cases, drawn conclusions about Maori society from information that has only the most tenuous relationship how Maori society operates.[35]

The social settings of the non-indigenous world into which Maori people were compelled to move – such as the school, the health system, the welfare system, the justice system – have at the same time provided researchers with a point of entry into Maori society. Essentially, this has been crisis research, directed at explaining the causes of Maori failure and supposedly solving Maori problems. On the basis of research carried out on the sites of these encounters, researchers sometimes made huge inferential leaps and generalizations about how the rest of Maori society functioned, and which elements of this society were inhibiting successful development.[36] To return to the story of Tane-nui-a-rangi and the three kinds of knowledge, these gifts were all essential to the survival and well-being of the group. Because knowledge was conceived from the beginning as being highly specialized, it had to be distributed among the members of the group. Individuals with specialist skills held them on behalf of the group. They were also dependent on other members of the group, with other types of knowledge, to carry out the various inter-dependent activities. When a researcher uses individual informants and interviews individuals in a one-to-one context, the resulting information may be a long way from the full picture. The connection of knowledge with *mana* could mean that an informant is not going to reveal too much, is not going to admit lack of knowledge but, conversely, is going to assert influence or a picture of dominance by what is revealed, and is going to give an individual view, from an individualist perspective, of group knowledge and activities. Although many people would argue that, under the influence of the colonial society, much of this tradition has been eroded, there is still a strong belief held by many Maori people that there is a uniquely 'Maori' way of looking at the world and learning. The growth of Te Kohanga Reo would seem to bear this out. The different ways in which knowledge is perceived by indigenous and non-indigenous is complicated further by the intersection with imperial power. They are not held to be equally valid or commensurate views of reality, let alone of research.

The colonization of Maori culture has threatened the maintenance of that knowledge and the transmission of knowledge that is 'exclusively' or particularly Maori. The dominance of Western, British culture, and the history that underpins the relationship between indigenous Maori and non-indigenous Pakeha, have made it extremely difficult for Maori forms of knowledge and learning to be accepted as legitimate. By asserting the validity of Maori knowledge, Maori people have reclaimed greater control over the research which is being carried out in the Maori field. 'Traditional' world views provide an historical example of the complexity of Maori beliefs and understandings of the world. They also provide ample examples of Maori efforts to seek knowledge, to organize it and to learn from it. It might be said that this historical knowledge is irrelevant in a contemporary context.[37] But from a Maori perspective, it is only as irrelevant as the thoughts of Western philosophers such as Plato or St Augustine, whose ideas have been of such central importance to Western epistemology. Maori knowledge represents the body of knowledge which, in today's society, can be extended, alongside that of existing Western knowledge.

Negotiating New Relationships with Non-indigenous Researchers

An illustration of the widespread ethical abuses of research is to be found in the 1988 research scandal which occurred in New Zealand over the treatment, and more especially non-treatment, of cervical cancer at National Women's Hospital in the 1980s. Similar abuses of research have been recorded – the Tuskagee project in the United States, for example, which involved a black male prison population in a project on syphilis. In brief, women with early signs of pre-cancer who were examined at the hospital were assigned to one of two groups without their knowledge or consent. One of those groups received treatment. The research came to be conducted as an ongoing project incorporated into institutional practices, almost as official policy. When two feminist journalists reported the study it produced a huge national outcry which eventually became the focus of an official inquiry. The nature of the research under investigation by the inquiry challenged the ethics of researchers in a public and dramatic way.[38] It was a moment in which the dominant non-indigenous society glimpsed some small part of a wider attitude and system of abuse by researchers with which indigenous people have been only too familiar.

Although many researchers involved in social science may confidently assert that their research does not endanger lives, many lessons can be learned from such an inquiry. Although most researchers would believe sincerely that they wish to improve the conditions of their research participants, this has not always happened. Research projects are designed and carried out with little recognition accorded to the people who participated – 'the researched'. Indigenous people and other groups in society have frequently been portrayed as the powerless victims of research which has attributed a variety of deficits or problems to just about everything they do. Years of research have frequently failed to improve the conditions of the people who are researched. This has led many Maori people to believe that researchers are simply intent on taking or 'stealing' knowledge in a non-reciprocal and often under-handed way. The Cartwright Inquiry motivated a more public discussion of research ethics. For Maori the inquiry simply reinforced an attitude of suspicion towards research although it also provided space to negotiate research with non-indigenous researchers much more explicitly. Researchers, for example, had to distance themselves from the experimental control research model used by the medical researchers under inquiry.

Research in itself is a powerful intervention, even if carried out at a distance, which has traditionally benefited the researcher, and the knowledge base of the dominant group in society. When undertaking research, either across cultures or within a minority culture, it is critical that researchers recognize the power dynamic which is embedded in the relationship with their subjects. Researchers are in receipt of privileged information. They may interpret it within an overt theoretical frame-work, but also in terms of a covert ideological framework. They have the power to distort, to make invisible, to overlook, to exaggerate and to draw conclusions, based not on factual data, but on assumptions, hidden value judgements, and often downright misunderstandings. They have the potential to extend knowledge or to perpetuate ignorance.

Culturally sensitive approaches to research cover a wide range of attempts to take heed of the problems and issues which concern the people involved in the research. For Maori, this has involved efforts by researchers to inform the 'researched' about themselves in a way which respects people. The challenge by Maori (and other groups) to the research community, demanding that they 'keep out' of researching Maori people or Maori issues, has led to several different approaches and strategies for carrying out further research. It did not mean that academics simply took notice of Maori and stopped all research, but that they sought other ways of thinking about their projects and proceeded with far more caution when entering the domain of Maori concerns.[39] There were different ways 'around the problem'. In a previously published paper I listed some of the following strategies which characterize the shifts towards becoming more culturally sensitive.[40] These are:

1   the strategy of avoidance whereby the researcher avoids dealing with the issues or with Maori;

2   the strategy of 'personal development' whereby the researchers

prepare themselves by learning Maori language, attending *hui* and becoming more knowledgeable about Maori concerns;

3   the strategy of consultation with Maori where efforts are made to seek support and consent;

4   the strategy of 'making space' where research organizations have recognized and attempted to bring more Maori researchers and 'voices' into their own organization.

These strategies have various consequences, positive and negative, for the researchers and the researched. They all involve different ways of making changes, although the first strategy of avoidance may not be helpful to anyone. In association with other shifts in social science theory and the development of feminist critiques of research, the move towards research which is more ethical, and concerned with outcomes as well as processes, has meant that those who choose to research with Maori people have more opportunities to think more carefully about what this undertaking may mean. This does not necessarily guarantee it, however.

Graham Smith has posited four models by which culturally appropriate research can be undertaken by non-indigenous researchers.[41] The first model he refers to as the *tiaki* or mentoring model in which authoritative Maori people guide and sponsor the research. The second model Smith refers to as the *whangai* or adoption model.[42] The *whangai* model differs from the *tiaki* model in that the *whangai* researchers are incorporated into the daily life of Maori people, and sustain a life-long relationship which extends far beyond the realms of research. Smith's third model is a 'power sharing model' where researchers 'seek the assistance of the community to meaningfully support the development of a research enterprise'. The fourth model Smith refers to as the 'empowering outcomes model', which addresses the sorts of questions Maori people want to know and which has beneficial outcomes.

All these models imply a culturally sensitive and empathetic approach, but go beyond that approach to address the issues which are going to make a difference for Maori. Russell Bishop critically discusses some of the problems associated generally with emancipatory research and empowering models of research.[43] As he has argued, espousing an emancipatory model of research has not of itself freed researchers from exercising intellectual arrogance or employing evangelical and paternalistic practices. This applies also to methods which appear to be qualitative or ethnographic. These approaches may sound more sensitive in the field, but often the assumptions behind the research focus and the translation into text can be just as problematic as other forms of research.

Another model of research is subsumed under the label of 'bicultural' or partnership research. Although Smith's four models could also be claimed as bicultural in some form, the latest interpretation of bicultural research involves both indigenous and non-indigenous researchers working on a research project and shaping that project together. Sometimes this involves non-indigenous researchers taking responsibility for interviewing non-indigenous participants, and indigenous researchers interviewing indigenous participants. In other projects it involves a more complex structuring of a research programme, its design and methodology. Teariki and Spoonley write that research as a partnership involves working through a process which is inevitably political.[44] They argue that research needs to be carefully negotiated, and that the outcomes of research need to be thought through before the research is undertaken.

Setting the Boundaries to Research by Non-indigenous Researchers

All of the above models assume that indigenous people are involved in the research in key and often senior roles. With very few trained indigenous researchers available, one of the roles non-indigenous researchers have needed to play is as mentors of indigenous research assistants. Increasingly, however, there have been demands by indigenous communities for research to be undertaken exclusively by indigenous researchers. It is thought that Maori people need to take greater control over the questions they want to address, and invest more energy and commitment into the education and empowering of Maori people as researchers. Some organizations, for example, have made it very clear that research is 'off limits'. The best-known of these is the Te Kohanga Reo National Trust. This anti-research stance has applied to all researchers. There are other kinds of limits also being set, as more Maori begin to work in the various fields of social science research. For example, many Maori now attend both national and international conferences and have been known to question and challenge the material of New Zealand academics on such occasions.[45] In education, there are increasing numbers of Maori academics, researchers, policy analysts and administrators who keep track of research on Maori, and who disseminate research results very quickly to the wider community. The more radical limits to non-indigenous research, however, are being set by the developing field of indigenous Maori research and the increasing numbers of Maori researchers in both the social sciences and physical sciences, and in the area of tribal histories and land claims. The development of new ways of thinking about indigenous Maori research, and approaches to the way this research should be framed, have emerged in the last decade under the rubric of Kaupapa Maori research. The following chapter will address this topic.

What I wanted to discuss in this chapter was the shift which occurred between Maori people being viewed as research objects and Maori people becoming our own researchers. This shift, I have argued, was not simply an evolutionary development. It came about through other changes, some of which occurred within Maori cultural politics, some of which were brought about by state intervention, and some of which occurred through the spaces opened up within the field of social science. I have not addressed individual disciplinary methodologies or methods, but have kept the discussion at a broader level of social science. Clearly there were significant changes in approach, which developed out of ethnographic research and other qualitative methods.

Notes

1 This was established through the Treaty of Waitangi Act (1975) to deal with claims by Maori that actions of the Crown from 1975 onwards had been prejudicial to them and had contravened the Treaty of Waitangi. This Act was amended by The Treaty of Waitangi Act (1985) which gave the Tribunal the right to hear cases which went back to 1840 when the Treaty of Waitangi, and the Maori version, Te Tiriti o Waitangi was signed. The Tribunal was expanded from three members under the 1975 Act to several teams of members who are hearing cases across the country.

2 Adorno, T. W. *et al.* (1976), *The Positivist Dispute in German Sociology*, translated by G. Adey and D. Frisby, Heinemann, London.

3 For a historical summary of critical theory in relation to education, see Blackledge, D. and B. Hunt (1985), *Sociological Interpretations of Education*, Croom Helm, London; Gibson, R. (1986), *Critical Theory and Education*, Hodder and Stoughton, London.

4 See Ranginui Walker's account of these events in Walker, R. (1990), *Ka Whawhai Tonu Matou. Struggle Without End,* Penguin, Auckland.

5 Bowles, S. and H. Gintis (1976), *Schooling in Capitalist America*, Basic Books, United States.

6 Carnoy, M. (1974), *Education as Cultural Imperialism*, D. McKay Co., New York.

7 And is itself inextricably part of the modernist project.

8 Fonow, M. M. and J. A. Cook (1997), *Beyond Methodology. Feminist Scholarship as Lived Research*, Indiana University Press, Bloomington.

9 Stanley, L. and S. Wise (1993), *Breaking Out Again. Feminist Ontology and Epistemology*, second edition, Routledge, London.

10 See, for example, Reinharz, S. (1992), *Feminist Methods in Social Research*, Oxford University Press, New York. Reinharz takes the reader through feminist methods for ethnography, survey research, experimental and cross-cultural research, oral histories, case studies and action research.

11 Ellsworth, E. (1989), 'Why Doesn't This Feel Empowering? Working Through the Repressive Myths of Critical Pedagogy', in *Harvard Educational Review*, Vol. 59, No. 3, pp. 297–324.

12 Lather, P. (1991), *Getting Smart, Feminist Research and Pedagogy With/ in the Postmodern*, Routledge, New York.

13 *Ibid.*, pp. 6–7.

14 Collins, P. H. (1991), 'Learning from the Outsider Within: the Sociological Significance of Black Feminist Thought', in *Beyond Methodology, Feminist Scholarship as Lived Research*, eds M. Fonow and J. A. Cook, Indiana University Press, Bloomington, p. 37.

15 *Ibid.*, p. 37.

16 The Treaty of Waitangi gave pre-emptive right to the Crown to purchase Maori land – that is, before any individuals or companies. This practice ceased under pressure from companies interested in settlement by British settlers.

17 According to Asher and Naulls, 'Since the signing of the Treaty of Waitangi in 1840 the Maori tribal estates have declined from almost 27 million hectares to about 1.3 million. And what remains is often in the form of fragmented holdings with a multiplicity of owners, predominantly absentee.' For further background see Asher, G. and D Naulls (1987), *Maori Land*, New Zealand Planning Council, Wellington, p. 46. Legislation which was used as a device to alienate the land included the Public Works Act 1908 which authorized the taking of European land for railways and roads, with right of objection and compensation. No notice was required to take Maori land until the Native Land Act 1909, which authorized the Governor General to take Maori lands for railways and roads, with no compensation. See Temm, P. (1990), *The Waitangi Tribunal,* Random Century, Auckland. There was a series of such acts of legislation which enabled the systematic stripping of land away from its owners.

18 *Ibid.*, p. 47.

19 According to Margaret Mutu, for example, her *iwi* (Ngati Kahu) had started talking about doing their own research in the early 1980s but had no funding to help them. Their case had its first hearing in 1987 and in 1995 is still being heard. Personal communication.

20 Egan, K. (1987), 'Literacy and the Oral Foundations of Education', in *Harvard Educational Review*, Vol. 57, No. 4, p. 446.

21 Salmond, A. (1985), 'Maori Epistemologies', in *Reason and Morality*, ed. J. Overing, Tavistock, London p. 240.

22 Smith G. H. (1986), 'Nga Kete Wananga – Akonga Maori: Maori Teaching and Learning', Maori Studies Department, Auckland College of Education, Auckland.

23 Best, E. (1934), *The Maori As He Was*, Maori Purposes Fund Board, Wellington, p. 93.

24 Pere, R. (1988), 'Te Wheke: Whaia te Maramatanga me te Aroha', in *Women and Education in Aotearoa*, ed. S. Middleton, Allen and Unwin, Wellington, p. 9.

25 Heuer B. (1972), *Maori Women,* The Polynesian Society, A. H. and A. W. Reed, Wellington, p. 55.

26 Fry, R. (1985), *It's Different for Daughters: a History of the Curriculum for Girls in New Zealand Schools 1900–1975*, New Zealand Council for Educational Research, Wellington, p. 156.

27 Drake, M. (1989), *The New Maori Myth*, Wycliffe Christian Schools, Auckland, p. 20.

28 Mita, M. (1989), 'Merata Mita On ...', in *New Zealand Listener,* 14 October, p. 30.

29 Every claim to the Waitangi Tribunal requires substantial amounts of research by Maori. This research includes searching through Native Land Court records,

archival research, written accounts of *whakapapa* (genealogies of tribes traced back to ancestors who arrived in Aotearoa by canoe and even further back to the creation of the universe), and the gathering of oral histories. In most cases this requires a team of researchers who have skills in Maori language, can find their way around legal documents, already have a sound historical understanding of the context, have the means to travel, are computer literate and can interpret different sorts of data.

30 In fact some, like Kendall, became very involved in discussions about Maori spirituality. See Binney, J. (1968), *The Legacy of Guilt: a Life of Thomas Kendal*, Oxford University Press, Auckland.

31 An English language account of one version of this story can be found in Buck P. (1949), *The Coming of the Maori*, Maori Purposes Fund Board, Whitcombe and Tombs Ltd., Wellington, pp. 443–72. Buck identifies the 'baskets of knowledge' as *kete uruuru matua* (peace and goodness), *kete uruuru rangi* (prayers and incantations) and *kete uruuru tau* or *tawhite* (war, agriculture, woodwork), p. 449. Another account is to be found in the manuscript by Te Matorohanga which was translated by Percy Smith as Smith, P. (1913), *The Lore of the Whare Wananga*, Polynesian Society, Thomas Avery, New Plymouth, New Zealand.

32 As well as three kinds of knowledge, Tane-nui-a-rangi also collected two *mauri* stones, Te Hukatai and Te Rehutai.

33 Teariki, C. and P. Spoonley (1992), *Te Whakapakari Te Mana Tangata – The Politics and Process of Research for Maori*, Department of Sociology, Massey University, Palmerston North, New Zealand.

34 Which is the point at which some definitions of reflexivity actually stop.

35 Which is the point made by Toby Curtis. Curtis, T. (1983), 'A Maori Viewpoint Related to Research in Education in Maori Education', republished in *The Issue of Research and Maori*, Research Unit for Maori Education, University of Auckland, Auckland.

36 See for example, Beaglehole, E. and Beaglehole, P. (1948), *Some Modern Maoris*, New Zealand Council for Educational Research, Wellington.

37 In fact, it is frequently said in letters to the newspapers that Maori knowledge, if such a thing can be said to exist, is irrelevant, heathen, backwards and wrong.

38 See for example, Coney, S. (1988), *The Unfortunate Experiment*, Penguin, Auckland. According to Coney, when this experiment was approved the ethical obligations were still framed by the Helsinki Agreement (1964, 1975, 1983) which developed in response to the clinical trials of Nazi doctors in concentration camps.

39 This is a very positive gloss as there are many anecdotal examples of researchers who just carried on with little regard for Maori concerns.

40 Smith, L. T. (1989), 'On Being Culturally Sensitive: the Art of Gathering and Eating Kina Without Pricking Yourself on the Finger', keynote address to the New Zealand Psychological Society Annual Conference, University of Auckland. Reprinted in *The Issue of Research and Maori*, Research Unit for Maori Education, University of Auckland. A *kina* is a sea urchin, very prickly on the outside and not very attractive on the inside, except to those of us who regard them as a summer delicacy.

41 Smith, G. H. (1992), 'Research Issues Related to Maori Education', in *The Issue of Research and Maori*, Research Unit for Maori Education, University of Auckland, Auckland.

42 Both terms, *tiaki* and *whangai,* define types of relationships which are considered

positive and appropriate under certain constraints.
43 Bishop, R. (1994), 'Initiating Empowering Research?' *New Zealand Journal of Educational Studies,* Vol. 29, No. 1, pp. 175–88.
44 Teariki, C. and P. Spoonley (1992), *Te Whakapakari.*
45 They will also challenge academics from other countries, especially if it is thought that they have ignored the situation of indigenous people in their own countries or, worse, misrepresented them.

CHAPTER 10

Towards Developing
Indigenous Methodologies:
Kaupapa Maori Research

What happens to research when the researched become the researchers?

As mentioned in previous chapters, research of Maori is marked by a history that has shaped the attitudes and feelings Maori people have held towards research. Research is implicated in the production of Western knowledge, in the nature of academic work, in the production of theories which have dehumanized Maori and in practices which have continued to privilege Western ways of knowing, while denying the validity for Maori of Maori knowledge, language and culture. We have also mentioned the general impact of Western research on Maori attitudes towards theory and academic knowledge, attitudes which have led some Maori at least in the direction of rejecting *all* theory and *all* research. One of the challenges for Maori researchers working in this context has been to retrieve some space – first, some space to convince Maori people of the value of research for Maori; second, to convince the various, fragmented but powerful research communities of the need for greater Maori involvement in research; and third, to develop approaches and ways of carrying out research which take into account, without being limited by, the legacies of previous research, and the parameters of both previous and current approaches. What is now referred to as Kaupapa Maori approaches to research, or simply as Kaupapa Maori research, is an attempt to retrieve that space and to achieve those general aims. This naming of research has provided a focus through which Maori people, as communities of the researched and as new communities of the researchers, have been able to engage in a dialogue about setting new directions for the priorities, policies, and practices of research for, by and with Maori. This chapter begins by discussing the ways in which Kaupapa Maori research has become a way of structuring assumptions, values, concepts, orientations and priorities in research.[1]

Research by Maori

At the outset it needs stating that not all those who write about or talk about Kaupapa Maori are involved in research. Kaupapa Maori has been applied across a wide range of projects and enterprises. Furthermore, not all Maori researchers would regard either themselves, or their research, as fitting within a Kaupapa Maori framework. There are elements within the definitions of Kaupapa Maori which serve the purpose of selecting what counts and what does not count. One can ask, for example, 'Can a Maori researcher who is anti-Maori carry out Kaupapa Maori research?' The answer, based on current definitions, is 'definitely not'. Another question is less easy to answer: 'Can a non-indigenous researcher carry out Kaupapa Maori research?' The answer on current definitions is more complex. Perhaps it might read, 'a non-indigenous, non-Maori person can be involved in Kaupapa Maori research but not on their own, and if they were involved in such research, they would have ways of positioning themselves as a non-indigenous person'; or the more radical interpretation might say, 'by definition, no, Kaupapa Maori research is Maori research exclusively'. From these two questions and answers, then, it is possible to say something more about what Kaupapa Maori research is, and what it is not.

Kathy Irwin characterizes Kaupapa Maori as research which is 'culturally safe', which involves the 'mentorship' of elders, which is culturally relevant and appropriate while satisfying the rigour of research, and which is undertaken by a Maori researcher, not a researcher who happens to be Maori.[2] This statement implies that other forms of research, that is culturally sensitive models, have not been satisfactory at the level of cultural safety. Irwin also grounds her work in 'a paradigm that stems from a Maori worldview'.[3] Russell Bishop writes that Kaupapa Maori 'addresses the prevailing ideologies of cultural superiority which pervade our social, economic and political institutions'.[4] Bishop's model is framed by the discourses related to the Treaty of Waitangi and by the development within education of Maori initiatives which are 'controlled' by Maori. By framing Kaupapa Maori within the Treaty of Waitangi, Bishop leaves space for the involvement of non-indigenous researchers in support of Maori research. He argues that non-indigenous people, generally speaking, have an obligation to support Maori research (as Treaty partners). And, secondly, some non-indigenous researchers, who have a genuine desire to support the cause of Maori, ought to be included, because they can be useful allies and colleagues in research. The issue of 'control' is linked, in Bishop's argument, with the goal of empowerment, 'In the context of research, empowerment means that

Maori people should regain control of investigations into Maori people's lives.'[5] Bishop also argues that Kaupapa Maori research is located within an alternative conception of the world from which solutions and cultural aspirations can be generated. This alternative conception draws from an alternative code. Both Irwin and Bishop argue for the importance of the concept of *whanau* as a supervisory and organizational structure for handling research. Bishop refers to this as a 'research *whanau* of interest'. Irwin refers to a '*whanau* of supervisors'. For both Bishop and Irwin, the *whanau* provides the intersection where research meets Maori, or Maori meets research, on equalizing terms. From these comments it is clear that under the rubric of Kaupapa Maori research different sets of ideas and issues are being claimed as important. Some of these intersect at different points with research as an activity. Some of these features are framed as assumptions, some as practices and methods and some are related to Maori conceptions of knowledge.

Graham Smith, who has written extensively about Kaupapa Maori initiatives, summarizes these by saying that Kaupapa Maori research:

1   is related to 'being Maori';
2   is connected to Maori philosophy and principles;
3   takes for granted the validity and legitimacy of Maori, the importance of Maori language and culture; and
4   is concerned with 'the struggle for autonomy over our own cultural well being'.[6]

Smith locates Kaupapa Maori research within the wider project of Maori struggles for self-determination, and draws from this project a set of elements which, he argues, can be found in all the different projects associated with Kaupapa Maori. The general significance of these principles, however, is that they have evolved from within many of the well-tried practices of Maori as well as being tied to a clear and coherent rationale.[7]

A Local Approach to Critical Theory

Most discussion about Kaupapa Maori is also located in relation to critical theory, in particular to the notions of critique, resistance, struggle and emancipation. The previous chapter, for example, situates Maori research within the anti-positivist debate raised by critical theory. Pihama suggests that,

> intrinsic to Kaupapa Maori theory is an analysis of existing power structures and societal inequalities. Kaupapa Maori theory therefore aligns with critical theory in the act of exposing underlying assumptions that

serve to conceal the power relations that exist within society and the ways in which dominant groups construct concepts of 'common sense' and 'facts' to provide *ad hoc* justification for the maintenance of inequalities and the continued oppression of Maori people.[8]

Bishop goes further to suggest that critical approaches to research have in fact 'failed' to address the issues of communities such as Maori, and that the development of alternative approaches by Maori reflects a form of resistance to critical theory. Bishop makes this point in the context of the debate between Ellsworth and Giroux, about the failure of critical pedagogy in relation to its emancipatory goals.[9]

Smith, however, argues that Kaupapa Maori is a 'local' theoretical positioning which is the modality through which the emancipatory goal of critical theory, in a specific historical, political and social context, is practised. This 'localizing' of the aims of critical theory is partly an enactment of what critical theory actually 'offered' to oppressed, marginalized and silenced groups. The project of critical theory held out the possibility that, through emancipation, groups such as Maori would take greater control over their own lives and humanity. This necessarily implied that groups would take hold of the project of emancipation and attempt to make it a reality in their own terms. Whilst Western academics may quibble about the success or failure of the emancipatory project, and question the idealism which lies behind it, there is a tendency to be overly 'precious' about 'their' project as a universal recipe that has to be followed 'to the letter' if it is to be effective. Furthermore, this stance assumes that oppression has universal characteristics which were independent of history, context and agency. At the level of abstraction, this is what has to be argued in a sense, but it can never be so on the ground. There is also a naïveté about the real-life 'dirtiness' of political projects, or what Fanon and other anti-colonial writers would regard as the violence entailed in struggles for freedom. The end result cannot be predetermined. The means to the end involves human agency in ways which are complex and contradictory. The notion of strategic positioning as a deliberate practice is partially an attempt to contain the unevenness and unpredictability, under stress, of people engaged in emancipatory struggles. The broader vision of Kaupapa Maori embraces that sense of strategic positioning, of being able to plan, predict and contain, across a number of sites, the engagement in struggle.

Another dimension of Kaupapa Maori research is to be found clustered around issues of identity. Bishop, Irwin, Pihama and Smith have all argued that being Maori, identifying as Maori and as a Maori researcher, is a critical element of Kaupapa Maori research. Whilst this position is anti-positivist, in that it is also saying that we look at the world through our grounding in Maori world views, most Maori researchers would also argue that being Maori does not preclude us from being systematic, being ethical, being 'scientific' in the way we approach a research problem.[10] This positioning of researchers and the views they bring to research has been well argued in terms of feminist research. Feminist research maintains its focus on issues of gender (not just of women), but has moved away from the idea that only women can carry out feminist research to one which is less essentialist.[11] Kaupapa Maori research, as currently framed, would argue that being Maori is an essential criterion for carrying out Kaupapa Maori research. At the same time, however, some writers suggest that we exercise restraint in becoming too involved in identity politics because of the potential these politics have for paralysing development.[12] This position is based on the specificities of our history and our politics. This does not, however, preclude those who are not Maori from participating in research that has a Kaupapa Maori orientation.[13]

This latter point connects with the concept of *whanau*, as raised earlier, as a way of organizing research. The *whanau* principle is one identified by Smith as an important aspect of Kaupapa Maori approaches. All Maori initiatives have attempted to organize the basic decision making and participation within and around the concept of *whanau*. It is argued that the *whanau*, in pre-colonial times, was the core social unit, rather than the individual. It is also argued that the *whanau* remains as a persistent way of living and organizing the social world. In terms of research, the *whanau* is one of several Maori concepts which have become part of a methodology, a way of organizing a research group, a way of incorporating ethical procedures which report back to the community, a way of 'giving voice' to the different sections of Maori communities, and a way of debating ideas and issues which impact on the research project. It also has a very pragmatic function, in that the *whanau* is a way of distributing tasks, of incorporating people with particular expertise, and of keeping Maori values central to the project. It would be at this level, for example, that non-indigenous people can be involved. The *whanau* then can be a very specific modality through which research is shaped and carried out, analysed and disseminated.

Whanau is one of several aspects of Maori philosophy, values and practices which are brought to the centre in Kaupapa Maori research. Tuakana Nepe argues that Kaupapa Maori is derived from very different epistemological and metaphysical foundations and it is these which give Kaupapa Maori its distinctiveness from Western philosophies.[14] In other words, there is more to Kaupapa Maori than our history under colonialism or our desires for self-determination. We have a different epistemological tradition which frames the way we see the world, the way we organize ourselves in it, the questions we ask and the solutions which we seek. It is larger than the individuals in it and the specific 'moment' in which we are currently living. The significance of Kaupapa Maori to Maori language is tied to the connection between language, knowledge and culture. According to Sir James Henare, one of the architects of Te Kohanga Reo, 'The language is like a cloak which clothes, envelopes, and adorns the myriad of one's thoughts. (Ko te reo te kakahu o te whakaaro te huarahi i te ao turoa o te hinengaro).'[15] The revitalization of Maori language has brought with it the revitalization of Maori forms of knowledge and the debates which accompany those knowledge forms.[16] Kaupapa Maori, however, does not mean the same as Maori knowledge and epistemology. The concept of *kaupapa* implies a way of framing and structuring how we think about those ideas and practices. Nepe argues that Kaupapa Maori is a 'conceptualisation of Maori knowledge'.[17] It is a way of abstracting that knowledge, reflecting on it, engaging with it, taking it for granted sometimes, making assumptions based upon it, and at times critically engaging in the way it has been and is being constructed.[18] There is the possibility within Kaupapa Maori research to address the different constructions of Maori knowledge. A good example of this is in the development of Maori women's theories about Maori society which question the accounts of Maori society provided by men, including Maori men, but which still hold to a position that argues that the issues of gender for Maori do not make us the same as white women.[19] The critical theory of Kaupapa Maori also applies, therefore, to Maori ways of thinking, and to Maori ways of doing things, but it does not deny either the existence or fundamental legitimacy to Maori people of Maori forms of knowledge. It seeks to understand these forms, however, on their own terms and within the wider framework of Maori values and attitudes, Maori language, and Maori ways of living in the world.

There is another feature of Kaupapa Maori research that is becoming increasingly important as research funding is restructured around government priorities and policies. The state is the largest funding institution for research in New Zealand. The restructuring which occurred after 1994 separated the policy-making functions of government from the allocation of resources for research. The largest amount of money is institutionalized through the Foundation for Research, Science and Technology. Other ministries and government departments still fund research but this research is in the form of 'purchases' of specific reports which fulfil the 'outputs' of the ministry concerned, and which, in many cases, are written over (rewritten) and subjected to government copyright. In this sense the research is not research; it is a purchased product which becomes owned by the state. It becomes debatable, then, as to whether the purchased product is worth taking seriously outside government. The restructuring of research connects with the wider restructuring of the state in line with neo-liberal economic policies. These have emphasized the importance of government objectives, of competition and contestability, of the separation of policy from funding, of 'outputs' which are 'purchased', and of outcomes.[20] This shift towards neo-liberalism, which has occurred in New Zealand over the last decade, has very profound implications for Maori cultural values and practices.[21] It also has major implications for Maori in terms of its re-inscription of positivist approaches to scientific research.[22]

Kaupapa Maori Research and Positivism

In terms of Kaupapa Maori research, the more important question is related to issues of social justice. The debate about this aspect occurs at several levels. Reconciling market-driven, competitive and entrepreneurial research, which positions New Zealand internationally, with the need for Maori to carry out research which recovers histories, reclaims lands and resources and restores justice, hardly seems possible. This is precisely why the debates around self-determination and the Treaty of Waitangi have been significant. The attempt by Maori to engage in the activities of the state through the mechanism of the Treaty of Waitangi has won some space in which Maori can argue for different sorts of research priorities. This space, however, is severely limited as not only has it had to be wrested from the state, but from the community of positivistic scientists whose regard for Maori is not sympathetic. Furthermore, the competitive environment created by economic restructuring makes Kaupapa Maori research a competitor for resources with positivistic research. The problem is not just that positivist science is well established institutionally and theoretically, but that it has a connectedness at a common sense level with the rest of society who, generally speaking, take for granted the hegemony of its methods and leadership in the search for knowledge. As far as many people are concerned, research is positivist; it cannot be anything else. Kaupapa Maori is a fledgling approach which is occurring within the relatively smaller community of Maori researchers, which in turn exists within a minority culture which continues to be represented within antagonistic colonial discourses. It is a counter-hegemonic approach to Western forms of research and, as such, currently exists on the margins.

Kaupapa Maori research is imbued with a strong anti-positivistic stance. The wider vision of Maori communities, however, is to include within research approaches to Maori all those researchers who are attempting to work with Maori and on topics of importance to Maori.

The outer edges of Kaupapa Maori are not necessarily sharply delineated although there is, at the political level, something 'at stake'. One of the strands of a burgeoning Maori research community is the development of Maori health research. This development provides one interface between the more positivistic medical science approaches to research, particularly epidemiology, and social science approaches such as sociology and policy analysis. The 'failure' of medical research to address the needs of Maori in health parallels the failure of educational research. Recognition of this has shifted some areas of health research towards, first, developing more culturally sensitive research, and, second, employing Kaupapa Maori approaches. These include the involvement of Maori researchers in large studies, and the establishment of Maori health research units and centres which focus on issues of Maori health, are managed and organized by Maori, and employ multidisciplinary approaches within a Kaupapa Maori framework.[23] Hence large-scale epidemiological survey work and ethnographic, qualitative studies sit alongside each other in the same centre. The connections between the two highlight yet another feature of Kaupapa Maori research. Getting the approach 'right' is the first and major issue; the second issue is employing the most appropriate methods and people. Sometimes a positivistic research task can be carried out by Maori researchers, but the questions it sought to answer, the problems it sought to probe and the data it sought to gather, have been priorities and debated by Maori working in a Kaupapa Maori framework. There are three different points to be emphasized here. First, there are politics attached to research which most researchers understand; quite simply, positivistic research attracts funding. Second, there are accountabilities and pre-research discussions which have already framed, and to an extent transformed, the approach to research. Third, most of the Maori health research units have developed strong ties with specific Maori communities.[24] These are reflected in the way the centres are constituted and the geographical areas in which they work.

There may be a question as to whether Kaupapa Maori research is its own paradigm. Irwin suggests that it is.[25] Others involved in Kaupapa Maori would be reluctant to engage in such a debate because it sets up comparisons with Western science, which is exactly what Kaupapa Maori is resisting.[26] Kaupapa Maori research is both less than and more than a paradigm.[27] It does set out a field of study which enables a process of selection to occur, and which defines what needs to be studied and what questions ought to be asked. It also has a set of assumptions and taken-for-granted values and knowledge, upon which it builds. In this sense it can be fitted into some of the ways a paradigm is defined. It is also, however, more than the sum of those parts. Kaupapa Maori research is a social project; it weaves in and out of Maori cultural beliefs and values, Western ways of knowing, Maori histories and experiences under colonialism, Western forms of education, Maori aspirations and socio-economic needs, and Western economics and global politics. Kaupapa Maori is concerned with sites and terrains. Each of these is a site of struggle. Each of these sites has also been claimed by others as 'their' turf. They are selected or select themselves precisely because they are sites of struggle and because they have some strategic importance for Maori. We are not at present interested in nuclear physics but we are becoming interested in genetic science.[28] There are sound reasons why we are interested in education, employment, health and history. Each of these domains situates us in crisis. They are more real and more pressing.

How Does Kaupapa Maori Research Proceed?

Kaupapa Maori approaches to research are based on the assumption that research that involves Maori people, as individuals or as communities, should set out to make a positive difference for the researched. This does not need to be an immediate or direct benefit. The point is that research has to be defined and designed with some ideas about likely short-term or longer-term benefits. Obvious as this may be, it must be remembered that, historically, indigenous peoples have not seen the positive benefits of research. The research approach also has to address seriously the cultural ground rules of respect, of working with communities, of sharing processes and knowledge. Kaupapa Maori research also incorporates processes such as networking, community consultations and *whanau* research groups, which assist in bringing into focus the research problems which are significant for Maori. In practice all of these elements of the Kaupapa Maori approach are negotiated with communities or groups from 'communities of interest'. It means that researchers have to share their 'control' of research and seek to maximize the participation and the interest of Maori. In many contexts research cannot proceed without the project being discussed by a community or tribal gathering and supported. There are some tribes whose processes are quite rigorous and well established. One tribe has allocated one day a month for dealing with external relations. Another tribe has a reputation for being rather fierce examiners of research projects. Many communities have a strong sense of what counts as ethical research. Their definition of ethics is not limited to research related to living human subjects but includes research involving the environment, archival research and any research which examines ancestors, either as physical remains (extracting DNA), or using their photographs, diaries or archival records.

One of the factors favouring the development of Kaupapa Maori research was the increasing involvement of young Maori researchers in projects in which they were employed as the minority group researcher. Support systems and mentoring processes which brought these researchers together for development, or for discussing issues, created an ever expanding group of young people who wanted a career in research but who were having enormous difficulties trying to advocate for Maori within projects which had employed them as token assistants. The support system brought together a group of people from very different research backgrounds. Through these meetings, and informal gatherings, discussions about research-related matters became a natural part of the meeting. Training issues emerged, ethical horror stories, and often very positive experiences were discussed. Some of the difficulties of interviewing elders were debated and problems relating to the writing of research. The bilingual dynamic within which many researchers were working was also a topic of discussion. Kaupapa Maori became in time an approach to training and supporting young researchers whose academic training had not prepared them for working inside their own communities and within their own value systems and cultural practices.

Setting Strategic Directions

At a conference of Maori health researchers in 1996, I raised the following list of priorities as a basis for discussion:

- determining as Maori our own research needs and priorities;
- defining the ways research should proceed;
- training of Maori researchers;
- discussion of culturally appropriate ethics;
- ongoing development of culturally sympathetic methods;
- continued collaboration with our own diverse *iwi* and communities of interest;
- development and dissemination of literature by Maori on research;
- continued reflection, evaluation and critique of ourselves as a community of Maori researchers;
- extending the boundaries for Maori (and for other indigenous peoples) of our own fields and disciplines;
- education of wider research community, including scientific, academic and policy communities; and;
- accountabilities to and outcomes for Maori.

The purpose of the list was not to say that this was the definitive list and order of priorities but to have people discuss and think about the broader project of Maori research. The participants at the gathering did discuss the priorities and took the list back to their own organizations and communities for further debate. The list encapsulates the wider debate occurring in relation to Maori research. Ten years ago such a debate could not have occurred within a gathering of Maori researchers. There were simply not enough researchers to hold a gathering. Recently, two years after the above list was first introduced, a meeting was held to discuss the strategic plans for Maori health research of a major research funding agency. The priorities raised in this original discussion paper informed much of the discussion. They had been discussed and used by different communities and health organizations to think about their own directions. The items on the list are still important, not just for health research but for all Maori research. Kaupapa Maori as an approach has provided a space for dialogue by Maori, across disciplines, about research. Maori researchers from the fields of health and medicine, justice and education, history, law, politics, architecture, planning and environmental management, along with tribal and community based researchers, can come together and discuss research in ways not always available to other communities. Maori interest in research has made research more interesting. Maori communities can engage in research in exciting ways if they are included in the research.

Discussions about the broader dimensions of research have been preliminary ventures into the domain of research. It has been like venturing into an alien domain. Maori researchers have sought to understand how and why research has provoked such fear and antagonism by indigenous peoples generally, and by Maori in particular. It has meant an 'indigenous participant observation' of research, of the culture and politics of research, of how it has been institutionalized and established in the colonies, of how research has been implicated in our own colonization. But it has also been about understanding the ways in which research can provide systematic ways of understanding our own predicaments, of answering our own questions, and of helping us as communities to solve our problems and develop ourselves. Engaging in a discussion about research as an indigenous issue has been about finding a voice, or a way of voicing concerns, fears, desires, aspirations, needs and questions as they relate to research. When indigenous peoples become the researchers and not merely the researched, the activity of research is transformed. Questions are framed differently, priorities are ranked differently, problems are defined differently, people participate on different terms.

Notes

1 Olssen M. (1991), 'Producing the Truth about People', in *Growing Up, The Politics of Human Learning*. eds J. Morss and T. Linzey, Auckland, Longman Paul.

2 Irwin, K. (1994), 'Maori Research Methods and Practices', in *Sites*, 28, Autumn, p. 27.

3 *Ibid.*, p. 28.

4 Bishop, R. (1994), 'Initiating Empowering Research?' in *New Zealand Journal of Educational Studies*, Vol. 29, No. 1, p. 175.

5 *Ibid.*, p. 176.

6 Smith, G. H. (1990), 'Research Issues Related to Maori Education', paper presented to NZARE Special Interest Conference, Massey University, reprinted in 1992, *The Issue of Research and Maori*, Research Unit for Maori Education, University of Auckland.

7 In this sense *kaupapa* means 'project' or plan.

8 Pihama, L. (1993), 'Tungia te Ururua, Kia Tupu Whakaritorito Te Tupu o te Harakeke: a Critical Analysis of Parents as First Teachers', MA thesis, University of Auckland, p. 57.

9 This debate began formally with a paper by Ellsworth, E. (1989), 'Why Doesn't This Feel Empowering? Working Through the Repressive Myths of Critical Pedagogy', in *Harvard Educational Review*, Vol. 59, No. 3, pp. 297–324. Ellsworth questioned many of the basic assumptions of critical pedagogy. This provoked a response by Henri Giroux and the broader issues of the debate are summarized more fully in Lather P. (1991), *Getting Smart, Feminist Research and Pedagogy With/in the Postmodern*, New York, Routledge, pp. 43–9.

10 Smith, L. T. (1995), 'Re-centering Kaupapa Maori Research', paper presented at Te Matawhanui Conference, Maori Studies Department, Massey University.

11 This is not uncontentious, in that some feminist groups would still argue that men, because they are men, cannot possibly articulate a feminist position or carry out feminist research. What I want to signal, however, is that feminist scholarship has moved from its early foundations and as a parallel the same possibility exists for Kaupapa Maori research.

12 For example, Kathy Irwin writes, 'There is still a destructive debate taking place in some quarters over who are "real" and, heaven forbid, "acceptable" Maori women.... Precious time is wasted debating amongst ourselves, who is and who isn't an "acceptable" Maori.' Irwin, K. (1992), 'Towards Theories of Maori Feminisms', in *Feminist Voices, Womens' Studies Texts for Aotearoa/New Zealand*, ed. R. du Plessis, Auckland, Oxford University Press, p. 3.

13 Nor does it preclude those who identify as Maori but cannot speak Maori language, those who are Maori but do not know their *whakapapa*, nor those who are Maori but have lived away from their *iwi* or *whanau* territories.

14 Nepe, T. (1991), 'E Hao Nei e Tenei Reanga: Te Toi Huarewa Tipuna, Kaupapa Maori, an Educational Intervention System', MA thesis, University of Auckland.

15 Cited in Nepe, 'E Hao Nei', p. 15.

16 See Salmond, A (1985), 'Maori Epistemologies', in *Reason and Morality*, ed. J. Overing, London, Tavistock.

17 Nepe, 'E Hao Nei', p. 15.

18 For example, those involved in Kaupapa Maori projects question attempts to mystify Maori knowledge or use either their identity and knowledge of *whakapapa* or Maori language as a way of excluding other Maori from participation in

decision making or other forms of involvement.

19 See for example, Te Awekotuku, N. (1992), 'He Whiriwhiri Wahine: Framing Women's Studies for Aotearoa', in *Te Pua* 1, University of Auckland, pp. 46–58.

20 For a further discussion of these points see Clark, J. (1995), 'The New Right and Educational Research', in *Input*, Wellington, New Zealand Association for Research in Education, Vol. 16, pp. 2–8.

21 For further discussion of this point refer to Smith, G. H. (1993), 'The Commodification of Knowledge and Culture', in *Overview*, Corso, No. 49, November, pp. 149–53 and Smith, G. H. (1994), 'Maori Culture for Sale', in *Polemic*, University of Sydney Law Society, Sydney, Friar Press, Vol. 4, No. 3, pp. 149–53.

22 For examples, see the guidelines and policies for the Foundation for Research, Science and Technology and their application forms.

23 Two such units, Te Pumanawa Hauora at Massey University and the Eru Pomare Research Centre at the Wellington Clinical School, are funded by the Health Research Council; another unit exists at the University of Auckland Medical School and other units operate inside existing centres, such as the Alcohol and Public Health Research Centre at the University of Auckland.

24 These include rural and urban communities and several *iwi* groups.

25 Irwin, K. (1994), 'Maori Research Methods and Practices', in *Sites*, 28, Autumn, p. 27.

26 See, for a further discussion, Smith, G. H. (1995), 'Falling Through the Cracks of the Constructivism Debate: the Neglect of the 'Maori Crisis' within Science Education', in *Access*, 14, soon to be published by ACCESS, Education Department, University of Auckland.

27 I am using the definition of paradigm by Kuhn, T. (1970), *The Structure of Scientific Revolutions*, second edition, International Encyclopaedia of Unified Science, Vol. 2, No. 2, Chicago, University of Chicago Press.

28 It is not that nuclear physics is not thought to have an impact on our lives – but this prospect is not yet as real for us as the advances currently being made in genetic engineering and the possibility which now exists under GATT for 'our' genetic material to be copied and patented.

Conclusion:
A Personal Journey

In February 1985, the general frustrations of Maori towards research were reframed in a discussion paper by Evelyn Stokes for the National Research Advisory Council. This paper was written for inclusion in the more general discussion relating to the formation of new national science objectives. Stokes's paper argues for the acceptance of Maori knowledge and values, for the desirability and social significance of more Maori research, and for the need to train Maori researchers. The importance of Stokes's paper was its audience and its timing. It was directed at the top policy level, where decisions were being made which would dictate the national priorities for research. Since then, those priorities, and the ways in which they have been institutionalized, have been radically restructured. The timing of the paper was therefore strategic because it put Maori research interests on the national science policy agenda. Several writers had already raised many of the same issues and had voiced these concerns at conferences and seminars. These occasions, however, tended to be hosted within various district disciplines, which did little to engage either the political realities of social science research or the attention of the few Maori who may have been in a position to carry out research.[1]

Later on in the same year I set out as a postgraduate student to interview a group of Maori women whose children were in Te Kohanga Reo. My daughter attended the same Te Kohanga Reo and the women were well known to me and had willingly agreed to be interviewed. I had found little help in the standard methodological guidebooks for the issues I would confront when I was a Maori carrying out research with other Maori. Very little in the discussions of cross-cultural issues was useful because I was not working cross-culturally. Much of the cross-cultural literature assumed that the researcher belonged to the dominant cultural group and was 'doing' research to, for, and sometimes with, a minority group. There were some studies that addressed the issues for

196

women researchers who were going to study in remote villages in Africa or South America. And, of course, there were the romantic National Geographic accounts of women who spent years studying primates in various isolated spots, which frankly did not appeal. This literature reinforced the idea that one needed special skills related to being culturally sensitive, and to effective ways of gaining entrance into the community being studied, and to gaining the confidence of 'informants'.[2] There was a limited availability of literature that related to critiques of methodological approaches and these were primarily by African American scholars rather than other indigenous people.[3] There was nothing which helped me think about and frame what I wanted to do within my own cultural context, or how I might go about doing some research in one of my own communities. Even previous research by other Maori academics appeared problematic to me, firstly because they wrote as if they were outsiders in their own world, and secondly because they were all men, fluent in Maori language and regarded as being deeply knowledgeable about Maori culture.[4] I wrote a paper as a preamble to my research project, setting out the issues I faced and attempting to articulate what it was that made those issues so problematic.[5]

I found as I moved around the communities with whom I was involved that while there was clearly a discourse which was anti-research and was very cynical about non-indigenous research there was also a great deal of support for the work that I was doing. People were genuinely interested in talking in a focused way about their lives. They were interested also in finding out what people who were just like them thought. I found that people entrusted me with information about themselves which was highly personal. I felt honoured by that trust, and somewhat obligated as well – in the sense of having to be very careful and very respectful about how I handled such information. Discretion was not something about which I had to be consciously mindful of before but it seemed to be an important skill in my working context as a researcher. After I moved from my graduate student status to employment as a health research coordinator I found even greater acceptance of my role as community-based researcher. It was a different role from the ones I had had before as a parent and teacher, and I discovered a very privileged role. I was invited to participate in community meetings about Maori health but did not get involved in the hot politics of community-based health. I was able to work between and within the different groupings of community health and education interests. I was asked to explain the intricacies of both government policy and health-related research. I was also expected to connect all the official information with what communities were trying to do themselves and with the way they talked about health. The community used an entirely different frame to make sense of official talk. This visibly exasperated officials who found themselves having to explain policies to people who did not agree with the basic assumptions on which policy was based, and who made every official accountable for the history of policies and relations with Maori!

I saw the strengths of communities and their ability to deconstruct official talk with ease. I saw their continuing belief in themselves, their positive outlook and optimism and their hope that maybe, one day, life would get better. In talking with people in the community I became interested in the questions which they were asking of health which were not being addressed by research. 'We know we are dying', someone said, 'but tell me why we are living?' 'Our health will not improve unless we address the fact that we have no sovereignty', 'We're sick of hearing what's wrong with us, tell us something good for a change', or, 'Why do they always think by looking at us they will find the answers to our problems, why don't they look at themselves?' The same questions were being asked of education and of justice. I too wanted to know why it was that community concerns were always reframed around standard research problems. How can research ever address our needs as indigenous peoples if our questions are never taken seriously? It was as if the community's questions were never heard, simply passed over, silenced.

I did not make a conscious decision about becoming a researcher, about deciding to become actively involved in the politics of research, or in the teaching of research, or in the practice of being a researcher. Somewhere within the process of becoming a researcher, however, I also thought a great deal about the role of research for Maori and my own role as a Maori researcher. The two issues, in my view, were connected yet also very separate. My defining of myself as a Maori or indigenous researcher seemed a natural thing to do. I was a Maori. I had been employed as a researcher on a project that needed to recruit Maori families into the study; my expertise was in developing the networks and the approaches to interviewing Maori families in community settings. I was the coordinator of the whole study, not just the part that related to Maori, and piloted all aspects of the questionnaire and interview schedules. As I read methodological writings, especially in relation to feminist methodologies, it seemed to me that the common sense prac- tices which Maori families and I as the researcher went through when- ever and wherever we met needed to be talked about and privileged as processes that were important.

In travelling around other places I have met indigenous people who have experienced similar histories as researchers. Their tertiary education was alienating and disconnected from the needs of their own communities. The more educated they became the more it was assumed that they would not want to return to their own communities. Assimilation policies in education were intended to provide one way roads out for those indigenous people who 'qualified'. Many did take that road and have never returned. There are many others, however, who choose to remain, to wear their identities with pride and work with and for their own communities and nations. In various places around the world there are small initiatives which are providing indigenous peoples with space to create and be indigenous. Research seems such a small and technical aspect of the wider politics of indigenous peoples. It is often thought of as an activity which only anthropologists do! As indigenous peoples we have our own research needs and priorities. Our questions are important. Research helps us to answer them.

Notes

1 Annual disciplinary conferences are often dominated by academic presentations and the 'political' nature of research is kept well away. In some cases it is regarded as a contaminant and people who raise or address political issues are seen as being polemicists! On the second point there were and still are very few Maori with post-graduate qualifications, which tend to be the prerequisite for most research positions. Even fewer of these attend conferences or belong to disciplinary societies.

2 I had always seen myself as belonging to the 'informant' community and thus felt well trained to inform on myself, but insufficiently trained to get others to do it for me! And of course, I 'read' what I was being told in the interviews, as if I were still a member of the 'informant' community, and was very conscious of the way the words being given me were being carefully selected and framed.

3 For example, Mitchell, J. (1982), 'Reflections of a Black Social Scientist: Some Struggles, Some Doubts, Some Hopes', in *Harvard Educational Review*, Vol. 52, No. 1, pp. 27–34.

4 None of which is how I saw myself.

5 The first of a series of papers, Smith, L. T. (1985), 'Te Rapunga Ki Te Ao Marama', Education Department, University of Auckland.

Index

Other titles from the University of Otago Press

The Welcome of Strangers:
An Ethnohistory of Southern Maori, 1650–1850
Atholl Anderson
PAPERBACK, ILLUSTRATED, ISBN 1 877133 41 8, $39.95
HARDBACK, ILLUSTRATED, ISBN 1 877133 59 0, $65.00

Te Mamae me te Aroha:
The Pain and the Love
Bill Dacker
PAPERBACK, ILLUSTRATED, ISBN 0 908569 89 0, $29.95

Four Generations from Maoridom:
The Memoirs of a South Island Kaumatua and Fisherman
Syd Cormack with Joanna Orwin
PAPERBACK, ILLUSTRATED, ISBN 1 877133 34 5, $29.95

When the Waves Rolled in Upon Us:
Essays in Nineteenth Century Maori History
Edited by Michael Reilly
PAPERBACK, ILLUSTRATED, ISBN 1 877133 20 5, $39.95

Traditional Lifeways of the Southern Maori
James Herries Beattie, edited by Atholl Anderson
PAPERBACK, ILLUSTRATED, ISBN 0 908569 79 3 $59.95

Patrons of Maori Culture:
Power, Theory and Ideology in the Maori Renaissance
Steven Webster
PAPERBACK, ILLUSTRATED, ISBN 1 877133 48 5, $39.95

Travels in Oceania
Dr Louis Thiercelin, translated by Christiane Mortelier
PAPERBACK, ILLUSTRATED, ISBN 0 908569 71 8, $34.95

Infectious Diseases:
Colonising the Pacific?
John Miles
PAPERBACK, 124 PAGES, ISBN 1 877133 26 4, $29.95